An Irishman's Cuttings

Aeonium lancerottense blooms in midsummer. (© E. C. Nelson)

Facing page:Tanglewood, near Glengarriff, County Cork; white-flowered St Dabeoc's heath with ferns. (© E. C. Nelson)

An Irishman's Cuttings

TALES OF IRISH GARDENS AND GARDENERS, PLANTS AND PLANT HUNTERS

E. CHARLES NELSON

The Collins Press

FIRST PUBLISHED IN 2009 BY
The Collins Press
West Link Park
Doughcloyne
Wilton
Cork

British Library Cataloguing in Publication Data

Nelson, E. Charles.
    An Irishman's cuttings : tales of Irish gardens & gardeners, plants
and plant-hunters.
    1. Gardening--Ireland--History. 2. Gardeners--Ireland--History.
    3. Plant collectors--Ireland--History.
    I. Title II. Irish garden.
    635'.09415-dc22

ISBN-13: 9781848890053

Design and typesetting by Burns Design
Typeset in Meridien
Printed in Italy by Printer Trento

CONTENTS

FOREWORD

A<small>N 'I</small>RISHMAN'S CUTTING', in garden parlance, is one that has well-formed roots before it is detached from the parent plant. Such a cutting is more certain to provide a robust, new plant than an ordinary slip which must first strive to form roots without parental succour. The earliest instance of the use of the phrase that I can trace is in an article about fuchsia, by Robert Fish, published in *The Cottage Gardener* on 7 February 1851. At the time Mr Fish, a Scot, was gardener to one Colonel Sowerby at Putteridge Bury near Luton in Bedfordshire; he was also a regular contributor to several horticultural journals.

> Many a sweet look, many a happy countenance, have I witnessed, produced by the receiving 'an Irishman's cutting'* of these lovely ladies' eardrops. Open-hearted, and open-handed gardeners, by the diffusion of these plants alone, have done something to refine, and soften, and purify the manners of the age.

The asterisk is in the original and indicated the following footnote: 'An Irishman's cutting is one with a nice root to it.' That that term, and not 'ladies' eardrops', needed explanation seems to indicate it was likely to be unfamiliar to the readers of *The Cottage Gardener* – lady's eardrop was one of the names for fuchsia current at that period.

Like the garden variety, the cuttings (of a different kind) in this book have deep roots in the gardens of Ireland and among plantsmen, of both sexes, who have Irish 'roots'. Each essay is an Irishman's cutting in another sense, having been first published in *The Irish Garden* magazine to which I have contributed since it was first published in 1992.

In making a selection of these wordy cuttings, I have tried to choose the most amusing and most interesting out of around eighty contributions to the magazine. Quite by chance, this has resulted in a distinctly Corkonian bias! In consequence of the process of selection, too, there is some overlap between the chapters. Most of the articles are only lightly altered from their original state – I have corrected obvious errors and sometimes added new facts. Only the 'Last Rose of Summer' chapter has an extensive addendum. As for the illustrations, these may not be exactly the images used in the originals because of availability or copyright. For many years, I was able to call on the generous help of Grace Pasley, who was one of the hard-working Botanical Assistants in the National Botanic Gardens, Glasnevin. She was an expert photographer and was ever-willing to assist in obtaining pictures but her untimely death in 2008, after a long struggle with cancer, has deprived me of that assistance and some of her photographs have had to be omitted.

The phrase I have chosen as the title of this anthology intrigues me. Its origins are 'lost' in garden history. Edward Augustus Bowles, whose name crops up in the following chapters, used it in the memorable trilogy about his Middlesex garden. In *My Garden in Summer*, he wrote this:

FOREWORD

We will leave the herbaceous beds, and go to the rock garden for Daisies. Here we find *Felicia abyssinica*, a fairy Daisy, with finely-cut foliage, that forms cushions of greenery like some extra good Mossy Saxifrage, and bears for months together soft, lilac-blue flowers in great profusion, but not hardy, so that a pot full of cuttings must go into a house every Autumn, to replace their deceased parents next Spring. It roots as it spreads, so there is no difficulty in propagating it, as one can always find Irishman's cuttings . . .

My Garden in Summer was published in 1914 and Bowles cautioned: 'Of course, if you are taking off a few to give to a visitor from the Emerald Isle, you must be careful to speak of Dutchman's cuttings or take the risk of adding one more insult to that distressful country.'

Time passes, but was it ever, is it an insult to talk about an 'Irishman's cutting'? Can the term really be deprecatory? We have Robert Fish's assurance that such rooted plantlets were tokens of generosity, and such 'newly rooted portions, around the old plants', to quote Bowles' definition, are a handy way of doing what all good gardeners should do: give their best and rarest plants away. The doyenne of Irish gardeners in the first half of the last century, Lady Moore, was always on the look-out for 'Irishman's cuttings' and maybe she was the person Bowles had in mind when he cautioned about using the phrase in the presence of a Irish plantsman – she and Bowles knew each other well and exchanged plants; even, dare I suggest, 'Irishman's cuttings'. Lady Moore's memorable request when she saw a plant she admired was this winsome one: 'Do you think that plant might have a little brother?' Graham Stuart Thomas, who reported Lady Moore's charming enquiry and whose friendship I am privileged to have enjoyed, was to point out that 'plants as a rule increase . . . and the giving away of manavilins is a blessed form of friendship in which we all take pleasure.' So whether the rooted pieces are Irishman's cuttings or little brothers or manavilins, they all connect the gardening network that has kept Ireland's gardens rich and exciting for decades on end.

Let me conclude with an apposite extract from an article by Frederick William Burbidge, who was the Curator of the College Botanic Gardens in Ballsbridge – he was a superlative writer too. In *The Garden* on 25 December 1886, his contribution was a kind of 'editorial' about snowdrops, one of his specialities:

A garden supplies food to our minds throughout all our varying moods and phases of feeling; it gives us Laurel wreaths or Cypress boughs for the old who precede us, as well as bridal garlands for the young who remain . . . A good garden is full of buried hopes and glorious resurrections; of swelling bulbs and rooting seeds of a thousand kinds; it is, indeed, the birthplace of miracles, which would be even more wonderful if less common, or if we had the power of seeing and of understanding the full and true value of simple things.

E. CHARLES NELSON
Outwell, Norfolk
2009

ACKNOWLEDGEMENTS

First and foremost, I owe gratitude to Mary Davies, Editor (latterly of garden history and book reviews) of *The Irish Garden*, and one of its founders, who took care of my articles and edited them so inconspicuously that I only noticed her interventions when preparing this book. Certainly, Mary improved my contributions and, overall, made the job of writing for the magazine a rewarding and pleasant experience. I am also most grateful for the several photographs which she has provided for this book.

Numerous others have assisted in divers way and I am most grateful to them: in no particular order and with profuse apologies to anyone I have forgotten:

– Mrs Wendy Walsh has permitted the reproduction of her watercolours and, of course, over the last thirty years has been a congenial colleague in the byways of Ireland's garden history.

– Bill King: for his collaboration in tracking William Robinson across the United States of America in 1870, and especially for his local knowledge of Salt Lake City. He is co-author of Chapter 3.6 about Robinson's transcontinental tip.

– Ed Perry: a fellow sea-beaner, for his photographs of nickars and Hans' hamburger bean.

– Colette Edwards, assistant in the library in the National Botanic Gardens, Glasnevin, has been most helpful in the time-consuming task of getting references and illustrations.

– the late Grace Pasley, also of the National Botanic Gardens, Glasnevin, produced excellent photographs herself and gave other invaluable help over many years; without her assistance many of the articles would have been rather bare.

– Mrs Heather Dobbin: for the photograph of her parents, Eileen and James Walker Porter.

– Allen Hall: for the Porter heathers.

– Mrs Theresa Andreucetti: for the photograph of Patrick B. O'Kelly.

– Dr Ted Oliver: for photographs of South African heaths.

– Richard Ramsden: for Thomas Drummond's mountain avens.

– Dr Keith Ferguson: for his slide of mistletoe in the long-gone College Botanic Garden, and for bringing *Brownea × crawfordii* from Kew to Dublin.

– Tony O'Mahony: for photographs of the cemetery that was Cork Botanic Garden.

– Neal Kramer for Brewer's mountainheath.

– the late Captain and Mrs Antony Tupper: for access to the papers of Charlotte Isobel Wheeler Cuffe.

ACKNOWLEDGEMENTS

– Hugh Langrishe: for the splendid photographic portrait of Lady Wheeler Cuffe.

– David Sayers: for making all the arrangements that allowed us to follow Shadow's footsteps through 'beautiful, laughing' Burma, even to the summit of Natmataung.

– Dr Steve Spongberg: for advice about Augustine Henry's map for *Davidia*.

– Mr & Mrs J. Connors: for assistance with my article about Miss Sheila Pim, and Philip Jacob and David Davison for facilitating the photographing of her portrait.

– Professor Bill Watts and Professor John Parnell (Trinity College, Dublin): for Coulteriana.

– Dr John Hall (Archivist, Ulster Medical Society): for the portrait of Sir Hans Sloane.

– the late W. E. G. Bagwell: for the photographs of W. E. Gumbleton and Belgrove.

– Stephen Besley: for Joseph Paxton's *Banksia*.

– Lieutenant-Colonel Philip Haslett: for William Robinson's photograph.

– Dr Philip Short: for advice about James Drummond.

– G. A. Kenyon: for the portrait of Professor Walter Wade.

– Tony Moreau: for assistance with various scanned images.

– The Tree Council of Ireland, and Dr Matthew Jebb (National Botanic Gardens, Glasnevin), for access to data on 'champion' *Cedrus libani* in Ireland, and Anne James for the dimensions of the cedar at Malahide Castle.

– for permission to use illustrations: Wellcome Library for the History and Understanding of Medicine, London; Ulster Medical Society, Belfast; Hunt Institute for Botanical Documentation, Pittsburgh; Beinecke Rare Books and Manuscript Library, Yale University; Royal Irish Academy, Dublin; Royal Horticultural Society of Ireland; The Linnean Society of London; The Heather Society; Royal Botanic Gardens, Kew; Natural History Museum, London; Trinity College, Dublin; National Botanic Gardens, Glasnevin; National Library of Wales, Aberystwyth.

My own photographs, taken over the past three decades, come from many different gardens in Ireland and Great Britain, and I am grateful for the friendship of the gardeners themselves.

Lastly, I am most grateful to The Collins Press for making this book of cuttings possible and for the care and attention given to its rooting.

ROSEMARY

1

THE IRISH GARDEN

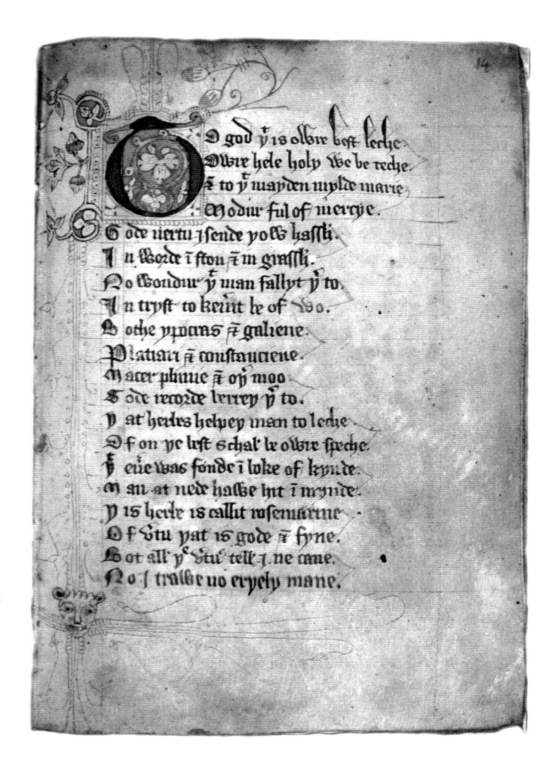

The first, beautifully decorated leaf of the original manuscript of the mediaeval verse-book entitled 'The virtues of herbs'. This version, comprising 273 lines, dates from the late 1300s or early 1400s. The manuscript is preserved in the Wellcome Library for the History and Understanding of Medicine, London. (© reproduced by permission of the Wellcome Library.)

1.1
ONCE UPON A TIME . . .

❧❦❧

SIX CENTURIES AGO, somewhere in the eastern part of Ireland, there is a scribe. He holds a goose quill in his hand. Sunlight pours through an unglazed window on to his simple, wooden desk; this is the only light, yet the best, for his work. There is a small vessel in front of him containing black ink, and a few sheets of fine vellum lie on the desk-top, each one carefully and neatly ruled with twenty barely visible lines. He starts to write, elegantly, line by line, for his is a beautiful hand, calligraphy as the Greeks say.

He is a learned man, trained in the arts of a physician as well as being skilled in writing and reading. He speaks English with a distinctive Irish lilt to it. He has just come home again to Ireland from England where he spent some time studying physic, especially phlebotomy, the skill of blood-letting. He also visited a few of the best gardens where he saw some herbs that were still so rare that they were grown only by the most favoured gardeners. He was greatly impressed by the plants, and the cures that they were said to provide, and took the time to learn about their cultivation. Now, before his memory fades, he is determined to write down what he learned including the wisdom of one Master Jon Gardener.

And so he begins to write, using the black ink. He has already emblazoned a gorgeous initial ℭ, brightly coloured in blue – . . . o god þᵗ is owre best leche, 'To God that is our best leech'. And so on, for another 271 lines, filling fourteen sides of vellum. He takes a long time to reach the end. Some lines have an elaborate initial in red, and other letters have billowing up-strokes in-filled with yellow. Each letter is inscribed with precision. There are times when he daydreams, perhaps about his garden, and then he doodles – a head here and a swirl there, in scarlet or purple. When he comes to the end he is happy to have remembered the whole

poem: Amen so bedde we snelle, 'Amen, so bid we snell', are its final English words. There is one more line to write, and then he can rest, satisfied that he has safely transferred to the vellum leaves these important verses – Explicit Gardbener.

He leaves the last vellum page to dry and, we may fancy, ambles outside into the neat herbar that adjoins his scriptorium, and sits down on the turf bench, savouring the scents of the herbs that grow around it: thyme, chamomile and lavender. His herbar is compact, regularly composed with gravelled paths and raised rectangular beds edged with bricks, the whole surrounded by a stone wall in the cracks of which grow small ferns and pellitory-of-the-wall which he often uses in medicines. A few paces beyond the wicket gate that leads out into the demesne there is a fish-pond; clumps of wild yellow irises have been planted around the edge and every summer white waterlilies float on the surface. The meadows are full of wild flowers and, when time allows, he loves to wander about looking for new herbs. He knows that he can rely on the meadows for St John's-wort, yarrow and cowslips, if he needs them for medicines. Nearby there are a few fields where beans and peas are grown, and others containing oats and barley.

Inside the herbar, the herbs and worts are tidily ordered in each carefully tended bed so that he can find the ones he needs easily when they are required. Some of the plants came from the local meadows and woods. The primroses finished blooming some time ago, but there are a few flowers left on the avens, and the strawberries sparkle with ripe berries. The hart's-tongue and polypody are unfurling new, bright-green leaves. He had brought these and others into the herbar to have them close at hand, and, of course, they grow so much more lushly than out in the wilds. Herb Robert is almost

COLEWORT

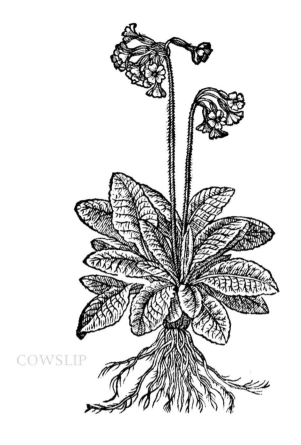

COWSLIP

PARSLEY

SAFFRON

Above: 'This herb is called rosemarine, Of virtue that is good and fine.' Rosemary has been used for countless centuries as a culinary, ceremonial and medicinal herb. This Mediterranean shrub was introduced into England in the reign of King Edward III, around 1340, and probably came to Ireland soon afterwards. 'The virtues of herbs' accounted for some of the old medical uses of rosemary – it was believed to prevent colds, cure baldness and headaches, cleanse the skin, and kill worms, and also to prevent nightmares, rejuvenate the elderly, and stop thieves from re-offending. (© E. C. Nelson)

Left: The reconstructed herb garden at Grey Abbey, County Down, in May 1994 with cowslips and woodruff in bloom. (© E. C. Nelson)

a weed, seeding itself everywhere, especially into the gravel paths. Teasel and clary look as if they will soon follow suit. Yet most of his herbs are only to be found in the gardens of monasteries and manor houses. The scribe has never seen teasel, clary and hollyhock in the locality, but they are so easy to grow as long as he is careful to gather their seed every year. The parsley has been doing well since he learned not to transplant it – Master Jon advised sowing parsley where it was to grow in March, and that has worked. Now he has no shortage of leaves and can even spare a hefty bunch now and then to add to the potage of leeks, colewort leaves, beans and peas which he so enjoys. Thinking of this, he remembers that he must soon sow some more colewort, for, again, Master Jon advised that this was the best way to have a continuous supply of fresh leaves for the kitchen. In four weeks' time he can lift and reset the seedlings in rows, and a fortnight later begin plucking the young leaves for potage. The bed for the worts is ready, well-dug, well-manured and without a weed in sight.

As well as learning how to cure the sick, our scribe had been taught how to graft plants, taking buds from the best varieties and then carefully transferring them to the stock. He enjoyed grafting and so had acquired some fine roses. He had been told that the one with many-petalled, rich crimson flowers was from the town of Provins, near Paris, and that the local apothecaries made conserves from the crushed, dried petals. He hopes to try it; as soon as the flowers are ready he will gather and dry them, meanwhile enjoying their lingering perfume.

Our scribe, like every gardener before and since, is especially proud of his most recent acquisition. In the warmest corner of the herbar, in a patch of its own, facing the noon-time sun and nicely protected from the north wind, are a few slips – he spoke of them as slivings – of a new herb that he brought from England, a gift from a fellow gardener. He knows he must be patient and allow the slips to strike root. If a black frost or a cold wind does not kill them, they will surely grow into fine plants from which he will soon harvest flowers and leaves for medicines. This new herb is called *Rosmarinus,* the dew of the sea, and is the main reason he spent so long learning Master Jon Gardener's poem by heart, and the reason he has written it down. He does not quite believe some of the claims made for it – could a thief really be stopped from re-offending by washing his feet in rosemary-scented vinegar? Yet, if it helps him keep his memory and quickens his senses, maybe he should try some of his 'own' medicine?

There is just one small problem with the poem, and that is the instructions about saffron. Master Jon advised planting the saffron bulbs in September, and then said you could harvest the flowers in September! He had done as instructed and taken a large dibber and placed the bulbs three inches deep. And they had bloomed in the spring. No chance whatever of gathering those flowers on the feast of St Simon and St Jude.

Still trying to puzzle this out, he returns indoors and gathers up the vellum leaves bearing poems on the herbs of Master Jon and on blood-letting, and the precious notes about herbal cures, arranges them and folds them neatly in two so they can be stitched to make a pocket-book . . .

The scribe's name is not recorded. He did not sign his work. Remarkably, almost miraculously, his hand-crafted book, now more than six centuries old, survives in the library of the Wellcome Institute in London. The vellum has darkened, while the colours of the inks have altered little. Very fine scrollings in purple and scarlet sparkle on the folios. The blue is brilliant. Only the yellow has faded. The neat script, in purest black, is still easy to read.

'The virtues of herbs of Master Jon Gardener' is the earliest book about practical gardening in the English language. Several scribes wrote down the poem, and one particular version retains the distinctive signs of the dialect of English that was spoken in medieval Ireland. In other words, this is also the first Irish gardening book. We do not know who its original author was, perhaps a master-gardener in one of the royal manors in England, but one thing is certain: he grew rosemary and coleworts, parsley and saffron. As for the anonymous scribe who spoke English with an Irish accent, I imagine he was a kindly doctor who loved dabbling in his garden when there were no patients to see. He could weed in peace and quiet, to his heart's content without anyone annoying him. Given his skill in calligraphy he most probably was a monk, living in one of the great monasteries such as Greyabbey, Mellifont or Jerpoint.

To handle this little pocket-book, to turn its vellum leaves and read what he wrote about roses and lavender, saffron and rue, is a remarkable privilege. Like any good book, savoured, it provokes daydreams. His herbar, if it ever existed, has vanished – except in our imaginations.

The apothecary's rose, *Rosa gallica* 'Officinalis', from Provins, was a famous medicinal plant and remains an excellent garden shrub.
(© E. C. Nelson)

1.2
'BY A LITTLE INDUSTRY BROUGHT TO PERFECTION': JOHN K'EOGH'S *GENERAL IRISH HERBAL*

When I was writing on this Subject, I had the Advantage daily of Viewing the Gardens belonging to the Right Honourable James Lord Baron of KINGSTON; wherein were Contained near two hundred different Species of Herbs and Trees. I was not acquainted with any Garden, which could ſhew ſo many, this was no ſmall advantage, or Conveniency to forward this Undertaking.

ONE OF THE ODDEST BOOKS about gardening and gardens in Ireland is not at first sight even about gardens and cultivated plants. It has even got a spelling mistake in its title. BOTANALOGIA *UNIVERSALIS* Hibernica, Or, *A General IRISH* HERBAL . . . , 'Printed and ſold by GEORGE HARRISON at the Corner of Meeting houſe Lane' in 'Corke', and published in 1735, was one of three 'curious' works written by the Reverend John K'Eogh. Intended to provide 'true descriptions' of the herbs, shrubs and trees 'naturally produced' in Ireland, it was certainly not a gardening manual but a herbal of the 'usual medical type'. K'Eogh has been damned as unreliable, especially because his accounting of native Irish plants is sometimes rather suspect.

However, as the author himself noted in the preface, he had opportunities 'daily' to study the plants growing in Lord Kingston's garden – Mr K'Eogh was in fact chaplain to Lord Kingston and also, according to the book's dedication, to the Earl of Antrim. So, no matter how untrustworthy his records of native species may be, *Botanalogia Universalis Hibernica* contains some nuggets of information about what a well-stocked Irish garden, at least one attached to a large house, contained in the early 1730s. On the other hand, it needs to be noted that K'Eogh's experience of Irish gardens was

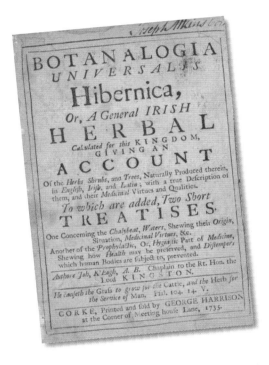

The title-page of John K'Eogh's herbal – the first word should have been spelled 'Botanologia' and is indeed correct elsewhere. K'Eogh ungraciously blamed George Harrison: 'By reason of the Authors distance from the Press, there are some ... Errors committed by the Printer, which I hope the Reader will excuse.' (Author's collection)

clearly rather limited, because there certainly existed at that period several containing many more than a mere two hundred different herbs and trees.

Baron Kingston's estate was at Mitchelstown in County Cork – 'it grows in the Lord Kingston's Garden in Mitchelstown' is an occasional refrain in K'Eogh's book. The less specific 'it grows in gardens' is much more common and together these comments allow us to reconstruct a vague notion of what was grown in the Mitchelstown demesne. The castle and garden which K'Eogh knew have long since vanished. The castle of his time was demolished in 1768 to make way for a Georgian mansion, which in turn was knocked down in 1823 and replaced by a Tudor-style mansion that was completely destroyed by fire in 1922. As for the garden, it was remodelled in the late eighteenth and early nineteenth centuries, and finally dismantled when the estate was parcelled out after 1922.

John K'Eogh leaves no doubt that there was a well-maintained and productive garden associated with Mitchelstown Castle in the early 1730s. This included a greenhouse, although the building would not have looked like a present-day one. While he did not state this greenhouse contained orange trees, he implies as much:

> Orange Trees grow Plentifully in forreign Counties, but of late years they have been tranſplanted here, which now by the Induſtry, and cultivation of curious Gentlemen, are in ſome Gardens brought to perfection . . .

The gardener charged with looking after Lord Kingston's oranges was clearly a skilful person: 'I have ſeen about ſeventy, or eighty [oranges], taken off of one Tree . . . as good as any I have ſeen brought hither from *Spain*, or the *Weſt Indies*'. Oranges were appropriate occupants of such a greenhouse, which would better have been called an orangery because it surely was built of brick, had a roof tiled with slates, not glass, and was probably fronted by double-casement windows. The orange trees will have been grown in large tubs that could be trundled out in summer to stand in the open air.

Oranges were not the only citrus fruits which 'by a little care and induſtry' flourished at Mitchelstown – not surprisingly there were lemons too:

> *Lemon-trees* are preſerved in this Country by ſeveral curious Gentlemen, in Green houſes, from the Inclemency of the Air, there are ſome of them to be ſeen in the Gardens of *Mitchelſtown* . . .

K'Eogh added, evidently from personal experience, that the leaves of the lemon trees have 'a very fragrant ſmell'.

A plant which K'Eogh named 'HERB ALOE or Sea Houſeleek' also grew in 'my Lord *Kingſton's* Green houſe.' Working out what this may have been proved quite simple because the Latin name that K'Eogh used, *Aloes Vulgaris ſive Sempervivum marinum*, was lifted straight from John Gerard's famous herbal, published a century earlier, in which it is described thus – 'Hearbe Alloe hath leaves . . . very broad, long, smooth, thick, bending backewards, notched in the edges, set with certain little blunt prickles . . . '. We would today call the plant *Aloe vera*, and it is certainly possible there was a plant of it growing in Mitchelstown during the 1730s.

Outdoors, the Mitchelstown gardens were planted with a range of medicinal and culinary herbs. One was 'licorice' which formed good roots 'as thick as a Mans finger, which is exceedingly pleaſant to the taſt'. The locally produced liquorice was much better than any that was imported, rather as home-grown greenhouse lemons were better than the imported ones which, K'Eogh noted, were never fully ripe.

ALOE VERA

'LADIES-MANTLE . . . had large, roundish Leaves, having eight Corners, finely serrated about the Edges, at their first Springing up, they are plaited or folded together . . . it grows in Gardens, and sometimes in Meadows, and Woods . . .' – judging by the description, John K'eogh knew this perennial well. (© E. C. Nelson)

Saffron grew 'to perfection' in Lord Kingston's garden, whereas scorzonera grew to 'great perfection'. The root of scorzonera, also known as Spanish salsify, was used as a vegetable, while presumably the red styles were harvested from the saffron crocus flowers for use in the kitchen and medicinally. Another plant 'particularly' grown in the Mitchelstown demesne was tobacco, but K'eogh makes no comments on its uses apart from his usual catalogue of medicinal ones: 'it prevents *Quinſies, Catarrhs, Megrims, Apoplexys,* and *Epidemical diſtempers* which proceed from the Malignity of the Air. Being externally applyed it cures *Itch, Scabs, Tetters,* and ſeveral other cuticular Eruptions.'

Occasionally K'eogh makes asides about other gardens that presumably he had visited, perhaps with Kingston's entourage. The myrtle, for example, was used for hedges at Lord Inchiquin's house at Rostellan on the eastern shore of Cork Harbour. Unconsciously illustrating the difference a relatively few miles can make in the climate of gardens, K'eogh remarked that myrtle was grown in the greenhouse at Mitchelstown. Bladder (or bastard) senna (*Colutea arborescens*) flourished in Robert

Fennell's garden near Mitchelstown – Fennell and Lord Inchiquin both subscribed for copies of K'Eogh's herbal.

The native Irish strawberry tree (*Arbutus unedo*) was exported from County Kerry in quantity during the seventeenth and eighteenth centuries because there are numerous records of it flourishing in Irish gardens as far removed from Killarney as Glenarm in County Antrim. John K'Eogh may have seen it in Kerry for his description of it is remarkably good (in parts):

> This is a ſmall tree, not much bigger than a Quince tree, the body thereof is covered with a reddiſh bark, which is rough and ſcaly, the Leaves are broad, thick, and ſerrated, the flowers are white, ſmall, & grow in cluſters, after which cometh the fruit like Strawberries, green at firſt, but afterwards yellowiſh, and at laſt red when ripe.

However he blundered by claiming that *Arbutus* blooms in spring – although there is a small chance that the exotic, spring-blooming *Arbutus andrachne* was grown at Mitchelstown.

One strange entry is for 'HONEY-TREE' for which K'Eogh provided the Latin name *Melianthus*. His enigmatic description includes the information that it bore a yellow flower 'which when gone, is ſucceeded by a Lump of Congealed *Honey*.' Whatever this tree was it grew 'commonly in My Lord *Kingſtons* Gardens in *Mitchelſtown*, where it is brought to great Perfection, with very little Cultivation or Induſtry.' I suspect he was referring to the honey-locust (*Gleditsia triacanthos*) although that is by no means certain. K'Eogh's names often have no modern counterpart and, to complicate matters further, he was sometimes confused by Latin names.

For the rest, we have to accept that the repeated 'it grows in gardens' referred to more than Mitchelstown. Among K'Eogh's more interesting comments are these. Vines, he noted, were planted in 'ſome Gardens, but ſeldom comes to any great perfection.' In his era, white poplar was 'planted

9

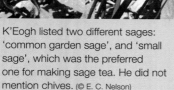

K'Eogh listed two different sages: 'common garden sage', and 'small sage', which was the preferred one for making sage tea. He did not mention chives. (© E. C. Nelson)

Rock samphire in the Burren. (© E. C. Nelson)

Maidenhair fern in the Burren. (© E. C. Nelson)

about Manſion houſes for Shelter, being of a quick growth.' Spanish (or sweet) chestnuts (*Castanea sativa*) were planted 'frequently . . . in Gardens, and Parks'. Potatoes, K'Eogh observed, are a 'very nouriſhing healthy food, which appears by the ſtrong [health], and robust Conſtitutions, of a vaſt number of the Natives who are almoſt intirely ſupported by them', which suggests that he did not much care to eat them himself.

As today, basil, borage, cabbages and peas, chervil and comfrey, dill and cucumbers, jasmine, leeks and onions, parsley and sage were all cultivated. Almonds, apples, walnut and fig trees are also noted. Plants that now would be considered purely of ornamental value – but were formerly also used medicinally – included cypress trees favoured because they were evergreen, peonies of several kinds, hollyhock, daffodils and lilies. K'Eogh noted white, red and damask roses.

John K'Eogh, a native of Strokestown in County Roscommon, was born about 1681, the second son of a renowned, scholarly cleric also called John who fathered twenty-one children, of whom only six survived into adulthood. Educated at Trinity College, Dublin, John junior followed his father's vocation and was ordained in the Church of Ireland. He married Elizabeth Jennings, and they had three sons and three daughters. After serving time as chaplain to Lord Kingston, K'Eogh obtained the living of the parish of Mitchelstown. No portrait is known to exist of John K'Eogh, who died in 1754, aged seventy-three.

Regarding native plants, I must defend him: K'Eogh was sometimes unreliable, but not always, and seems to have had an excellent knowledge of the plants of northwest County Clare, of the Burren and the Aran Islands. Rock samphire (*Crithmum maritimum*) he knew grew on rocks 'by the Sea ſide

The squirting cucumber (*Ecballium elaterium*) photographed in Crete – did K'Eogh really find it at Moycarnon in his home county? When ripe, the cucumber-like fruits explode and squirt out the seeds. (© E. C. Nelson)

Above, both photographs: 'DROPWORT . . . grows in gardens, and wild in the *Barony* of *Burrin*, in the *County* of *Clare*, flowering in *June* and *July*' – a plant photographed where K'Eogh reported the species, in the eastern lowlands of the Burren. (© E. C. Nelson)

very plentifully in the Iſles of Aaron, and in the weſt of the County of *Clare*' – no one knowing those localities could fault that. Writing about 'true' maidenhair fern (*Adiantum capillus-veneris*), K'Eogh stated that 'it grows on ſtone walls, and Rocks, the beſt in this Kingdom, is brought from the rocky mountains of *Burrin* in the *County* of *Clare*, where it grows plentifully, from thence it is brought in ſacks to *Dublin*, and ſold there.' He was the first to report dropwort (*Filipendula vulgaris*), which happens to be restricted to a relatively small part of the low-lying limestone of east Clare and southwest Galway. Another plant he described was squirting cucumber (*Ecballium elaterium*) – the description is accurate so he presumably saw it, especially bearing in mind that he noted it was grown in gardens (it was used to alleviate, among other complaints, the pain of gout), and was to be found 'in ſeveral places wild, as in *Moycarnon* in the County of Roſcommon.' No Irish botanical work has mentioned it since, but the barony of Moycarnon was not far distant from K'Eogh's home town. But wherever did he get the idea that the castor-oil plant (*Ricinus communis*) grew in the Burren, unless it was utter confusion about the name '*palma Christi*', which was also used in Gerard's herbal for the early-purple orchid which abounds in the Burren?

Eighteenth-century authors could never resist the chance to sermonise, and the Reverend Doctor John K'Eogh was no exception. He was prompted by the pleasant taste of home-grown liquorice and the bountiful orange trees, to remark: '. . . ſo you ſee, how by a little Induſtry, the moſt *Exotic* plants, may be brought to perfection, in this Country, which demonſtrates, what a fertile, prolific Land, we live in . . . '.

1.3
'CHARMING VIEWS EVERY WAY: & SWEET INEQUALITIES': DESIGN DESK 1765

IN 1765, the Very Reverend Thomas Paul had a tricky problem with the design of his garden, so he wrote to Joseph Spence, Esq. of Byfleet, Sussex to seek his assistance.

Dear Mr Spence

I take the liberty of sending this letter through our mutual friend Colonel Slaughter.

My wife and I want to create a new garden but are at a loss how to set about it as we don't want anything that is going to need an army of gardeners.

Enclosed is a very rough plan of the existing garden which extends for about 300 paces towards a small river. It's not level, but slopes this way and that.

We want something that will blend into the landscape which hereabouts is like a basket of eggs with little hummocky hills and watery places in between.

My wife is very fond of roses, so we hope you will include some in the plan.

No doubt the Colonel will be able to answer any queries you have.

Your humble and obedient servant
Thomas Paul

Nothing much has changed in almost two and a half centuries. Today we do just the same thing, except that adding a digital photograph or two helps to give the garden designer some extra clues about the tricky problem. In 1765 things were only a little different; there were no cameras of any kind but Mr Spence still needed to get to know the lie of the land.

Joseph Spence's client was the Dean of Cashel. At the time, Thomas Paul was also rector of the parish of Aughnamullen, in the Diocese of Clogher; its parish church lies between Cootehill and Ballybay in County Monaghan. The Dean and his wife obviously wanted to establish a new garden adjacent to the house they lived in. They had around 50 Irish acres of land (about 80 statute acres) encompassing the house, all of it set as pasture. There was also a kitchen garden on the 'foreside' of the house and, evidently, it served its role more than adequately.

To get the project started, Thomas Paul sent a sketch plan of the existing garden to Spence. The plot was not quite two Irish acres, facing north, bounded on the east and west by straight hedges and with another hedge across the centre. The land sloped towards a 'very pretty' trout stream, although the view of the stream from the house was probably obscured by a curving hedge along the stream bank: when asked if the water was visible from the lower rooms of the house, the Dean replied that it was, although that does not necessarily mean it could be seen at that time. It was not exactly an exciting garden.

Spence responded with a series of questions, and Paul duly supplied answers.

Q: 'What Views; on each side? What pleasing walk, on the left hand, at bottom?'

A: 'Charming Views every way: & Sweet Inequalities.'

It is not hard to imagine the landscape around: drumlins, lushly pastured, with little loughs, or bogs, in the hollows between.

Q: 'What the size, swiftness, color, and course of the river?'

A: 'A very pretty clear stream, with trout.'

Spence wanted to remove the hedge along the stream to open up the view, and so he asked whether the stream itself could serve as a 'fence' between the garden and the field opposite. 'Yes', replied the Dean.

Apr: 13, 65.
40 f. to 1 Inch

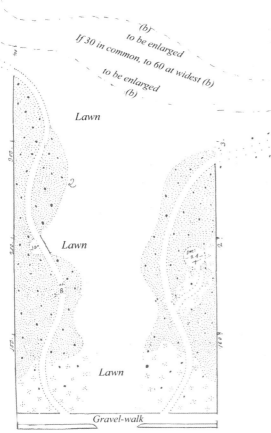

Joseph Spence's draft plan for Thomas Paul's garden in County Cavan. The clusters of dots close to the house represent 'studs'; the stippled areas are the 'groves'. Based on the original manuscript in the Beinecke Rare Books and Manuscript Library, Yale University.

Above: Wild broom was to be planted in the garden. (© E. C. Nelson)

Left: The native wild cherry, with its white blossoms, is a much neglected tree – Joseph Spence appreciated its value. (© E. C. Nelson)

Having got the answers he needed, Spence did some thinking and responded on 13 April 1765 with a plan for a new-look garden. To begin, he proposed a gravel walk, 200 feet by 20 feet running east/west in front of the house. From this, two serpentine paths, one either side of the garden, wound towards the stream which, Spence proposed, should be widened to 60 feet. The hedge was to be removed. Within the garden Spence suggested an irregularly shaped lawn: he had earlier asked:

Q: 'Whether the lawn-part might not be fed at times by Sheep: with a careful boy?'

The Dean's splendidly ambiguous reply was 'Yes, or rather, Two' – boys or sheep?

The winding paths were to go on beyond the garden proper. The one on the west side, Spence suggested, should be carried on along the stream and then around the field – 'or round all Mr Dean's fields, if several', and eventually return to a small garden door that would allow anyone out for a stroll back on to the gravel in front of the house. The same was thoughtfully suggested for the eastern path, 'so that Mr Dean might have a dry walk in half an hour after a shower, all around his domain whenever he should choose it'. These outer pathways would not be mere grassy lanes. They would have trees planted along them to give shade 'as well as ornament'. Near the stream, a variety of willows would be planted: weeping willow, yellow-barked Dutch willow and swallow-tail willow. Away from the water's edge, oaks, beech and firs were proposed.

The mock-orange is another shrub with fragrant flowers in summer.

Mezereon is a beautifully perfumed winter-flowering shrub.

So much for paths. Now to the main garden's plants. This was to be no colourless garden! In fact, Joseph Spence's planting plan seems to come right out of the post-Robinsonian era – but William Robinson's book *The Wild Garden* would not be published for another century. Spence wanted a mixture of shrubs with scattered trees to form the plantations – he called them groves – on either side of the lawn. A summer house, reached by a short, winding path, could be concealed in the eastern grove. Nearest to the main house, he wanted the best available flowering shrubs: a wonderful mixture of perfumed lilacs and mock-orange (*Philadelphus*), with guelder-roses, laburnum, double-flowered peaches and cherries. Intermingled with these would be trees such as mountain ash and strawberry tree, with broom, laurels and other evergreens. Farther from the house, in the part of the garden close to the stream, Spence suggested locust (*Robinia pseudoacacia*), larches, almonds and wild white-blossomed cherries, with Scots and Weymouth pines, silver firs and more evergreens.

The lowest and most pleasing things, should be scattered in or very near the margins. The most pleasing wild flowers should be supplied largely, all about the groves, but particularly so towards the walks and margins. Primroses, violets, cowslips, wood strawberries, etc.

Native wild flowers in a Cavan rectory garden! Spence was brimming over with ideas, and did not end there. He wanted studs for roses, jasmine and honeysuckle. The studs were tall, supporting tripods or cones, maybe made from hazel or willow. He was very specific about what he wanted done – this was not a formal garden with everything and its mirror-image precisely placed.

Here a damask rose with two jasmines. There a Provence rose with a couple of white mezereons. A cabbage rose with two Dutch honeysuckles in a third. A moss rose, alone, in a fourth: and so on. With as much variety as can be.

He was enjoying this, and it would be very fragrant – jasmines, honeysuckles and mezereons (*Daphne mezereon*) would pour their perfumes into the Ulster air.

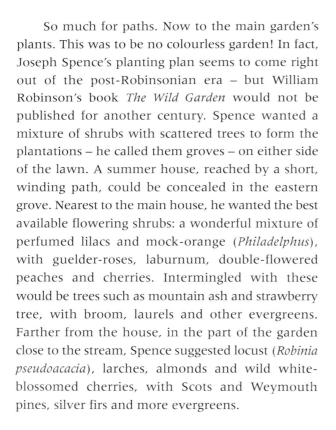

Joseph Spence's list of shrubs included moss roses, so called because the flowers and stems are 'mossy'.

Above: Spence suggested different roses, including the "Rosa Mundi", *Rosa gallica* 'Versicolor'. (© E. C. Nelson)

Centre: For lingering perfume in the evening, the native woodbine or honeysuckle is hard to beat. (© E. C. Nelson)

Right: Cowslips were among the 'most pleasing wild flowers' that Spence recommended 'all about the groves'. (© E. C. Nelson)

This variety might be greatly helped by planting one of the afore-named red roses (Damask, Provence, Cabbage, or Moss) with a white rose, in one stud. Two whites with a red in another: and two reds with a white in a third. The same alternative might be tried with Rosa Mundi and with the yellow rose, if you can get good ones. And the jasmines, white or yellow; or with white and red mezereons.

Then down to practical matters. The studs were to be set either in circular beds at least 4½ feet in diameter, or in ovals, which would be dug and kept clean by hoeing. The edges of the beds were to be not less than 10 to 12 feet apart to allow for mowing the lawn between them – the practicalities were thought of, too.

Having coped with the plants, Joseph Spence concluded with a more conventional proposition. Bearing in mind the very pretty hill in the upper part of the field to the west of the garden, he wrote:

> If this would deserve a building on it better, the summer house mentioned for the grove might be omitted there, and built on that hill, and the walk might wind up to that summer house or temple, towards its conclusion, and down from it to the gravel-walk door.

Did the rector and his wife follow Joseph Spence's blueprint? We simply cannot tell. This is the kind of garden that leaves no trace after two centuries and more. This rectory garden, if it flourished, lacked many of the fashionable ornaments of most large eighteenth-century Irish gardens – grottos, allées, temples (although one was suggested in place of a summer house). It was in many ways before its time.

Postscript. Everything written about this garden is contained in Joseph Spence's papers; only the introductory letter from Dean Paul is due to the present author's imagination. In 1837 the Ecclesiastical Commissioners reported that Aughnamullen glebe house was built in 1775 by Thomas Paul, at the cost of £848 14s 0¼d, paid out of his private funds. This 'handsome and commodious' glebe house had 40 acres of grounds. As it was built ten years after Spence was consulted, it might be concluded that the garden Spence designed was for another house owned or leased by the rector and his wife before this glebe house was built. It may, of course, have been on the same site; this is suggested by the coincidence in the figures provided to Spence, which indicate that in 1765 the Pauls' residence had 40 acres attached.

1.4
'THE PRETTIEST ORANGERY IN THE WORLD'

WHEN MRS MARY DELANY arrived at her new home, Delville, in the village of Glasnevin to the north of Dublin at around 11 o'clock on the morning of Wednesday 28 June 1744, she was most impatient to see the place. 'Never was seen a sweeter dwelling,' she wrote to her sister. Three weeks later, Mary penned a longer description of the garden while admitting that 'describing it puzzles me extremely.' There was a bowling green at the back of the house, and a little brook, fruit trees, roses, and lots more, as well as a 'full view of Dublin harbour.' She continued, almost breathlessly:

> On the left hand of the bowling-green is a terrace-walk that takes in a sort of a parterre, that will make the prettiest orangery in the world, for it is an oval of green, planted round in double rows of elm-trees and flowering shrubs with little grass walks between them, which will give a good shelter to exotics.

Mrs Mary Delany.

'Orangery' was not a new word in English – it had been around for a while, borrowed from the French, and spelled, at first, 'orangerie'. It originally was applied to any part of a garden where orange trees were grown. Be all that as it may, Mrs Delany's exclamation that the Delville parterre 'will make the prettiest orangery in the world' is the third example quoted in the *Oxford English Dictionary* of the word's use. Gradually, 'orangery' came to mean something more specific – an airy building specially built so that orange trees, and other tender exotics, could be grown in cold climates.

The golden apples of the sun

To us today, piles of oranges in greengrocers or supermarkets are not objects of romance – they are mundane. On the other hand, orange trees are still a little mysterious and romantic, and you still need a frost-free glasshouse to keep them in during the winter – global warming has not progressed so far that oranges and lemons can be kept outdoors all the year round in Ireland.

Oranges are not native plants and did not grow anywhere in Europe in ancient times yet legends about golden apples – χρυσομηλιά, chrysomelia – suggest that the Ancient Greeks at least possessed a skimpy knowledge of oranges long before they were introduced to cultivation around the Mediterranean. Greek myths relate that trees bearing fabulous golden apples grew in the garden of the Hesperides, who were three beautiful nymphs, situated at the western corner of the world. The golden-apple trees had been a gift from Gaia to her daughter Hera when she wed Zeus,

Delville House in the village of Glasnevin was the 'best belov'd retreat' of Mary Delany and her second husband, Dr Patrick Delany. This house was demolished in the mid-twentieth century.

king of the gods. The trees were guarded by Ladon, a ferocious, hundred-headed, never-sleeping dragon, and it was the unfortunate Heracles' eleventh task to steal those golden apples.

Growing oranges for their fragrant blossom and juicy fruits became a European passion after the mid-sixteenth century, and that passion had dramatic consequences not only for horticulture and its technology but also for architecture.

Oranges come in many flavours, sweet, sour and all grades in between. Where did these fruits originate? They have been so widely cultivated for so long that, like most other domesticated plants, the wild originals have been lost sight of in a welter of cultivated varieties. Recent genetic studies indicate that the progenitors of cultivated oranges, lemons and other citrus fruits were probably indigenous to the warmer parts of southeastern Asia, the islands of Melanesia and Australia. The 'wild' lemon, for example, apparently arose in southeastern Asia and, while known to the Arabs by the tenth century, took another two centuries to reach Europe. The sour Seville orange perhaps comes originally from Cochin-China (Vietnam) – it also spread westwards towards Europe and thence, on one of Columbus' voyages, to the New World. The sweet orange followed; some inferior varieties were grown in Mediterranean lands by the late fifteenth century. The Chinese being such experienced and

skilful gardeners had selected better, sweeter forms, which the Portuguese plundered and brought to Europe in about 1520. We do not know when the first orange trees were grown in Ireland – perhaps in the late 1600s. In the early 1720s lemon and orange trees were being imported from Holland by the Huguenots based in Portarlington.

At the end of the sixteenth century, John Gerard, the great Elizabethan herbalist, wrote that 'Citron, lemon and Orange trees do grow especially on the sea coasts of Italy . . . there is also great store of them in Spain . . .' but the gardeners of north-western Europe had an almost intractable problem: the orange tree is a subtropical plant so there was no hope of a bush thriving during foggy, frosty winters. Each tender orange tree had to be cosseted and protected from cold and damp, yet when this was done well they bore fruit abundantly.

Orange butter and orange-flower bread

Let us return to Delville, 'best belov'd retreat' of Mrs Delany and her husband, the Dean of Down, Dr Patrick Delany. We do not have an exact record of when Mary Delany acquired the trees with which to create the pretty orangery but we can be certain they had arrived by 1748.

The Delanys often entertained. A procession of visitors is reported in Mary's letters. Sometimes she mentioned what was served for lunch. Delville had

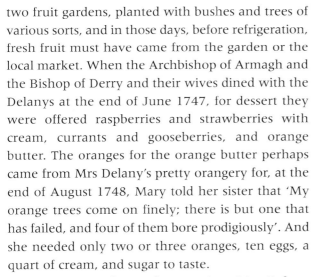

The flowers of the orange are opening in spring just as the fruit set by the previous year's blossoms are ripe. (© E. C. Nelson)

Ripe oranges – were these the golden apples of the Hesperides? (© E. C. Nelson)

two fruit gardens, planted with bushes and trees of various sorts, and in those days, before refrigeration, fresh fruit must have came from the garden or the local market. When the Archbishop of Armagh and the Bishop of Derry and their wives dined with the Delanys at the end of June 1747, for dessert they were offered raspberries and strawberries with cream, currants and gooseberries, and orange butter. The oranges for the orange butter perhaps came from Mrs Delany's pretty orangery for, at the end of August 1748, Mary told her sister that 'My orange trees come on finely; there is but one that has failed, and four of them bore prodigiously'. And she needed only two or three oranges, ten eggs, a quart of cream, and sugar to taste.

Just as we do not know when Mrs Delany acquired her orange trees, we do not have any exact information about how she managed them. They must have been kept indoors in the winter but it seems that there was no special greenhouse for them. The Delanys sometimes took tea in their orangery, enjoying the fragrance in more ways than one. In another of her letters, Mary mentioned that she had been in the kitchen helping to make 'orange-flower bread of my own orange flowers, of which I am not a little proud.' I have not traced a contemporary recipe for orange-flower bread, but the heavily fragrant flowers must have infused the bread with a wonderful aroma, and they would have been freshly picked.

Orangeries and glasshouses

'I am now considering about a green house, and believe I shall build one this spring; my orange trees thrive *so well* they deserve one': so Mrs Delany wrote to her brother in January 1751. Yet that is a trifle odd, for less than a month before she had 'taken a run along my portico walk into the greenhouse' where she picked an 'orange-leaf and a yellow Indian jessamine' to send to her sister: 'I wish they may not lose their sweetness before they kiss your hands.' Possibly that greenhouse was bursting at the seams, and the orange trees needed more space – not long after this Mary sought advice on pruning them.

Gardeners, being an ingenious breed, set about erecting houses to protect their orange trees with enthusiasm and flair. At first they constructed little huts for the trees, and lit fires in them to keep the oranges warm in winter. But oranges do not like living in dark, smoky sheds even for a few months each winter. Grander buildings were needed – architects were called in and special houses were designed. The newfangled orange-houses had

19

south-facing, high casement windows that let in as much light as possible. In these grand edifices – orangeries – little else was grown but the precious orange and lemon trees.

A typical eighteenth-century orangery, such as the fine one at Marino Point on the shores of Cork Harbour, had a slate roof but that only darkened the orangery, so when roofs of glass could be built, orangeries lost their slates and evolved into greenhouses and conservatories. The most elaborate orangeries were beautiful buildings, centrally heated, with flues incorporated into their north walls. The trees were grown in huge containers that could be moved outside in summer, so that the oranges could enjoy the clear air and bright sun. The tubs were trundled back indoors when winter beckoned and the plants settled down in the warm, bright orangery, well protected from frost. Few other exotic plants have received so much attention. No other plant has lent its name to an entire class of buildings.

And so again to fragrant Delville, 'blissful seat'. We have no evidence that the Delanys constructed an elaborate orangery. Indeed, in June 1751, Mary's thank-you to her brother indicates she – or at least her gardener – had recently hauled the orange trees out for the summer.

> I thank you for your kind hint about my orange-trees; when is the proper time for trimming them? I have lost one of the variegated sort; it died of an apoplexy – was in appearance healthy when I brought it out the 20th May with the rest of my trees, and in a day or two it dropped. I have not the heart to trim them now – they are so thick budded to blossom.

The next summer Mrs Delany revealed that she was adept at budding and grafting – the term she used was 'inoculate': 'I have just inoculated two orange trees of my own raising and have planted 26 myrtles in my orangerie.' This seems to indicate that the 'oval of green, planted round in double rows of elm-trees and flowering shrubs', now also had a myrtle hedge. And the oranges must have gone on

The eighteenth-century orangery at Marino Point, County Cork, shortly after restoration in the late 1970s. (© E. C. Nelson)

thriving because in 1759 Mary wrote: 'You talk of candied orange flowers; pray is it clear candy. If it is, I should be excessively glad of the receipt.'

Oh that I were an orange tree, That busy plant!

Oranges, as Mary Delany learned, are useful, busy plants, evergreen and ornamental, with opening flowers and ripe fruits at the same time. They yield aromatic leaves, juicy fruits and fragrant flowers. The peel can be candied; the juice is refreshing; the whole is delightful as marmalade. The flowers are pure white and long-lasting, perfect for scenting breads and cakes, and for romantic wedding bouquets: in the nineteenth century, in the 'language of flowers', orange blossom was transmuted into a symbol of chastity and bridal festivity.

Mary Eales' receipt for orange butter from her book *The Compleat Confectioner*; a third edition was published in 1742 and may well have been used by Mary Delany.

To make Orange-Butter
Take the rind of two or three Oranges, and boil them very tender; then beat them very fine in a Mortar, and rub them thro' an Hair Sieve; then take a Quart of Cream, boil it, and put in the Yolks of ten Eggs, and the Whites of two; beat the Eggs very well before you put then in the boiling Cream; stir it all one Way, 'till it is a Curd; then whey it in a Strainer; when it is gold, mix in as much of the Orange as you think will make it taste as you wou'd have it; then sweeten it as you like it.

1.5
'WHEN THE SWIFT APPEARS, TURN OUT THE GREENHOUSE': CRANMORE AND JOHN TEMPLETON, ULSTER'S PIONEER PLANTSMAN

❧❧❧

NO PORTRAIT OF JOHN TEMPLETON is known, but a word-picture can be formed. He was, wrote the Reverend Thomas Hincks, very modest and unassuming, not prone to 'vain and ostentatious displays' like the great Swedish naturalist, his hero, Dr Carl Linnaeus. I can imagine John in his garden, in a sober frock-coat, dark britches and white stockings, the usual attire of gentleman during the late eighteenth-century, carefully weeding the flower-beds by hand, taking cuttings of his recent acquisitions, ensuring that the bud-wood and stocks of the grafts that he made were well-matched, and tending the pots of newly sown seeds. A hands-on gardener, to be sure.

Cranmore House in the early 1850s; lithograph by A. McQuillan of an original drawing by E. M.

The garden surrounded his family home at Malone, which in the 1790s was little more than a tangle of country lanes rather than a posh suburb of Belfast. The property boasted some very fine sweet chestnuts that had been planted in the 1600s, and these particular trees gave the house one of its names, for it was called either Cranmore – from the Irish, *crann mór*, great tree – or, when it was expedient, Orange Grove. How large the garden was we do not know, but we can say that it was full of the most interesting plants available. John Templeton was also the archetypal, acquisitive, adventurous plantsman, a 'breed', one might say, that seems to flourish in Ireland's northern counties.

Born in Belfast in 1766, John began to take an interest in gardening when he was about twenty years old 'and soon made his flower-garden an object of attention'. In 1793, according to Mr Hincks, Templeton laid out an experimental garden in what was formerly an orchard and osiery. A stream was redirected to pass through the new garden; this probably formed the serpentine pond that survived long after John's death. A rock-garden was created. Into this place Templeton brought 'from various parts of the world, rare and useful plants, which he endeavoured to naturalize in this climate'. That is the nub of his pioneering horticulture.

He had his own methods for germinating seeds. 'I never apply artificial heat', he wrote. 'In sowing seeds I think great numbers are lost by sowing too deep'. So he sowed seeds on the surface of the soil: 'Nature sows on the surface and leaves to chance the covering of them by leaves or Moss.' Following this principle, John put a thick wad of chopped moss over freshly sown seeds; he knew that this would keep the soil in the pots moist even in summer – 'all the watering that is necessary, is just to keep the [soil] dark color'd' – while in winter the moss blanket 'prevented the plants from being affected with frost'.

Just as we don't know what John Templeton looked like, we have no contemporary images of his

Dog's tooth violets were planted under the trees at Cranmore. (© E. C. Nelson)

The Australasian tea-tree, *Leptospermum scoparium*, was among the recently introduced, southern-hemisphere plants that John Templeton treasured. (© E. C. Nelson)

garden – he was no mean botanical artist but he did not leave us any views of Cranmore. It is most unlikely that the garden was a formal one, because the sorts of plants John acquired were not the ones that lend themselves to formality – indeed there were so many different plants that formality would have been impossible. Cranmore's plant-list has such a present-day ring about it that I fancy John's garden would not look out of place today. There were magnolias including the wonderful bull-bay (*Magnolia grandiflora*), an array of sun-roses (*Cistus*), such alpine delights as spring gentians and *Hepatica nobilis* in variety (including 'double red' and 'single white'), shade-lovers like dog's-tooth violets (*Erythronium dens-canis*), not to mention rhododendrons, numerous roses, phloxes, red-hot pokers, daffodils, day-lilies and heathers.

Over the years he grew at least a dozen different azaleas, two dozen species of bellflowers (*Campanula*), fifteen different crocuses including the saffron crocus, eighteen distinct irises and as many different lilies, and a dozen peonies including the moutan from China. Saxifrages were a particular favourite – nearly three dozen are named, and quite a few of these were varieties of native Irish species. As for trees, there was a grove of larch, and numerous specimen maples, limes, elms, yews and oaks,

along with ten different pines, and the famous, slow-growing variety of Norway spruce, *Picea abies* 'Clanbrassiliana', from Lord Clanbrassil's demesne at Tollymore near Newcastle in County Down. In 1813, Templeton obtained a young plant of the eastern North American swamp-cypress (*Taxodium distichum*) from a local nurseryman and, after planting it at Cranmore, tied a piece of horse-hair rope around its trunk 'to prevent snails from climbing up'.

The Cranmore garden also produced fruit and vegetables, undoubtedly for the family's use – John had married Katherine Johnson on 21 December 1799, and the couple eventually had a son and four daughters. The list of fruits is impressive: raspberries, strawberries, gooseberries, greengages, plums, cherries, currants, black grapes and, although some of the orchard had become a flower garden, pears and apples in variety. Potatoes, peas, beans, 'yellow Dutch' and 'Swedish' turnips, early purple broccoli, lettuce, kale, cabbages (the varieties 'sugar loaf', 'early dwarf York', 'Pomfret', 'Penton or Portuguese' included) were grown in the Barn Garden.

To John Templeton it seems that all plants were interesting and worthy of cultivation. He was not averse to bringing in plants from local ditches, or from Ulster's mountains, bogs and coasts. For example, at Greyabbey, County Down, in 1793,

John found a plant of native bog rosemary (*Andromeda polifolia*) which had beautifully ridged, five-sided bells, brighter and larger than usual, with a dark stripe along each ridge. It was one of the jewels of Cranmore, regularly propagated from cuttings – 'I have had it in my garden', he wrote shortly before his death in 1825, 'where it has not altered'. There was a crowberry (*Vaccinium vitis-idaea*) too, from a bog near Ballynahinch, which was unusual in having serrated, wavy leaves – I wonder if it might still grow thereabouts? For a few years at least John carefully cultivated a white-flowered harebell found on the Newtownards Road – it was in bloom on 1 August 1812. But his famous find was the Irish rose, a natural hybrid between the dog rose (*Rosa canina*) and the burnet rose (*Rosa pimpinellifolia*) which he thoughtfully named *Rosa × hibernica*. Templeton discovered this growing 'On the Road side going from Belfast to the Village of Hollywood' in about 1793. He propagated the rose, presumably either by cuttings or grafting (at which he was clearly adept), and gave young plants to such notables as the London nurserymen William Curtis and Samuel Dickson. It's a lovely, simple rose and still survives in a few gardens, although the original colony at Holywood has long since been exterminated.

Not all the native plants that John brought to Cranmore survived. One casualty was cowbane (*Cicuta virosa*), a highly poisonous member of the carrot family: 'Having brought some of this plant [from the Blackwater] to a pond in my Garden 2 tame Widgeon totally destroyed it without suffering the least injury from 2 or 3 plentifull meals.' The widgeons seem to have enjoyed a charmed existence at Cranmore for around a decade, and John was amused to observe them courting one another.

What of the plants the widgeons didn't snack on? It is very likely that John Templeton was the first to grow several newly discovered Australian plants out of doors in Ireland, including gum-trees (*Eucalyptus*), bottle-brushes (*Callistemon*) and mimosa (*Acacia*) as well as an uncounted number of other exotics. It was John Templeton, I am sure, who discovered the joy of growing *Fuchsia* outside

The Irish rose, *Rosa × hibernica*, was discovered by John Templeton at Holywood, County Down; it survives today in gardens but has been exterminated from its original habitat.
(John Templeton's original illustration)

and getting larger, more highly coloured blooms than on pot-bound specimens grown indoors. As for *Camellia*, also grown out in the open-air, one of the shrubs he planted was still alive at Cranmore in 1856 and so was around six decades old.

Thoughtful, observant, enquiring, he reasoned out horticultural techniques for himself from what he knew about Ireland's native plants. For example, noticing that established deciduous trees provided sufficient shelter to protect less hardy subjects – brambles and bracken growing under such trees stayed green longer than plants out in the open – he planted many of his new acquisitions, raised from seed, in sheltered situations beneath trees and, remarkably, many thrived. Templeton, remember, did not have the Internet or a vast array of well-written, illustrated gardening manuals to consult – for many plants he had no information whatsoever, perhaps not even a name, certainly no fund of hard-won knowledge garnered by other gardeners. He had to take risks with his precious seedlings and young cuttings. How to be successful

Above: Cranmore House in ruins, January 1992. (© E. C. Nelson)

Far Left: Southern heath, *Erica australis*, was one of several heathers grown out of doors at Cranmore; it is a Mediterranean species. (© E. C. Nelson)

Left: The Irish rose, *Rosa × hibernica* (© E. C. Nelson)

with the cultivation of many exotic plants was, in the 1790s, as much 'uncharted territory' as the places whence they came – Botany Bay and the Cape of Good Hope, for example. In February 1793, he wrote:

> I am confident that if many plants that are now found too tender for our climate, were planted under the thick shade of trees, they would be found sufficiently hardy to stand our winters. I have at present a small Passiflora cærulea, climbing on a tree covered with ivy, that stood a frost when ice was 3½ inches thick, and which killed a large plant against a south-facing wall. I have likewise a plant of the Ficus stipulata which has grown against a large Chestnut tree, last winter and this, without seeming at present affected with the Cold, an Erica tubiflora of near four feet high has stood out so far of this winter, by having some Broom branches stuck about and over it.

To have grown any of the Cape heaths – heathers native to the Cape of Good Hope in southern Africa – outside, getting one to four feet in height with only a wigwam of broom for protection against frost, was no small achievement. Templeton's *Erica tubiflora* was most probably *Erica curviflora* which bears tubular, yellow, orange or red flowers that are curved.

John had a keen interest in the weather, and gauged the severity of a winter by the thickness of the ice – it was never more than an inch thick during the 'uncommonly mild' winter of 1788–89, but on 22 December 1796, at 8.30 in the morning, 'Ice on a pond in my Garden 2 inches thick, bore 7 stone Weight' – the temperature was then 12° Fahrenheit below freezing. The three-and-a-half inches of pond-ice which signalled the end to the passionflower suggests a very severe frost.

When a few clicks of a computer mouse will provide detailed weather reports for Botany Bay and sundry other places, we may wonder what the gardener two centuries ago, without the benefit even of a local weather forecast on radio, did to predicate the destruction of plants or anticipate the arrival of warmer weather? Watch the birds!

> When the woodcock, fieldfare, and other winter birds of passage, appear unusually soon and in uncommon numbers, we have every reason to expect a severe winter . . . We should accordingly provide ourselves with shelter, food, and suitable raiment; and the attentive gardener, protection for his tender plants. But when the swift appears, let him turn out the inhabitants of his green-house.

1.6
'. . . 'MONGST THE GREEN MOSSY BANKS & WILD FLOWERS': CORK BOTANIC GARDEN 1808–1828

A ROUND TWO CENTURIES AGO, near Evergreen and not far from 'the banks of my own lovely Lee', there was a remarkable botanical garden in which you would have seen the painted lady anemone-flowered dahlia for the first time, some native butterworts, and cauliflowers sporting straw hats. Yet that place is almost forgotten, one of Ireland's 'lost' gardens, probably because it flourished for no more than twenty years.

In fact, the garden still exists, an oasis of green, sheltering some interesting weeds, left-overs from cultivation no doubt – the Caucasian crested field-speedwell and Oxford ragwort, for example. Remarkably, too, in the collective memory of the citizens of Cork, the locality continued to bear its short-lived title long after that botanical garden ceased to be. It was not unusual for notices in Cork newspapers, until the 1890s at least, to include such announcements as: 'Funeral . . . for the Botanic Gardens . . . at 3 o'clock. R. I. P.'

This garden story starts in the first decade of the nineteenth century when a Presbyterian clergyman and keen amateur naturalist, Thomas Hincks, persuaded the 'respectable inhabitants of Cork' to establish the Cork Institution, an organisation modelled on the Dublin Society. The Institution came into being in 1802 and in 1806, driven on by Hincks, its members began to discuss forming a botanical garden 'in which agricultural improvement will be particularly attended to, without, however, neglecting whatever may appear useful in botany.'

'Our business is now a Gardener'

Thus, in 1808, six years after it was formed, the Cork Institution took a lease on some suitable land 'in the rich tract between Friars Well & Evergreen, leading towards Ballyphehane bog.' Lying to the southeast of the city, the plot comprised nearly six Irish acres (four hectares), then mainly under grass but divided also into a cabbage field, a small flower garden and a central walled garden. There was a 'good pump' so water was not a problem. Hincks quickly set about the task of finding a suitable gardener to superintend the new garden. 'We wish to have one well versed in Botany & Gardening – so as to be capable of directing & instructing, & we wish to have such a person as soon as possible', Hincks wrote, in a letter to James Mackay, the young Scot who had been in charge at the new Trinity College Botanic Garden in Ballsbridge, Dublin, for the previous few years. Mackay was ideally placed to help, because he had many friends and contacts back home in Scotland – and Scotland was the place that provided the most skilful gardener-botanists of the period. Hincks was able to set down the new gardener's general responsibilities: 'He would have a greenhouse to superintend, some fruit trees, a shrubbery & perhaps a small nursery – to have all Irish plants . . . and perhaps an aquatic garden.' After some negotiations, early in June 1808, James Drummond, who came from the county of Angus in eastern Scotland, was selected. Hincks wrote again to Mackay:

> I should like to know what quantity of coal and candle you think necessary, that we may offer accordingly . . . We have a house on the ground containing a kitchen and some out-offices – a sitting room of tolerable size on the first floor with one or two small bedrooms – and 2 garetts. We shall have this repaired and made neat and comfortable. We shall also furnish it in a neat but plain manner. We shall not wish to be extravagant, neither would we be deficient in what is reasonable.

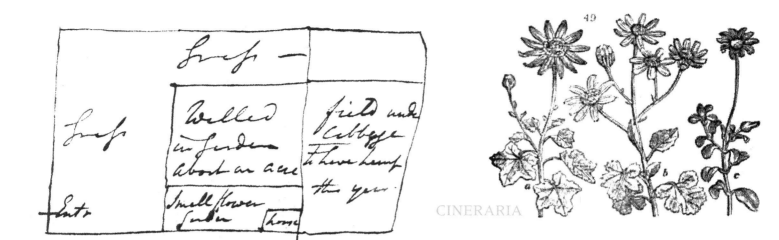

CINERARIA

The Cork Botanic Garden was established at Evergreen on a site that had a walled garden, a house and small flower garden, a cabbage field and lots of grass; a sketch plan by the Reverend William Hincks. (By courtesy of the School of Botany, Trinity College, Dublin)

Thus, the 21-year old Drummond, 'a long headed young Scotchman with a broader dialect that I ever before heard, and . . . an excellent Botanist', arrived in Cork during the summer of 1808 and began to make his mark. Within a short time he had clearly made much progress – the garden was described in 1809 by one visitor as 'extensive and judiciously laid out'. Another took a slightly different view:

> . . . to judge of the future by what has been already effected promises to do great credit . . . The ground is extensive, well situated, though not having the advantage of any bog or marsh land. . . It is well arranged and well managed as Mr Drummond the chief Gardener seems fully equal to the duties of his situation.

'Sweet Ladies' Traces'

The garden did not occupy all of James Drummond's time. He began to explore the countryside for plants, probably at first to help establish the living collection of native species. He used the garden network too, obtaining plants from whoever was willing to donate them, including his nurserymen friends. The Cork countryside provide a few notable gems. The lovely large-flowered St John's-wort (*Hypericum calycinum*) familiar as the so-called Rose of Sharon, which is an excellent ground-cover plant, evidently was already well established in the county. James found it 'in great abundance 3 miles from Cork in the way to Bandon', and he must have brought some roots back to Evergreen. Hincks sent flowering material on to London and there a specimen was painted for illustrating the *English Botany* of Sir James Edward Smith. In Drummond's opinion, at that time, the St John's-wort was 'perfectly wild' – he later changed his view writing that 'I have some doubts on the subject'. Its habitat on the Bandon road was destroyed soon afterwards.

Another significant find was not in flower in July 1809 when Drummond happened upon it. However, he 'brought roots of this newly discovered species to his garden' and in the spring of 1810 the plants blossomed. By comparing the flowers, twice as large as those of the common species, Drummond realised he had found the large-flowered butterwort (*Pinguicula grandiflora*) one of the gems of the flora of the southwest of Ireland. 'I first observed this beautiful plant . . . in bogs near Macromp, and since, in many other parts of Cork

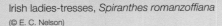

Irish ladies-tresses, *Spiranthes romanzoffiana*
(© E. C. Nelson)

Part of St Joseph's Cemetery today. (© Tony O'Mahony)

and Kerry.' Again specimens were despatched by Hincks to London to be painted for Smith's flora, and in later years Drummond sent plants of this insectivorous native to other gardens. Not bad going for just two years, but there were more interesting plants waiting Drummond's eagle-eye.

Piecing together the fragments of the tale, while James was botanising near Castletownbere in west Cork during the summer of 1810, he noticed an orchid with lovely white flowers arranged in a three-row spiral. They were in a 'marshy spot of ground by the sea shore' on the northern shore of Bantry Bay. He dug up some plants – not then regarded as a disreputable activity. Each one had a pair of thick, fleshy roots about three inches long that tapered to a blunt tip – these roots were downy, he noted. Drummond 'sent home several plants hoping to propagate it – but rats destroyed the roots', although enough material remained for Hincks, once again, to despatch specimens to Sir James Smith. The pressed and dried, rat-nibbled fragments survive to this day, testimony to Drummond's discovery of 'Proliferous Ladies' Traces', now dubbed Irish

lady's-tresses (*Spiranthes romanzoffiana*), a beautiful orchid that has since cropped up, but is still very rare, in other western and northern counties.

'They have very bad vegetables in Cork'

I cannot imagine that that response, prompted by his interview with the Commissioners of Irish Education Inquiry on 27 September 1826, did anything to endear James Drummond to Cork's resident market-gardeners. Yet, throughout his time as curator of the Cork Institution's Botanic Garden, he had tried to follow the original precept that the Reverend Thomas Hincks had expressed – 'In short we want to improve the county . . .'. In the 1820s the Brussels sprout was not grown in Cork – Drummond introduced the vegetable. 'They have very bad vegetables in Cork, and it would be desirable to introduce some good kinds . . . I have introduced from England a great many things, new and valuable fruit trees and other things.'

He made various experiments, reported in contemporary horticultural periodicals and repeated in books for years to come, on the cultivation of

E.D.Smith delt

Watts sculpt

London.Published by Thomas Kelly 17 Paternoster Row 1839.

Large-flowered St John's-wort: this is the illustration prepared from specimens sent to London from Cork. James Drummond found the shrub, which is an excellent ground-cover, beside the road to Bandon and originally thought it was a native plant but later realised it was an escape from cultivation. (By courtesy of The Linnean Society of London ©)

Large-flowered butterwort was discovered by James Drummond near Macroom; he grew it in the Cork Botanic Garden and the specimen sent to London was the basis for this hand-coloured engraving. (By courtesy of the Hunt Institute for Botanical Documentation, Pittsburgh ©)

Facing page: *Dahlia variabilis* 'Bella Donna', the painted lady anemone-flowered dahlia raised in Cork Botanic Garden by James Drummond before 1828. (Reproduced by courtesy of the Hunt Institute for Botanical Documentation, Pittsburgh ©)

vegetables. Drummond 'of the Cork botanic garden, protects cauliflower-plants during winter by planting them in excavations made in the common soil in the garden, and covering with frames thatched with long straight wheat-straw. He uncovers constantly in mild weather, whether nights or days.' He tried planting red-apple potatoes in single and in double drills, and in beds, to see which method of cultivation was best and yielded the best crop.

But the Commissioners were not impressed nor convinced that the garden run by a dedicated and determined Scot was worth the money the government gave to the Cork Institution.

'Painted Lady Anemone-flowered Dahlia'

Ornamentals were as important as the vegetables and those plants which Drummond had to grow for the use of the Institution's lecturers. In his evidence to the Commissioners, he stated: 'I have raised a good many plants from seed; I raised a very beautiful dianthus, which I distributed about in different places.' Nothing else is recorded about the 'very beautiful dianthus' which was a carnation of sorts. There were exotics from Australia in the greenhouse – wattles and gum-trees – as well as the familiar 'florist's cineraria' which Drummond liked to raise from seed because of the 'fine double and single varieties, of different colours' that he obtained.

He seems to have had a fondness for members of the daisy family, and also for roses. Drummond's 'thornless rose', now extinct, alas, was much admired after he had sent it to the Horticultural Society of London's garden at Chiswick. Called *Rosa alpina* 'Speciosa', in June and July it bore semi-double flowers 'of a very brilliant carmine, fading to pale rose'. Drummond had raised it, and it was supposed to be a hybrid between *Rosa alpina* and *Rosa indica*. A second rose, received at Chiswick from Cork, with dark red, medium-sized flowers appearing in June, was called *Rosa dicksonii* – for a while it was claimed that James Drummond had discovered it in Cork, but in fact it had come to him from Glasnevin and had indeed originated in England.

That's not all – to my great surprise I recently unearthed information about another plant that originated in the Cork Botanic Gardens. *Dahlia variabilis* 'Bella Donna', it was called – the 'Painted Lady Anemone-flowered Dahlia'. The anemone-flowered varieties were 'raised and first brought into notice by Mr. Drummond, of Cork, and are now rapidly spreading into every garden of note in the kingdom', according to Charles McIntosh when he published the first account of this rather handsome plant. 'Bella Donna' was painted for McIntosh by Edwin Smith and the plate, dated May 1829, was published in one of the rarest books about garden plants – McIntosh's *Flora & Pomona*. A plant of the anemone-flowered dahlia varied in price from half-a-crown to one pound – that's around €100 in present-day money. But by 1829 Drummond had sold his stock, packed up his goods and chattels, closed his seed shop on Parliament Street, locked the entrance of the Botanic Gardens for the last time, and left with his wife and young family for a new life in one of the most remote places on Earth – the Swan River Colony on the west coast of Australia. But that's another story . . .

Cork Botanic Garden, starved of cash, was not viable, despite the hopes of its founders. The lease was given up, and a new purpose found for the acres. A little over a decade later, in his book, *Scenery and antiquities of Ireland*, W. H. Bartlett wrote:

> The Cemetery, near the village of Evergreen, stands on the place formerly occupied by the Botanic Garden. The walks, which are tastefully arranged, are adorned with flowers and shrubs, intermingled with the weeping-willow and the dark cypress . . .

For many more decades, a cedar of Lebanon spread its branches over the site, a last reminder of Drummond's domain.

1.7
FORTY SHADES OF GREEN AND WHITE

VARIEGATED PLANTS are not to everyone's liking. Indeed the gardening world is divided into two implacable camps: those who love them and those who loathe them. Some variegated plants are abominations, and should have been composted at birth. Others, however, even to a sceptical gardener, can be useful and attractive when properly sited within a garden, helping to lighten dark corners, providing focal points, or as background plants against which some dark flowers and foliage are better displayed.

In gardens new variegated plants pop up frequently. They can be chance seedlings among batches of otherwise plain green seedlings, or they can occur as 'sports', for example as a variegated shoot on a green-leaved shrub. Most variegated seedlings probably die before anyone sees them because they are usually (but not always) weaker plants than their fellow all-green ones. As for 'sports', these can sometimes be propagated but, again, many variegated shoots are weaker and often do not root. All the same, numerous variegated plants have been propagated and then have proved to be garden-worthy.

Among chance variegated seedlings is the speckled Lenten rose that Rosemary Brown noticed and which she carefully tended. *Helleborus* 'Graigueconna', named after her garden at Bray, County Wicklow, grew into a handsome clump, its leaves finely mottled with white, pale green and dark green. Remarkably, when its seeds are sown, a small proportion of the seedlings 'come true'.

Much more easy to obtain is a plant that is admirable when it is well grown and carefully placed. *Sisyrinchium striatum* 'Aunt May' is believed to have come from Ireland, but its Irish history is not known. The story goes that Mrs Ludovic Amory obtained the plant in Ireland and brought it over to her own garden at Chevithorne in Devon. There it was spotted and propagated and some of it was planted by Jimmy Platt in the garden at Knightshayes, home of Mrs Amory's nephew, the British politician Sir John Heathcote Amory. For a while it was called *Sisyrinchium striatum* 'Variegatum', but this name was not acceptable and so it was named after Mrs Amory – she was affectionately known as Aunt May – and introduced into the trade. The upright fans of grey-green, sword-shaped leaves are streaked with cream, and its yellow flowers look well against this foliage. Dead leaves that turn black should be removed.

Another admirable perennial with variegated foliage is *Acanthus mollis* 'Lady Moore'. Its origins are also obscure although Lady Moore grew it in her

Helleborus 'Graigueconna'; the original plant. (© E. C. Nelson)

Sisyrinchium striatum 'Aunt May'. (© E. C. Nelson)

Acanthus mollis 'Lady Moore'. (© E. C. Nelson)

Only the newly emerging foliage of *Galega* × *hartlandii* is variegated. (© E. C. Nelson)

Rathfarnham garden, whence it passed to other gardeners including Rosemary Brown, David Shackleton at Beechpark, County Dublin, and the Walkers at Fernhill, Sandyford. When plants were propagated and then offered for sale at Fernhill in the 1980s, the plant needed a label, so Mrs Sally Walker, 'tongue in cheek', stuck 'Lady Moore' on the label and thus christened it. This deciduous perennial forms a hummock of slightly prickly leaves that when young are so heavily spotted with white as to appear silvery grey.

The goat's-rue, *Galega × hartlandii*, is a good perennial too. It is named after the extraordinary Cork nurseryman, William Baylor Hartland, who, among other things, was a great self-publicist. To him, Cork was the centre not just of the world but of the horticultural universe! His main interests were apples and daffodils, but he also introduced this goat's-rue, a member of the pea family. Here is Hartland's own description of the plant. 'It appears in March with silver variegated foliage which it keeps into the month of May, then in June it sends forth a quantity of blue and white bicolor blooms, the colour of the wisteria.' The flowers are held in upright spikes, like small lupins, on strong, tall stems. This was a chance seedling in Hartland's nurseries at Ard Cairn, Cork. Frederick Burbidge, of Trinity College Botanic Garden in Ballsbridge, Dublin, reckoned it one of the best summer border plants for colour, but the editor of *The Garden* commented in 1904 that 'we care little for this yellow in the leaf, as the flowers are quite sufficient colouring'. A white-flowered cultivar is also available.

As for shrubs, there is a clutch of handsome Irish ones. Pride of place may be said to go to another native of County Cork, *Azara microphylla* 'Variegata'. It has small leaves bordered with cream, which from a distance give a well-furnished plant a pale, fluffy appearance. Add to this, tiny, discrete flowers that are wonderfully fragrant, with a scent like vanilla or, to some, chocolate, and you have a good garden shrub. It needs a sheltered spot, and is really best when grown against a background of dark evergreen foliage. *Azara microphylla* 'Variegata' originated in the garden of the eccentric Cork

gardener, William Edward Gumbleton. 'Gumbo' (to use his pet name) lived at Belgrove, outside Cobh, and had an amazing garden crammed full of the choicest plants. He is remembered as the man who would tour even the Glasnevin Botanic Gardens with a walking cane in his hand which he would use to demolish any plant he did not like. 'Tush, utter tush', he would exclaim. His variegated *Azara* must have had a precarious birth, but thankfully it was spared the cane and now can be grown and admired.

Similar in many ways (though not in its history) is the variegated myrtle from Glanleam on Valentia Island. The leathery leaves are grey-green with irregular cream margins. The overall colour of a shrub is darker than that of an azara because the foliage often has a purple tinge. The flowers are white, like those of the common myrtle. The Glanleam myrtle has a bewildering number of names, and the current one depends on the botanical opinion of each author. In *An Irish Florilegium*, which contains a portrait of the myrtle by Wendy Walsh, I called it *Myrtus apiculatus* 'Glanleam Gold', while now it is usually listed as *Luma apiculata* 'Glanleam Gold'. The original plant still grows at Glanleam.

Likewise, the original plant of *Griselinia littoralis* 'Bantry Bay' is alive and well on Ilnacullin (Garinish Island) at Glengarriff in the far west of County Cork. Murdo Mackenzie, head gardener on the island for many years, spotted this as a 'sport'. He carefully removed all the plain green shoots and gradually the variegated part gained strength and vigour and is now taller than his cottage. The foliage shows the reverse variegation to the shrubs previously mentioned. The centre of each leaf has a broad flash of cream, leaving the margin patterned irregularly with green. Given that the foliage of *Griselinia* is a glossy, pale green, the overall effect from a distance is of a yellow shrub. This needs a sheltered position, and suffers from late frosts that blacken and kill young growth.

More hardy are the Irish hollies. *Ilex × altaclerensis* 'Lawsoniana' is over one century old and still a splendid cultivar: it has gained the prestigious Award of Garden Merit from the Royal Horticultural

Luma apiculata 'Glanleam Gold', a variegated evergreen with small leaves. (© E. C. Nelson)

The foliage of *Griselinia littoralis* 'Bantry Bay'. (© E. C. Nelson)

The original shrub of *Griselinia littoralis* 'Bantry Bay' on Ilnacullin, Bantry Bay, County Cork. (© E. C. Nelson)

Pittosporum 'Silver Queen' was one of the first plants released by the Slieve Donard Nursery. (© E. C. Nelson)

Society of London. The almost spineless leaves have dark-green margins and their centres display irregular patches of gold and pale green. This came from the Hodgins' nursery at Cloughjordan in County Tipperary. *Ilex* × *altaclerensis* 'Lady Valerie' originated in the garden of Sir Basil and Lady Goulding at Enniskerry, County Wicklow, and was named and introduced by Dr Neil Murray. The leaves have a twist to them, and there is a large golden blotch in the centre. While it resembles 'Lawsoniana', 'Lady Valerie' is a brighter plant and well worth acquiring. (Incidentally, 'Ripley Gold' is indistinguishable from 'Lady Valerie'.)

Neil Murray was also responsible for naming and introducing *Pittosporum* 'John Flanagan', and a subsequent sport which he called 'Little John'. John Flanagan was Neil's right-hand man for many years. His *Pittosporum* was a 'sport' on the well-known 'Garnettii', but has leaves that are subtly variegated – the bright green margins surround a paler green middle which is veined with cream. 'Little John' has much smaller leaves with very wavy margins, with the same colouring scheme, a paler, irregular central patch and translucent creamy-green veins. There are several other variegated Irish cultivars of *Pittosporum*, including the old but still unbeatable 'Silver Queen' that was an early introduction by the Slieve Donard Nursery of Newcastle in County Down. Its leaves are silvery grey-green, margined with white.

As far as trees are concerned, a variegated ash was found at Hillsborough, County Down, in the 1830s, but it is no longer grown. A variegated sycamore released by the Daisy Hill Nursery of Newry survived in the 1980s only as a solitary tree in the National Botanic Gardens, Glasnevin; it has since been propagated. There is a variegated beech from Birr Castle, evocatively called 'Birr Zebra' and its leaves are indeed striped. You will not be able to obtain plants of Richard Hartland's variegated giant redwood, *Sequoiadendron giganteum* 'Aureum' – it may even be extinct – and anyway you will need quite a large garden to accommodate it although it is said to be slow-growing. The young shoots are amber coloured, turning deep golden yellow. And another Award of Garden Merit has gone to *Thuja plicata* 'Irish Gold' (*Thuja plicata* 'Zebrina' of Irish gardens), which is listed by many nurseries. Its shoots have pale bold flecks, giving the whole tree a distinctive golden hue.

I could go on listing variegated plants of Irish birth or with Irish connections: St John's-worts, sea hollies, laurels and extinct forget-me-nots. Still thriving are *Heuchera* 'Helen Dillon', its leaves speckled and figured with cream, and *Omphalodes cappadocicum* 'Starry Eyes' with its very unusual variegated blue flowers. In all about sixty variegated cultivars have been named and introduced from Irish gardens. Many of them mercifully have 'passed away'. No doubt others will appear to take their places!

Omphalodes cappadocicum 'Starry Eyes'. I remember well the day I was first shown photographs of this lovely plant by Eithne Clarke. She brought me some offsets and I grew these and passed divisions on to several friends with clear instructions not to pass the plant to any one else. Sure enough, as I expected, 'Starry Eyes' was soon being grown everywhere! (© E. C. Nelson)

33

1.8
A GARLAND FROM AN IRISH GLEBE

The Glebe House, with the rose 'Buff Beauty'. (© E. C. Nelson)

Narcissus 'Wendy Walsh' was raised at Broughshane, County Antrim, by Mrs Kate Reade, and was named at my suggestion. (© E. C. Nelson)

THE GLEBE HOUSE in what used to be north County Dublin, one of those distinctive former rectories that are scattered around Ireland, sits four-square within a grove of beech trees. In front there is a gravelled carriage-sweep and tennis lawn, to the rear a cobbled yard and some outbuildings with an entry leading into a haggard. A mixed orchard, a vegetable and fruit garden, and the main grove of beeches arc to the west. Until the late 1990s, the Glebe House was the home of John and Wendy Walsh. Wendy is a keen gardener as well as the doyenne of Irish botanical illustrators, and her books, particularly *An Irish Florilegium* and *An Irish Flower Garden* subtly influenced the garden.

Some years ago I suggested to Wendy that she should paint a garland and she took up the idea with enthusiasm. There was no grand design, merely that the informal gathering of flowers, fruits and foliage should reflect Ireland, a true anthology of an Irish garden. In the same way, there was no grand design for Wendy's garden. It was as informal as any fascinating garden should be, and wild in the sense that happy plants were allowed to spread freely. There were mixed shrubberies, a pool, glades for woodland plants and, everywhere, the offspring of subjects from Wendy's watercolours.

Painting even a 'postage stamp' plant portrait is not accomplished in an hour. Each of the water-colours for *An Irish Florilegium* took at least one whole week's work. Sometimes, a painting finished, there was no point discarding the still-fresh shoot, so Wendy frequently recycled her models into cuttings: nothing was wasted and no opportunity to add to the garden was overlooked.

The haggard and beech wood

The Irish garland is a good starting point for a ramble through the Glebe garden, beginning in the former haggard where a patch of delectable asparagus throve. By the wall stood the yellow-blossomed, ferny leaved *Rosa × cantabrigiensis*. Beside the asparagus Wendy had planted her 'own' daffodil. *Narcissus* 'Wendy Walsh', raised by Kate Reade at Broughshane in Northern Ireland, has a short trumpet shading softly from pink through apricot and yellow to green. Nearby was the double Irish primrose 'Elizabeth Dickey' which was found on a roadside near Ballymoney, County Antrim, many years ago.

Primroses grew wild under the beeches, mingling with wild violets, lesser celandines and bluebells. In a west-facing border a large clump of the antique auricula 'Old Irish Blue' (1) flourished.

Rosa × cantabrigiensis in the haggard. I was given this rose from my grandparents' garden, and passed on cuttings to Wendy Walsh. Years later, I was able to get cuttings from her when I moved house – 'The best way to keep a plant is to give it away!' (© E. C. Nelson)

A patch of Mrs Alice Lawrenson's St Bridgid's anemones kept it company. *Primula* 'Guinevere' (2) has bronze foliage and yellow-eyed mauve-pink flowers on purple stems; it is a robust, old primrose and thrives in many Irish gardens. Joining 'Guinevere' and 'Old Irish Blue' in Wendy's garland is *Primula nana* (3), a Himalayan native more familiar as *Primula edgeworthii* which name honours Michael Pakenham Edgeworth who hailed from County Longford. It was one of his discoveries during the 1840s, and because it does not enjoy muggy Irish winters must be covered by a sheet of glass to keep the rain off. Wendy grew it in a raised bed that also sported *Omphalodes cappadocicum* 'Starry Eyes', another Irish cultivar, with sky-blue flowers rimmed with lavender-blue.

By the haggard gate, in a narrow bed that caught the afternoon sun, *Schizostylis coccinea* 'Mrs Hegarty' flourished. This pink-flowered river-lily turned up before 1919 in Blanche Hegarty's garden at Clonbur, County Galway. A few paces further on, leaning against the west wall of the house, was an unheated glasshouse containing a vine, yet there was also room for the lovely sky-blue *Tweedia coeruleum* (4), introduced in the 1840s to the Glasnevin Botanic Gardens by John Tweedie who also sent us the pampas grass from Argentina.

The wild flowers in the vegetable garden

A cherry laurel hedge sheltered the vegetable garden, where sea kale, leeks and raspberries often had unusual companions. Club sedge, *Carex buxbaumii* (5), is now extinct in the wild in Ireland but a small offshoot, obtained from Glasnevin, excelled itself beside the sea kale spreading like bishop's weed. Likewise, the wild leek, *Allium babingtonii*, from Galway Bay, which has grey leaves and stems and bulbils as well as flowers, became a bit of a nuisance. The native blue-eyed grass, *Sisyrinchium angustifolium* (6), also romped away when made redundant from the artist's studio. One of its habitats is County Kerry. There were lusty clumps of exotic African harebells, including the dwarf, hardy one from the Drakensberg, *Dierama dracomontanum* (7), which was a parent of the famous hybrids raised at the Slieve Donard Nursery. Another South African bulb with Irish connections, the amber blossomed *Crocosmia masoniorum* 'Rowallane Yellow', increased prodigiously in the vegetable patch.

One of the projects that Wendy and I collaborated on as the garland took shape was a book about the Burren, and one of its wonders is the maidenhair fern (*Adiantum capillus-veneris*) (8); for many years Wendy grew this fern in her glasshouse. Shrubby cinquefoil (*Potentilla fruticosa*) in its wild, yellow-blossomed Burren form, grown from left-over slips, also enjoyed the vegetable garden's rich soil.

The borders at the Glebe House

A rustic arch led into shrubberies and informal borders centred on a magnificent *Magnolia wilsonii*; in June, bowl-shaped blooms of perfumed alabaster hang from the branches. Some of the shrubs close by had Irish associations. The Chilean myrtle (*Luma apiculata*) flourished here. A mature bushy tree has a spectacular cinnamon bark and glossy, dark-green foliage that is an excellent foil for pure white flowers. Its Irish offspring, 'Glanleam Gold' (9), has delicately mottled cream and green leaves. While Wendy did not often entertain variegated things, the variegated tutsan, *Hypericum androsaemum* 'Mrs

The garland of Irish plants: © Wendy F. Walsh. (Reproduced by permission, from the author's collection)

Cyclamens spreading under the red-flowered hawthorn; the flowers are replaced, in season, by a dense, variegated carpet of heart-shaped leaves. (© E. C. Nelson)

Wilson's magnolia, from China, has hanging blooms unlike most other magnolias, which have flowers that sit erect like goblets. (© E. C. Nelson)

Gladis Brabazon' (10), is a valuable plant for dim, dry corners in shrubberies. This mysteriously reappeared in Irish gardens during the 1970s, having formerly grown at Glasnevin during the 1930s.

Beside the magnolia in the summer of 1997 were statuesque, 8-feet-tall Himalayan lilies, *Cardiocrinum giganteum*, attended by the fluffy plumes of the plume poppy (*Macleaya cordata*). Both plants were introduced by Irish travellers. Lord Macartney from County Antrim and Sir George Staunton from County Galway brought the plume poppy out of China in 1794, while Edward Madden of Kilkenny sent the giant lily to Glasnevin in the 1840s.

During spring a carpet of violets and wood anemones spread under the magnolia including the splendid blue *Anemone nemorosa* 'Lucy's Wood'. This makes a striking companion for the jet-black *Viola* 'Molly Sanderson' (11). Columbines, false spikenard (*Smilacina racemosa*), with martagon lilies and *Scilla peruviana* succeeded the wood anemones and violets as spring melds into summer.

Wendy's had a small, choice collection of roses. 'Buff Beauty' was a centrepiece of the mixed border to the east of the house. Nearby was 'Daisy Hill', a pale pink with lolloping shoots, which was raised at Newry, County Down, around 1900. About the same time, the deliciously fragrant 'Souvenir de St Anne's' (12) happened as a 'sport' on 'Souvenir de La Malmaison' in the Ardilauns' Dublin garden, St Anne's. Its pure pink flowers open almost flat, and a well-grown bush will blossom from May to December. Two centuries ago, with the plume poppy, Macartney and Staunton introduced *Rosa bracteata* (13) which produces lemon-perfumed, white flowers with yellow stamens towards the close of summer. The Irish rose, *Rosa × hibernica* (14), is a natural hybrid between the dog and burnet roses, with flowers like those of the dog rose and pear-shaped, dark red heps; it has been exterminated in its original habitat but, fortunately, survived in the gardens of connoisseurs.

Autumn fruits and winter flowers

The beech trees surrounding The Glebe House have two prime seasons – spring when the leaves are light, fresh green, and autumn when they are gilded and brown. The first signs of autumn were the spear-like buds of *Amaryllis belladonna* in the cobbled yard. Under an old red-blossomed hawthorn was a veritable stumpery of huge cyclamen corms – they looked like gnarled tree roots, but when September dawned they sprouted the densest coronets of magenta, pink and white. *Cyclamen hederifolium* leaves by themselves are handsome, creating a patterned carpet all year round. *Sternbergia lutea* bloomed profusely by the

This pale variant of *Cyclamen coum* grew under the beech trees; in the background is a patch of deep-coloured *Cyclamen repandum*. (© E. C. Nelson)

The rose 'Daisy Hill'. (© E. C. Nelson)

Iris lazica 'Turkish Blue' was collected by Wendy's son, Michael, during a university expedition to northern Turkey in 1968. It thrives is gravel and rubble. (© E. C. Nelson)

front steps, the yellow flowers echoing the St John's-wort, *Hypericum* 'Rowallane Hybrid' (15). A keepsake from *An Irish Florilegium*, this shrub, over four feet tall, is often at its best in early autumn. In a sunny nook, and overhanging the kitchen window, grew the holly-like, semi-evergreen *Itea ilicifolia*, a demure shrub with scented, creamy catkins in late summer. This was introduced from China by the redoubtable Dr Augustine Henry who also provided the pressed specimens from which *Hamamelis mollis,* Chinese wych-hazel, was named. He collected for the first time as well the dwarf sweet-box, *Sarcococca humilis* (16), an evergreen shrub with tiny, fragrant, white flowers in winter.

Winter and early spring flowers are Wendy's favourites, both as subjects to paint and as garden plants. Snowdrops including *Galanthus* 'Straffan' (17), Lenten roses in variety, and crocuses were naturalised at The Glebe House. At the foot of one beech two cyclamens, *Cyclamen coum* and *Cyclamen repandum*, were very content, while the starry-blossomed pale blue *Ipheion uniflorum* (18), another of Tweedie's sendings from Argentina, was cosy at the corner of the house under a winter-flowering jasmine. Beside the pool, on a rocky mound, Wendy had her own distinct clone of the winter-flowering *Iris lazica* with long-stemmed, rich blue blossoms held well above the foliage.

The art of gardening

The flowers that paint best, as Wendy has observed, are not always the showiest: 'Sometimes the inconspicuous ones are the ones that make the better painting'. Like the garden of the Glebe House, this Irish garland contains both conspicuous flowers and those inconspicuous, yet equally entrancing plants that often are the hallmark of the best gardeners, the choicest things that require painstaking cultivation. And the garland is a gathering of exotic and native Irish plants – in a word, a florilegium – because both have received equal attention from this artist in her own garden.

2

HOME-GROWN
PLANTS

2.1
THE SHORT-STYLED BRISTLE-FERN FROM KILLARNEY

EXTINCTION IS FINAL, irreversible, despite what the science fiction movies suggest. None of us, and no one in the future, is likely to see a great auk or a dodo, to mention just two celebrated species. Within the plant kingdom, perhaps a third of all the orchids that have been named no longer exist. Several cycads, the palm-like relatives of conifers, have not been seen for many decades in the wild. Gardeners can fairly be accused of assisting in the extinction of such plants because they wanted to grow them, and botanists, amateur and professional, are not blameless. Today collecting living plants from the wild for cultivation is often illegal and, even when not forbidden, is frowned upon, while collecting for scientific purposes is often only allowed by special permit.

Ireland's native flora has not suffered many extinctions because few of our wild plants have the same allure for gardeners as a cycad or a tropical orchid. Only one Irish species, the Killarney fern, has a history of remorseless collection. Looking on the bright side, it has managed to cling on precariously in half a dozen counties, and nowadays is protected by law throughout the island.

Sometime around 1804 Dr Whitley Stokes, Professor of Medicine in Trinity College, Dublin, and a Miss Fitton – either Elizabeth or her sister Sarah Mary – were botanising in County Wicklow and visited the waterfall at Powerscourt. They found a solitary plant of a fern that seemed new and gathered a specimen for identification. A little afterwards, James Townsend Mackay, a young Scottish gardener who had come to Dublin in 1803 as assistant to Dr Robert Scott, Professor of Botany in Trinity College, was visiting Killarney and on Torc Mountain he found a fern that he did not recognise. When he returned to Dublin, Mackay sent his fern post-haste to Dr James Edward Smith, the

The Killarney fern still grows in some of its old haunts including dark, damp nooks, where little else will grow, in almost inaccessible places at Torc Waterfall. (© E. C. Nelson)

distinguished President of the Linnean Society of London, who, deciding that it did not match any hitherto named species, published a description and illustration and named it *Hymenophyllum alatum*. Smith was wrong. Mackay's Torc fern, and the one Miss Fitton and Dr Stokes had found at Powersourt, were, in fact, the same as a species that had been collected in Madeira and had been described in 1804 and named *Trichomanes speciosum* by Carl Ludwig von Willdenow.

James Mackay had gathered specimens both for pressing and cultivation – he brought at least one living plant back to Trinity College. Years later he recorded that he had succeeded in growing the new fern 'to perfection, by placing the pots in which it is planted in the Green-house under a hand-glass.' He went even further, inscribing one sheet with a pressed specimen as follows: 'I was the first to cultivate it under a hand glass before Mr Ward's publication on his glass cases or boxes'.

Mackay's back-hander to Mr Ward is a reference to Nathaniel Bagshaw Ward who in 1842 published a famous little book entitled *On the Growth of Plants in Closely Glazed Cases* – and so, henceforth, glass containers, looking like fish tanks, in which plants are cultivated have been called 'Wardian cases'. Ward's was one of the most influential horticultural books of the early Victorian era. In fact, he had already published articles on the subject; the first, printed in *The Gardener's Magazine* in 1834, was headed 'On growing ferns and other plants in glass cases in the midst of the smoke of London; and on transporting plants from one country to another by similar means'. That is the crux of the matter – plants that would grow in dark places were desirable as ornaments in suburban drawing-rooms because they could be incarcerated in Wardian cases. And so a new fashion started which developed into a mania – and that led to the near-extinction of one of our native ferns then known as the short-styled bristle-fern or *Trichomanes radicans*.

There were many social factors in play that led in the mid-1850s to the full flowering of the 'Victorian fern craze', or pteridomania (from *pteris*, a fern). In his fascinating history of the craze, David Allen noted the coincidence of the start of pteridomania with a sudden change in clothing style – men started to wear black – and with the fashion for intricate and elaborate designs. Ferns suited the mood of those times; they were plain, sombre, yet produced delicate fronds that formed a mass of green filigree.

However, the assault on the short-styled bristle-fern was started by the botanists and collectors of pressed specimens, not by the cultivators. During the first four decades of the nineteenth century, some new sites for the fern were discovered and it was soon obvious that the Killarney area was the headquarters of this fern within both Ireland and Britain. Published reports alerted fern hunters to this unusual, indeed 'very rare' fern, and those who sought to have complete collections of the ferns of Great Britain and Ireland had to obtain specimens. By the early 1840s the plant had disappeared from Powerscourt Waterfall. The Torc station, to quote one of the greatest of Victorian fern authorities, Edward Newman, 'has been visited . . . by many botanists and tourists; among the latter tribe

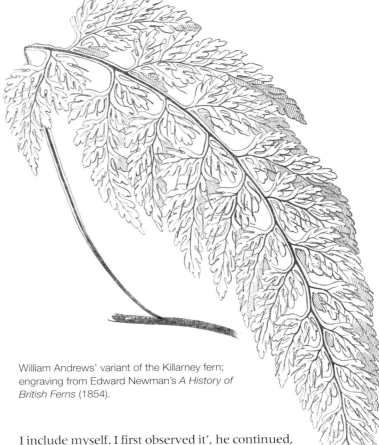

William Andrews' variant of the Killarney fern; engraving from Edward Newman's *A History of British Ferns* (1854).

I include myself. I first observed it', he continued, 'to the left of the seat whence visitors usually take their first view of the cascade.' Being readily accessible, the plant was soon eliminated from Torc too. In June 1844, James Mackay wrote to Sir William Hooker, Director of the Royal Botanic Gardens, Kew, saying that the fern had become 'so scarce' around Killarney that 'Mr Herbert of Muckross has applied to me for a plant to shew to any friend that may enquire for it, & has dismissed from his service a man who used to act as guide, for having completely destroyed it for the purpose of selling it as 5/- each frond.'

Thus the short-styled bristle-fern had become an integral part of the burgeoning Killarney tourist industry. It added to the botanical allure of Killarney, already famous as the habitat of the strawberry tree and ancient yews. Soon it was incorporated in the designs of the furniture made in the area, and before long its name changed to the 'Killarney Fern'.

The discovery during the autumn of 1842 by William Andrews of a patch of the fern displaying

The Killarney fern as depicted in Ann Pratt's *Ferns of Great Britain* (1855).

substantial differences from the Torc plants, seems to have exacerbated the pillage. Andrews' find was considered at least a new variety and it was promptly named *Trichomanes radicans* var. *andrewsii*. Having been given a name signalling its distinctness, Andrews' Killarney fern became as desirable as, if not more desirable than, the original because of its larger fronds – the plunder doubled because collectors had to have each and every variety. Within less than two years Andrews' variety was virtually extinct. In 1844, Mackay was:

> sorry to say [the fern] has been nearly all taken away last autumn from Mr Andrew's new station by a Dublin collector . . . I understand that large tufts of it have been sent to various people in England and elsewhere by the person who brought it to Dublin or some of his friends.

Professor William Harvey, who visited Killarney with Francis Whitla in 1845, wrote: 'We visited the defaced station of Andrews' Trichomanes & Whitla was pathetic over the spot. The plant still exists there, & after some years – if no further robbery be committed – may again cover the rock.' The robbery did not cease; extinction ensued.

Professional collectors were not the only culprits. It is astonishing to us that men as knowledgeable, respectable and concerned as Harvey and Nathaniel Ward are implicated in the annihilation of the Killarney fern. When Anne Pratt published a fine illustration of the species, its particular story was told by none other than Ward.

> Some years since, when I had the pleasure of visiting Killarney with Dr. Harvey, we determined to find out, if possible, another locality for [the fern] . . . We were landed accordingly on the south side of the lake, amid a mass of [Royal Fern], and after making our way up the stream a few hundred yards . . . Dr. Harvey, who was in advance, called out, 'Eureka – Eureka!' I hastened onwards, and saw a sight which might have repaid a much more lengthened and laborious search. In the

inside of a natural cave . . . the [fern] was growing in its native beauty. One specimen, with a creeping rhizome three or four feet in length, and containing forty-eight perfect fronds, we divided, and my portion is now in the hands of your artist.

Through the latter half of the nineteenth century botanists, fern 'enthusiasts' and 'peasants' alike continued to stalk the Killarney fern across MacGillycuddy's Reeks, with an enthusiasm fuelled by the knowledge that it was lucrative, dead or alive. In the early 1890s whole plants were sometimes hawked around the Killarney hotels. Dr Reginald Scully, author of *Flora of County Kerry*, recalled seeing 'a peasant' carrying a large box full of the fern, which had been gathered near Sneem – he wanted five pounds for the boxful but could not find a willing buyer. However, when the man started selling the fern piece by piece he quickly sold bits for from half a crown to seven shillings and sixpence depending on size. Scully remarked ruefully: 'that box, no doubt, represented the total destruction of another station.' In 1896 Dr Scully and Nathaniel Colgan published the second edition of *Cybele Hibernica*, a standard account of the distribution of plants in Ireland, and in this listed places where the Killarney fern had been found up to that time. The list is sprinkled with such comments as 'Seen on Turc [Mountain] as late as 1889, but seems to have been nearly, if not quite, exterminated in the districts of Killarney and the Reeks', and, in conclusion, 'Formerly abundant in parts of Kerry, but now become very rare there, and is most probably exterminated in many of the localities given above.'

What made the Killarney fern so desirable to Victorian collectors was its facility to survive in Wardian cases in dark, smoky city rooms, yet few of the fragments sold to tourists would have survived long enough to be planted. While the species did not present insurmountable horticultural problems, those pieces, deprived of constant moisture, will soon have shrivelled and died. Indeed, none of our native plants is as well adapted for growth in the

43

dim light of sunless nooks and crannies as *Trichomanes speciosum*. Not until one has had the immense privilege of seeing the Killarney fern in its natural habitat can one really appreciate how it seems to favour the darkest places where no sunlight penetrates even on a summer's day. Very few other plants can grow in the half-dark – perhaps only golden saxifrage flourishes in such Stygian gloom.

The Killarney fern's dark green, translucent, deeply divided fronds were 'evergreen', often living for three and more years. In cultivation, if conditions were ideal, well-furnished plants were soon formed as long as some simple rules were observed. A Wardian case was the first essential but the principal conditions for success were 'an equable temperature, moisture, and a kind of diurnal twilight'. Writing in 1872, Frederick Burbidge, on of Mackay's successors as curator of Trinity College Botanic Garden, advised that the Killarney fern:

> grows very nicely in a close humid plant-case. It should be grown in a shallow pan in nodules of peat and sandstone, with a little sphagnum moss intermixed. Cultivated beneath a glass shade, it forms an interesting ornament to any apartment.

Robert Callwell of Herbert Place, Dublin, a friend of William Andrews, planted his 'in pure maiden earth, or virgin mould' through which had been mixed charcoal, and within three years had such a luxuriant specimen that he had to transfer it to another container. Coconut fibre was sometimes added to the soil too, while Burbidge recommended that 'a few lumps of sandstone may be used to vary the surface.' Even in the darkest room, the beautiful and elegantly cut fronds of a flourishing Killarney fern could 'sparkle like golden dew-drops after being sprinkled with pure soft water', according to Burbidge.

The challenge of growing the fern was not just taken up by amateurs – in the botanic gardens at Glasnevin, Ballsbridge (Trinity College) and Belfast, plants were displayed with great pride. At Glasnevin, when the Curvilinear Range was completed, a special Killarney Fern House was built behind it, entirely shaded from the sun – it is still there. In 1878 an anonymous writer exclaimed that:

> nothing in the whole garden struck us more than [this] small house, one side of which is literally matted from top to bottom with one or two British [filmy ferns], interspersed with luxuriant examples of [the Killarney Fern] – a sight almost worth a journey from London to Dublin to see!

Wardian cases came in many shapes and sizes; these models were illustrated by Frederick Burbidge in his book *Domestic Floriculture, Window Gardening and Floral Decorations* (1874).

2.2
BLUE THUNDERBOLTS AND WOODEN ENEMIES

WHAT WEIRD NAMES folk give to wild and garden flowers. My good friend the late Miss Evelyn Booth and I wanted to name a particular new variety 'Wooden Enemy', but it just did not seem proper. Some gardeners without a sense of humour might have misunderstood. Anyway it was such a lovely shade of sky-blue that the silly name was soon abandoned in favour of 'Lucy's Wood'.

Lucy's Wood is a copse in County Carlow, outside the town of Bunclody, and was the original home of a handsome wood anemone – say it quickly: wood anemone! Evelyn Booth, a keen gardener and expert botanist, found it, removed a few pieces to her garden, and there the blue anemone flourished. Evelyn's house was also named Lucy's Wood, so the wood anemone's name marked its double origins. *Anemone nemorosa* 'Lucy's Wood' has good broad petals so that the flower has a full appearance.

Blue wood anemones are not uncommon in gardens – in the wild they are very uncommon. Several cultivars have reputed Irish origins. One of the oldest, named 'Robinsoniana' after the irascible, famous William Robinson of 'wild garden' fame, is said to be Irish. He related the story of its discovery himself, telling how he saw it in the University Botanic Garden, Oxford, and was told it had been sent to the curator, William Baxter, by 'a lady from Ireland'. It then acquired the name 'Robinsoniana', after its champion. The petals are backed with fawn rather than pale violet as is more usual in the blue-flowered wood anemones.

'Blue Bonnet' also has Irish links. In his book *My Garden in Spring*, the great English plantsman Edward Augustus Bowles – he is always known as 'E. A.' Bowles – said that it had been found in Wales, whence it was 'taken to Daisy Hill, Newry, where Mr. Smith's magic wand makes everything grow'.

Anemone nemorosa 'Lady Doneraile'.

Anemone nemorosa 'Lucy's Wood'.

The garden at Lucy's Wood, Evelyn Booth's home, outside Bunclody. (All photographs © E. C. Nelson)

Thomas Smith's nursery was indeed well known for wood anemones. Bowles wrote that 'Blue Bonnet' was 'the latest of all the [wood anemones] to flower, and is very distinct in appearance, being more waxy . . . it lasts on till the middle of May in shady nooks, and I have never noticed it flag with the warmer temperature.' 'By far the largest of the blue wood anemones and not only the largest, but much later than any of the others' was what Smith wrote when he included it in Daisy Hill catalogues around 1905.

Another wood anemone of 'good substance' is 'Lady Doneraile'. Again Bowles stated that this was found in Ireland – presumably at Doneraile, County Cork – by Viscountess Doneraile, a lady known for her interest in gardening and plants: 'A wonderful anemone. The flowers when open face upwards so that they resemble miniature sunflowers.' I grew it in my garden at one time and it certainly was a robust anemone with a stout rhizome; the stems rose about 20 centimetres tall and bore large, pure white flowers which could be over 4.5 centimetres in diameter.

There are some varieties that cannot be traced nowadays, and I don't even know what they looked like. 'Captain Riall's Variety' presumably hailed from Old Conna, Bray, County Wicklow; it was in the Glasnevin Botanic Gardens about 1920 whence it was distributed to gardeners in Antrim and Cardiff. 'Mucklagh Variety', again from its name, must have come from Mucklagh in County Wicklow, the garden of The O'Mahony. It was also grown in Glasnevin about 1915 and was distributed widely, even to the Royal Botanic Gardens, Kew, in April 1916. It is possible, indeed probable, that 'Mucklagh Variety' was the pale grey-blue flowered wood anemone from Wicklow described in the 1910s. There was also one called 'The O'Mahony' – or was it the same?

Anemone nemorosa 'Levingei' was around in the late 1800s; its flowers were 'of a pink shade . . . one of the loveliest flowers of spring'. This came from somewhere in 'the west of Ireland'. As the name is surely a clue, this may have been collected by Harry Levinge of Knockdrin, Mullingar, County Westmeath, after whom a delicate Himalayan fern *Pseudophegopteris levingei* was named. Patrick O'Kelly, the inimitable nurseryman and amateur botanist who lived in the Burren, sold this anemone in the 1890s – significantly he was a close friend of Levinge and often joined him in local botanical explorations. Perhaps this pink wood anemone came from the County Clare.

'Currey's Blue' and 'Currey's Pink', I believe, are synonyms of 'Lismore Blue' and 'Lismore Pink'

respectively. These surely are the forms known to Bowles, who received them from Miss Fanny Currey, who is better known as one of Ireland's pioneering daffodil breeders. She was described as 'a woman of many accomplishments, proficient in riding, shooting and fishing, besides being clever with her pencil', and a fine watercolour artist.

Some folk believe that picking a wood anemone will bring bad luck, and that is the origin of the name 'thunderbolt' (which, come to think of it, would be a fine name for a white one). Pick a wood anemone and a thunderstorm will rise and 'Lad, you'll be struck by the thunderbolt'! Whatever the connotations of 'granny's nightcap' are I do not know, but that's what they call it in Somersetshire. I prefer two names which Dr Molly Sanderson of Ballymoney, County Antrim, devised. 'Green Dream' and 'Green Fingers' were christened by Dr Molly. She had obtained both as unnamed plants from Sweden from her friend Tage Lundell (there is a lovely *Clematis* bearing that gardener's name). These anemones have no stamens in the middle of their flowers, just small green bracts resembling diminutive tufts of parsley. The flowers are thus somewhat odd – green and white, not white and gold.

I don't think of wood anemones as enemies, although when they are happy in a garden they will spread rapidly. They like dappled shade and a good loam into which leaf-mould has been liberally forked before the rhizomes are planted. Leave them alone and they will romp about, delighting you every spring. And, don't pick them – they will look lovelier in the garden.

Anemone nemorosa 'Robinsoniana'. (© E. C. Nelson)

2.3
MY LOVE'S AN *ARBUTUS* – STRAWBERRY TREES

My love's an arbutus
By the borders of Lene . . .

THE STRAWBERRY TREE, *Arbutus*, is one of the glories of southwestern Ireland. Strawberry trees slant out from the rocky shores of Lough Leane and the other lakes of Killarney, as the poet Alfred Perceval Graves described.

To see the Irish strawberry tree is its wild nobility, take a trip to Killarney in the winter, not summer. The oak, ash and birch have dropped their leaves so that the few native evergreens stand out. Holly bushes glisten in the sun, their twisted, glossy leaves acting like small mirrors. Along the woodland margins and on the rocky lough shores, the strawberry tree, a more sober evergreen than the holly, is equally conspicuous. Its rough trunk is reddish brown.

So slender and shapely
In her girdle of green; . . .

A true evergreen, unlike most of our other native trees, *Arbutus unedo* is a most peculiar plant, bearing flowers and fruits at the same season: autumn.

But though ruddy the berry
And snowy the flower
That brightens together
The arbutus bower . . .

The flowers are pearly white, flushed with green and pink, and the fruits are scarlet like perfectly round strawberries.

Strawberry trees also inhabit the borders of the Mediterranean Sea and so were familiar to the Ancient Greeks. According to a Greek myth, the goddess Gaia changed her three-limbed son Geryoa into a strawberry tree. According to an ancient Irish myth, the Tuatha Dé Danann brought fruits of the strawberry tree from Tír Tairngire, the Land of Promise, and a few fell to earth in Killarney where they sprouted and flourished. Other legends implicate early Christian monks.

Shrubs or trees that are in full bloom in the autumn are not that common, so our native strawberry tree is a valuable addition to the garden bridging the gap between the late summer flowers and the true winter ones. The flowers slowly swell to maturity, beginning in September, and they continue to bloom as long as the autumn is mellow. They are clustered in miniature chandeliers, each individual blossom being a small, translucent urn. Hanging beside these will be clusters of round, warty-skinned fruits that were formed the previous autumn and have taken a full year to ripen. If the weather has been rough many of the young fruits will be stripped off, so a good fruiting year is one that has been gentle throughout.

The strawberry tree: © Wendy F. Walsh, reproduced by permission (author's collection).

Not only is the strawberry tree one of the few native plants that we regularly allow into our gardens, it is also the one with the longest history as a garden plant. One of the earliest records of this tree as an inhabitant of Killarney reports the export of saplings to adorn gardens in England. That was during the reign of Queen Elizabeth I. About the same time, strawberry trees must also have been planted in Irish gardens, far from Killarney, because in 1650 there was a large tree at Ballymount near Dublin, and other giant specimens were recorded in the 1700s. In May 1752, Mrs Mary Delany was staying with the Usher family at Mount Usher in County Wicklow and wrote to her sister Anne, Mrs

A strawberry tree at Lough Leane, Killarney; this was the tree depicted by Wendy Walsh on the cover of *Trees of Ireland, Native and Naturalized* (1993). (© E. C. Nelson)

Dewes, describing the local strawberry trees all of which had once been deliberately planted:

> This country is particularly famous for arbutus (the strawberry tree) and myrtles, which grow in common ground and as flourishing as in Cornwall. Myrtles are so plentiful that the dishes are garnished with it, and next Xtmas the gentlemen in this neighbourhood are agreed to adorn Wicklow church with myrtle, bay and arbutus instead of ivy and holly. I tell them it is well I am *not* to be *one* of their congregation – I should be tempted to commit sacrilege! The arbutus bears fruits and flowers (like the orange tree) at the same time, and is in its full glory about Xtmas; the berries are as large as the duke cherry and of a more glowing scarlet, the surface rough like a strawberry . . .

On Christmas Day 1793 the great strawberry tree in the Cuninghame's demesne, Mount Kennedy, County Wicklow, was in 'full beauty of foliage berry and blossom *at once*', according to Samuel Hayes. It was a monster tree with a trunk 13 feet 9 inches in girth. There is no tree of such a size in Ireland today.

Strawberry trees have inhabited Ireland for thousands of years. We know this because pollen of *Arbutus unedo* has been found in peat deposits considered to have formed about 6,000 years ago. So the legends that St Finnian or one of his monks (or even the Tuatha Dé Danann) brought the strawberry tree from continental Europe are fanciful. The tree is not confined to Killarney and County Kerry. There are scattered colonies throughout south Kerry, and also in west Cork around Glengarriff and Skibbereen, and a very isolated one of the shore of Lough Gill, County Sligo.

Place-names, it is argued, record that the strawberry tree was more widespread in the west of Ireland in bygone era. Tracing one of the plant's Irish names, *caithne*, suggests that it flourished once in County Clare at Derrynacaheny, which means the oak wood of the strawberry tree, near Ennis. Following another name, *cuinche*, which is Anglicised as quin, perhaps indicates that strawberry trees once grew in County Waterford at Cappoquin, and on Quinsheen Island in Clew Bay, County Mayo.

As a garden plant, the strawberry tree is easy to grow, and hardier than its natural range suggests. There are two very old trees in the National Botanic Gardens, Glasnevin, which have withstood the rigours of Dublin's weather for probably two centuries. And the soil in Glasnevin is not the best! What is required is a well-drained loam. Strawberry trees will die if their roots become waterlogged. The soil can contain lime although this is not essential. Some protection from cold, dry winds is best, especially at the sapling stage. Otherwise strawberry trees, when established, will withstand quite hard frosts.

A handful of cultivars of *Arbutus unedo* are readily available, as well as the 'ordinary' species. You do not have to choose one of the named cultivars – almost any strawberry tree will provide pleasure. One of the most desirable is *Arbutus unedo* f. *rubra* which had distinctly red flowers, but be

Top left: Winter in Killarney National Park; the evergreens, mostly strawberry trees, stand out. (© E. C. Nelson)

Top right: The flaking bark of *Arbutus × andrachnoides*. (© E. C. Nelson)

Left: *Arbutus × andrachnoides* is a hybrid arising when the autumn-flowering *Arbutus unedo* and the spring-blooming *Arbutus andrachne* have cross-pollinated: it has cropped up in gardens but also occurs in the wild where the two species cohabit. (© E. C. Nelson)

Below: In autumn *Arbutus unedo* carries both flowers and fruits. (© E. C. Nelson)

Above: *Madroña*, *Arbutus menziesii*, is the species of strawberry tree that is native to the Pacific coast of North America.
(© E. C. Nelson)

Right: The peeling bark of *madroña* (© E. C. Nelson)

warned, this is a variable plant – before purchasing one you should check its flowers. The best will have translucent rosy-pink bells – the flowers on many 'ordinary' strawberry trees can be tinged with red so avoid those that are only flushed red, hinting at pink. 'Compacta' and 'Elfin King' form quite small, bushy shrubs rather than trees; 'Elfin King' is a good cultivar, and flowers and fruits abundantly even when young. There is a large, old plant of 'Quercifolia' in the National Botanic Gardens. It has irregularly lobed, rather unshapely leaves and does not flower profusely, so it is just a curiosity. 'Glasnevin' has narrow foliage – the original grows in the Botanic Gardens near the Cactus House.

Other cultivars have been recorded and a few are still cultivated but are rarely available for sale. There is a double-flowered one, but it is not attractive and may be confined properly to specialist collections.

The variegated one, known at the beginning of the 1800s and then sold by at least one Irish nursery, appears to be extinct.

While I have a great affection for our native strawberry tree, if I was choosing one *Arbutus* for a garden, I would forgo the wild plant and choose instead the hybrid *Arbutus × andrachnoides*. The reason is simple: the bark of a healthy tree is the most glorious colour, rich red especially when wet. Even on the dullest, dank Irish autumn day, *Arbutus × andrachnoides* is outstanding. There is a handsome tree behind the Great Palm House at Glasnevin. The one that used to grow in Rosemary and John Brown's garden at Bray, alas, succumbed to storms a few years ago. It had been planted at the end of a vista and made a striking focal-point.

Arbutus × andrachnoides is a hybrid resulting from the crossing of *Arbutus unedo* and the eastern

Mediterranean species *Arbutus andrachne*. Although the latter blooms in spring and the Irish species blooms in autumn, both may have occasional out-of-season blooms so hybrids can be formed in nature. In fact *Arbutus × andrachnoides* is known in the wild, in Cyprus. It flowers in autumn and will also have flowers in spring, but being sterile never has fruits.

Arbutus andrachne is not at all common in Irish gardens, and is definitely frost-sensitive when a sapling. It blossoms in spring, and produces very small, red fruits in the succeeding autumn. The bark is cinnamon-coloured and smooth.

Arbutus has an extraordinary pattern of distribution, suggesting that it is a very ancient genus. There are the two European species already mentioned, and *Arbutus canariensis* which is confined to the Canary Islands. Remarkably there are about a dozen species in western North America ranging from British Columbia into Mexico. The most familiar of the American strawberry trees is the madrone or *madroña*, *Arbutus menziesii*. Its leaves are leathery and dark green, much larger than those of the Irish tree. *Madroña* flowers in May, at the same time as the dogwoods, producing erect, dense spikes of white flowers. The blossom is followed by small orange-red fruits. *Madroña* has a reputation for being difficult. It is a woodland plant and perhaps is best planted in a shaded place where it will have room eventually to form a tree, in a humus-rich, lime-free soil. The bark is also cinnamon-coloured like that of the Chilean myrtles, and like that of *Arbutus × andrachne* peels to show streaks of young green bark underneath.

Other species are in cultivation. *Arbutus canariensis*, the Canary Islands strawberry tree, is decidedly tender and only suitable for the mildest southwestern gardens. Its leaves are large, soft and often hairy, and the flowers are pale green with a pink tint. In the University Botanic Gardens, Cambridge, I have seen a fine shrub of *Arbutus texensis*, which evidently is not tender although it comes from Texas as its name indicates, perhaps as long as the wood is well ripened in the summer sun. Its foliage has splendidly subtle tones of grey and red and blue.

Returning home, there is no doubt that '*My love the arbutus . . .*' is a very remarkable tree. Its wood has been used to make charcoal, and was employed in the famous Killarney marquetry. It is still greatly prized by woodturners. The best uillean pipes are made from the strawberry tree. In southern Europe its strawberries are gathered and used to make liqueurs and can even be eaten. Some say they are dry and tasteless, but in the sunnier climes of southern Europe they can be sweet and tasty.

> *Alas! Fruit and blossom*
> *Shall scatter the lea,*
> *And Time's jealous fingers*
> *Dim your young charms, machree.*
> *But unranging, unchanging,*
> *You'll still cling to me,*
> *Like the evergreen leaf*
> *Of the arbutus tree.*

So plant an arbutus in your garden. You'll be charmed, *machree*!

2.4
A SAINTLY HEATHER

ONE OF IRELAND's most beautiful native plants, one that is also greatly admired by gardeners, bears the name of a luminary of the Early Celtic church. St Dabeoc's heath, otherwise *Daboecia*, is almost unique among flowering plants in being named after a saint – at least, in the sense that both its botanical (Latin) name and its everyday name are derived from the saint's name.

Who was Dabeoc? There is no simple answer! There is more than one Dabeoc recorded in the annals, and to complicate matters Dabeoc is the same name as Beo-aedh, or rather the diminutive of it, just as Billy is the diminutive of William. This led to the suggestion that the most likely patron of the heather was Beo-Aed, Bishop of Ard Carna in the present-day county of Roscommon, whose festival day is 8 March, because his diocese was the nearest to the native habitat of the heather.

The notable Irish naturalist Dr Robert Lloyd Praeger favoured a better-known saint, Dabeoc of Lough Derg in County Donegal. This Dabeoc lived at about the turn of the fifth century. The annals of the

St Dabeoc's heath, *Daboecia cantabrica*, on the coast near Clifden in Connemara, County Galway.
(© E. C. Nelson)

Irish Church do not enlighten us greatly about him, but, according to one source, he was the youngest of ten saintly sons of Brecan, who ruled part of southern Wales and gave his name to Breconshire and the Brecon Beacons. Dabeoc's grandfather was an Irish prince named Bracha, who was in turn the grandson of Caelbadh, King of Ireland, who was slain in AD 357. What makes Dabeoc of Lough Derg so significant is that he founded the monastery on the far-famed island where St Patrick is said to have had his vision of the Otherworld. St Dabeoc died in 516 and tradition relates that he was buried on Saint's Island, now a place of devotional pilgrimages. How this Donegal saint could have become the patron of the heather that is found native in Ireland only in Connemara and south Mayo is a veritable mystery – even in AD 500 it is most unlikely the heather grew as far north as Donegal, and it is rather improbable that Dabeoc himself ever set eyes on it.

The first inkling of the association with Dabeoc was recorded in 1700 by the Welsh naturalist and antiquary Edward Lhuyd (or Lloyd). Lhuyd travelled through Ulster, Connacht and Munster collecting information about the Irish language and antiquities, and also spent some time exploring the countryside for plants. He took back to Britain pressed specimens of a heather that he described

ST DABEOC'S HEATH

White-flowered plants of St Dabeoc's heath have been known in the wild since the early 1800s, and the variant was soon introduced into cultivation. (© E. C. Nelson)

The bell-like blossoms of St Dabeoc's heath, with the yellow flowers of tormentil. (© E. C. Nelson)

Daboecia cantabrica 'Charles Nelson' has 'double flowers', each one packed full of extra 'petals'. (© E. C. Nelson)

as having flowers like a harebell and leaves like rosemary. He also noted that in Connacht 'sometimes ye women carry sprigs of it about them as a Preservative against Incontinency'. The prevalent meaning of the word incontinence has since altered a little – when Lhuyd wrote he clearly meant that it was believed to reinforce a young woman's self-restraint in sexual appetite (to paraphrase the *Shorter Oxford English Dictionary*). One subsequent commentator quipped that Lhuyd had omitted to say how this was achieved or how effective it was! The name of this invaluable heather, Lhuyd recorded, was *fraoch Dabeog*, St Dabeoc's heath.

More than half a century later, the great Swedish botanist Carl Linnaeus, the man who invented the modern system of plant names, listed St Dabeoc's heath as *Erica daboecii*, reversing the vowels o and e. This error was repeated in the 1790s when Professor Thomas Martyn first noted the name *Daboecia* in his edition of Philip Miller's *The Gardener's Dictionary*, and David Don perpetuated the misspelled name in his review of the heather family published in 1834.

St Dabeoc's heath was introduced into gardens not from Ireland but from another of its wild habitats, northern Spain. Dr William Bowles, a native of Cork who was Superintendent of Spanish Mines, sent seeds of the heather from Spain to London in 1763, and Peter Collinson, a very keen gardener, raised seedlings.

Today there is a splendid array of cultivars of St Dabeoc's heath available to gardeners, and from May to November it is possible to have this elegant, dwarf shrub in bloom in the garden (bear in mind that it requires lime-free soil). The flower colour ranges from ruby to rich purple and pure white. The foliage is usually dark, glossy green, but varieties with lime-green and even variegated foliage are available. Don't plant them singly; the best effect is achieved by mixing colours so that a patch of the heather has white, purple and red flowers intermingled.

Top left: The original plant of *Daboecia cantabrica* 'Charles Nelson' growing beside a boreen at Carna in County Galway; it was still alive in 2000. (© E. C. Nelson)

Top: *Daboecia cantabrica* 'Praegerae', the red-blossomed clone, found by Mrs Praeger in Connemara. (© E. C. Nelson)

Left: *Daboecia cantabrica* 'Celtic Star': this is the wild, original plant, which grew on the Errislannan Peninsula, Connemara. (© E. C. Nelson)

There are numerous white-blossomed cultivars, and one of the best to look for is 'David Moss', which can bloom from June to October and has glossy, dark leaves which provide an excellent foil for the flowers. It is not of Irish origin, having arisen in north Wales. Otherwise, plants labelled *Daboecia cantabrica* 'Alba' (or var. *alba*) are of mixed origin and may indeed be rather inferior ones. A very striking variety is 'Bicolor' – its history is not known but it has been in cultivation for a century and more. The flowers can be beetroot, or white, or striped in beetroot, pink and white, and flowers of different colours can even appear on the same shoots. It is a real oddity, and has 'sported' a pale shell-pink one named 'Donard Pink' after the Slieve Donard Nursery that once marketed it.

The best of the red-blossomed varieties is 'Waley's Red', a robust shrub with ruby bells that came from Spain. I regard 'Praegerae' as equally good, although it has a reputation for being tender and will lose its leaves during hard winters and then look rather scruffy. 'Praegerae' was found by Mrs Hedi Praeger, Dr Lloyd Praeger's wife, in Connemara in September 1938. She took some cuttings that were successfully rooted at the National Botanic Gardens, Glasnevin, whence the plant was later distributed to nurseries.

Among other varieties that have been found in the wild in Connemara and subsequently propagated by cuttings are the remarkable 'Celtic Star', which has purple bells enclosed by fleshy, almost scarlet sepals; 'Cleggan' notable for its lime-green foliage; 'Doris Findlater'; and (leaving

Daboecia azorica growing in the wild in the Azores. (© E. C. Nelson)

modesty aside) 'Charles Nelson' with remarkable, puffy, double flowers. Mr and Mrs David McLaughlin of Omagh found 'Celtic Star' and several years after finding it they were able to show me the original plant still growing on a rocky, windswept knoll on the Errislannan Peninsula, south of Clifden. Miss Maura Scannell, of the National Botanic Gardens, spotted 'Cleggan' at Coorhoor Lough south of Cleggan in 1975, and for many years it was kept in the native species collection at Glasnevin. 'Doris Findlater' is another oddity, having erect, not hanging, flowers of ruby-red, and it was a chance find by Miss Doris Findlater, and her sister Sheila, on the Bog Road near Roundstone. As for my namesake, the original plant remained (at least until 2000) where I discovered it by the edge of a boreen near Carna.

Daboecia cantabrica is one of the glories of the Irish flora. Although it is a delight to see it growing in gardens, I will always maintain that it is at its best when mingled with dwarf gorse and bell heather in the shadow of Croagh Patrick or the Twelve Pins. You can try to recreate the effect in your garden, but I'm sure it will not be nearly so splendid as on a natural, wild heathland.

There are two species of *Daboecia*. The familiar one from western Ireland is native also in western France, northern Spain and the northernmost parts of Portugal; its name *Daboecia cantabrica* signals the fact that it was first reported in the later 1600s from Cantabria in the north of Spain. The other species is *Daboecia azorica*, and, as its name suggests, it occurs only on the remote islands of the Azores in mid-Atlantic. *D. azorica* inhabits the volcanic cones of the islands of Faial and Pico where it forms great patches in very well-drained, gravelly soil. The Azorean plant is more slender than the Irish one, and its flowers are smaller and usually bright ruby red.

Until recently it was thought to be extinct in cultivation, but we have now discovered several clones of it, one in England and one in the United States, that are hardy, so true *Daboecia azorica* may soon become available commercially again.

The secret of success with it is likely to be very sharp drainage – if you are lucky enough to obtain the true plant, grow it in a trough or container filled with the sort of gritty, lime-free soil that is suitable for 'alpines'.

When two species, isolated in the wild, are grown close together in gardens hybrids often result, and the cross-pollination of these two heathers has indeed yielded a 'race' of hardy hybrids that make superb subjects for heather beds, tubs and containers. The first time the hybrid was detected was in North Wales, but it seems not to have been propagated. Later it cropped up in Scotland, so it is now named *Daboecia × scotica*. 'William Buchanan' and 'Jack Drake' were the two original Scottish cultivars, and both deservedly have gained the Royal Horticultural Society's Award of Garden Merit. 'William Buchanan' has crimson flowers, while those of 'Jack Drake' are ruby coloured. The bells of 'Silverwells' are pure white. Again these are best grown in mixed groups to give a mosaic of flower colours.

The heathers from Connemara mentioned in this article were all propagated from a few cuttings carefully removed from the original shrubs which remained intact in the wild. As heathers are easily propagated from cuttings, half a dozen non-flowering shoots, about 7 centimetres long, will suffice to establish plants in cultivation.

2.5
DR O'KELLY, I PRESUME?

Patrick O'Kelly and his sister, Mrs Mary Casey.
(Reproduced by courtesy of Mrs Theresa Andreucetti)

The shell of Glenarra House, Patrick O'Kelly's home, in the valley south of Ballyvaghan, County Clare, photographed in the late 1980s.
(© E. C. Nelson)

HAD YOU VENTURED to Ballyvaghan or Lisdoonvarna in, say, the 1920s and needed a guide to show you some of the botanical delights of the Burren, you would almost certainly have been advised to ask for Dr O'Kelly – Dr Patrick Bernard O'Kelly of Glenarra. He would have guided you around, just like the present-day guides, taking you perhaps to some of his favourite, out-of-the-way haunts. He might even have tried to tempt you to buy the odd souvenir of your visit, a clump of gentians, perhaps, or a few of his own special orchids.

Patrick Bernard O'Kelly, born near Ballyvaghan in 1852, was a big man, a real character, a gem of the first water (to use one of his own favourite phrases). He was a bachelor farmer who lived all his life in the heart of the Burren. His house, now ruined, lies in the middle of Ballyvaghan valley, and the neglected garden still contains a display of daffodils and Italian cuckoopint (*Arum italicum*) every spring.

O'Kelly was a Clare man through and through, but unlike his contemporaries, who perhaps took little more than a passing interest in the wild flowers of the region, he discovered that he could make a bit of a living out of the gentians, ferns and orchids that abounded in his neighbourhood. He also loved plants: there is no question about it. We don't know how his interest in flowers and other wild plants developed, but by the 1880s P. B. O'Kelly was well known to gardeners, especially that special breed who had a passion for ferns. The Burren is a ferny place. Hart's-tongue ferns grow in the shelter of every one of the cracks that criss-cross the limestone pavement. Rustyback ferns sprout from the walls and the pavement; their small fronds have silvery golden backs and sinuous margins. Maidenhair ferns, with fan-shaped leaflets, colonise the seepage lines where water continually trickles out of the limestone.

O'Kelly certainly admired ferns, and, because he was so familiar with them, was able to spot those freaks and monstrosities by which fern enthusiasts were besotted. Sometime around 1884, somewhere out in the broad pavement of the Burren, eagle-eyed O'Kelly found a hart's-tongue fern that was very strange – indeed unique. On the plain green back of the fronds there were tiny plantlets, miniature ferns, growing in piggyback fashion. (Some well-known ferns, the kinds that grow happily on a windowsill, have this characteristic; they reproduce by budding tiny plantlets that can be removed and grown on into mature ferns.) O'Kelly's piggyback hart's-tongue, given the name *Phyllitis scolopendrium* 'Cristatum O'Kelly', was illustrated in *The Gardeners' Chronicle* in 1884 and was marketed by Abraham Stansfield, the English fern nurseryman. And then it vanished. No one has seen the like of it since.

Perhaps that remarkable find, and the undoubted small fame that followed, was the spark that converted plain Mr O'Kelly into a professional plant-hunter and nurseryman, and eventually earned him the sobriquet 'Dr O'Kelly'. He did not give up his farm, but within ten years he had established a thriving business supplying native Irish plants to acquisitive gardeners in Ireland, Britain and farther afield.

In a short time O'Kelly was offering fifty different sorts of rustyback ferns. These were not dramatic plants like the piggyback hart's-tongue; the differences between the individuals were probably quite small, but the fern enthusiasts lapped them up. Pteridomania – the craze for growing ferns and their extraordinary, often ugly mutants – had not yet died in Ireland. He also found a handsome polypody that is still in cultivation; its name, a mouthful and a half, is *Polypodium cambricum* (Semilacerum Group) 'Falcatum O'Kelly'. Moving on, O'Kelly began to look for unusual hart's-tongues, and eventually he claimed to have 700 different ones: 'This is the largest collection of the hart's-tongue fern in the United Kingdom', he exclaimed. There is some powerful exaggeration there – but P. B. O'Kelly knew how to tempt his customers!

Top: Hart's-tongue ferns in a scailp in the Burren. (© E. C. Nelson)

Part of the price-list for 1904–1905, from P. B. O'Kelly's printed notepaper.

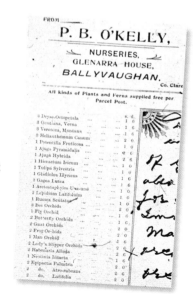

57

Far Left: Spring gentians: 'It is the only known flower in existence that exhilarates the mind and heart of the fair sex.'
(© E. C. Nelson)

Left: O'Kelly's orchid.
(© E. C. Nelson)

In the early 1890s, he published a handsome catalogue of all the plants he had for sale. For a man who was probably self-taught, he was superb at writing plant descriptions. He was lyrical about the spring gentian:

The flower is heavenly-blue. It is the queen of all known alpine plants in the whole world. No collection complete without this gem of the first water. It is the only known flower in existence that exhilarates the mind and heart of the fair sex.

Under a engraving of sheep and lambs ('Where sheep may safely graze') was the headline *Catalogue of choice hardy perennials, alpine and herbaceous plants & evergreen shrubs from Burren Nurseries and Botanic Gardens*. Truth to tell, there was no botanic garden – it was the Burren.

Maidenhair ferns were nine pence a piece. Large tufts of Burren gentians cost four shillings a dozen. White-blossomed spring gentians were priced at five shillings a plant.

Undoubtedly O'Kelly obtained most of his plants in the wild, but he was not ravishing the countryside. While he was digging up plants for sale, there is no evidence that he did any damage to the populations of wild flowers, including orchids, that grow in the Burren. He supplied an eager market, in days before conservation was a byword. I have seen the records of such reputable institutions as the University of Cambridge Botanic Gardens, the Royal Botanic Gardens, Kew, and our own National Botanic Gardens – in each there are entries for several years in succession for maybe fifty or a hundred gentians supplied from Ballyvaghan.

P. B. O'Kelly was well known in botanical as well as horticultural circles in Ireland and overseas in the early part of the last century. He contributed substantially to our scientific knowledge of the plants of the Burren region by sending properly labelled and documented pressed specimens of the flora to botanists. In the Burren itself, the few people who remember him still speak highly of his knowledge of the local wild flowers. His greatest contribution was to make known the existence of a white-flowered orchid which for many years was believed to be unique to the Burren.

O'Kelly called it *Orchis immaculata*, which can be translated as the unspotted or the unstained orchid. It has pure white flowers and a lingering fragrance, and he reported that there were millions of them. There still are! It is one of the great joys of a summer day in the Burren to see a boreen lined with the white spires of O'Kelly's immaculate orchid. This is a plant that frustrates botanists; they cannot agree about it. Is it a species? Or a subspecies? Or just a local variety, or a western form? But that does not matter for the name that George Claridge Druce, the Oxford botanist, gave it still sticks no matter what the orchid's exalted or lowly status may be – *Orchis o'kellyi* has become *Dactylorhiza fuchsii* subspecies *o'kellyi*.

There has to be a moral to this story. Attitudes have changed. Today, no one would tolerate a nurseryman who dug up wild plants for sale – it is contrary to all the best practices of present-day gardeners, botanists and nurserymen, for whom conservation is as much a concern as the growing of handsome plants. Patrick O'Kelly, were he alive today, would I am sure be as respectable and honourable a man as he was in his own time. He might still show visitors around the Burren and he would certainly still contribute to our knowledge of its exceptional flora by making records and taking photographs, but not by wholesale collection of specimens. Instead, if he chose, he could propagate gentians by seed from cultivated stock, and for orchids use a state-of-the-art propagation unit to grow them from tissue-cultured plantlets.

'Dr O'Kelly', who died in 1937 aged eighty-four, was a learned man but he never went to university, and he did not have a doctorate. He is unique among Ireland's home-grown plant hunters because he belonged to the Burren, stayed there, and explored his native territory. I would love to have met him – maybe he would have given me a little plant of that extraordinary hart's-tongue fern, and let me into the lost secret of where he found it, and, perhaps, brought me to the exact spot. And we could have walked across the pavement to admire his living memorial, the sweetly-scented, pure white orchid that blooms every year in the Burren.

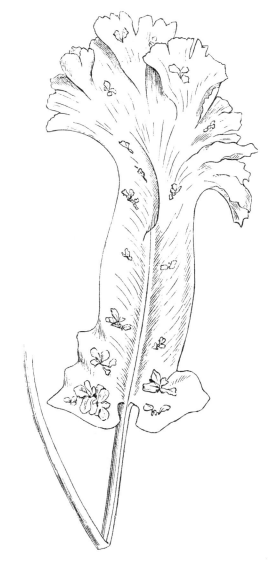

O'Kelly's hart's-tongue fern; engraving from *The Gardeners' Chronicle*.

2.6
THE ARCHBISHOP OF DUBLIN'S MISTLETOE

KISSING UNDER THE MISTLETOE at Christmastide is not a time-honoured, indigenous Irish tradition! Mistletoe, like the Christmas tree and the poinsettia, is an alien, imported from abroad by two very reputable gardeners who deliberately set out to 'forge Mother Nature's signature'.

Mistletoe is a very odd plant. It defies all the rules. You cannot sow its seed and then pot on the seedlings. You cannot take cuttings, dibble them into some compost with a touch of rooting hormone, and expect a cluster of little rooted plants in a few months' time. You can't grow it in a mixed border – it just doesn't have roots like other self-respecting shrubs. You cannot even graft it, like an apple tree, although it looks as if that would be the way to proceed.

Mistletoe is a oddity because it is a parasite – it depends on another plant for all its water and essential mineral salts. Yet, unlike some parasitic plants, mistletoe does have green stems and leaves and so it can utilise sunlight to manufacture sugars – as botanists say, it can photosynthesise. It is not too fussy about what plant acts as its beneficent host although we tend to have the notion that it prefers apple trees.

For a very long time, at least two millennia in fact, mistletoe has had a good reputation, enhanced by its strange habits, as a medicinal plant. The Roman naturalist Pliny the Elder, who died on 25 August AD 79 during the catastrophic eruption of Vesuvius which destroyed Pompeii and Herculaneum, wrote about mistletoe in his encyclopaedia *Historia Naturalis*. He reported that the best mistletoe grew on oak – such a mistletoe yielded berries from which the most potent ointment for wounds, sores and swellings could be concocted. 'Some persons have a sort of superstitious notion', Pliny added, 'that mistletoe

will be all the more efficacious if the berries are gathered from the oak at new moon, and without the aid of iron.' Women who 'make a practice of carrying it about them' will conceive more easily, he asserted, and he gave us the story of the druids: 'Having made all due preparation for the sacrifice and a banquet beneath the trees, they bring thither two white bulls, the horns of which are bound then for the first time. Clad in a white robe the priest ascends the tree, and cuts the mistletoe with a golden sickle, which is received by others in a white cloak.'

Mistletoe comes to Ireland

Viscum album, the archetypal mistletoe with translucent white berries, is not a native plant on this island. Like the wild rhododendron, mistletoe is an alien, an invader, but we don't worry about it because almost every mistletoe grows out of sight high up in tall trees. As I will relate, mistletoe became established here in the mid-1800s after a large number of consignments of mistletoe berries were imported by a rather curious archbishop of Dublin.

We can be certain that mistletoe did not grow naturally in Ireland until modern times because there is no sign of its pollen in the ancient peat that forms Ireland's bog. There was not any mistletoe known to Irish botanical writers in the early 1700s although towards the end of that century a solitary old mistletoe-infested apple tree grew at Kilmainham, outside Dublin.

While the botanists could not find mistletoe growing wild in Ireland, gardeners decided to rectify this woeful omission by Mother Nature. As we know, gardeners are never thwarted by supposedly impossible plants – the more difficult the plant, the more alluring it is! The Belfast naturalist and enthusiastic gardener John Templeton tried growing it. On 12 March 1812 he 'Stuck Mistletoe [seeds] on Chestnut & Apple trees some of which I covered lightly with Cow dung'. We have no information about his success, but he does not mention mistletoe again in his diary, and even today mistletoe is not common around Belfast. James Townsend Mackay, Curator of the Trinity College Botanic Garden at Ballsbridge in Dublin, had a go about this time too. He was certainly successful in establishing one plant on an apple tree – in the 1840s, David Moore, who had been an undergardener in the College Garden, recorded that he was not aware of any mistletoes in Ireland except in Dublin '. . . where three plants have been established for a considerable period—one, in the College Botanic Garden—another, in the Royal Dublin Society's Botanic Garden [at Glasnevin]— and a third, growing on a thorn, near Kilmainham.'

Addressing the Royal Dublin Society in the middle of March 1845, David Moore recalled that his friend Mackay had placed mistletoe seeds on trees 'on many subsequent occasions . . . but was only successful the one time'. The College's mistletoe was the best Moore knew, but eventually it killed the apple tree it was infesting and so died itself. Other mistletoe plants must have sprung to life, for there was mistletoe in the College Garden as late as the 1960s when the garden was dismantled and replaced by hotels.

Mistletoe in Glasnevin

David Moore, then curator of the Royal Dublin Society's Botanic Gardens, Glasnevin, took up the mistletoe challenge and he had powerful support. Let him speak for himself.

> I would beg here to be excused for introducing the name of his Grace the Archbishop of Dublin, to whom the Royal Dublin Society, as well as myself, are indebted for affording the means of bringing this subject before you. His Grace, (who, it is well known, takes much interest in the natural history of both plants and animals,) wishing to introduce the mistletoe more generally through Ireland, has for that

Dr David Moore (National Botanic Gardens, Glasnevin; reproduced by permission).

purpose, had parcels of the seeds sent from England during the last four of five years, when some of them were kindly presented to the Botanic Gardens, on each occasion.

Indeed, the records of the Glasnevin Gardens confirm that a package of mistletoe berries came from the Archbishop in April 1844 – the others referred to by Moore are not recorded. Moore continued: 'In place of one miserable plant, as before, there are now nine living plants in the garden, in various stages of growth, from one to four years; some growing on thorn trees, some on apple trees and one on elm.' Thus the establishment of an abundant, thriving colony of mistletoe in the Glasnevin Botanic Gardens was due to Moore's skill as a horticulturist and the persistence and generosity of an archbishop.

Archbishop and gardener

The Most Reverend Dr Richard Whately, Church of Ireland Archbishop of Dublin, is now largely

The Most Reverend Dr Richard Whately, Archbishop of Dublin; watercolour by William Brocas (c. 1794–1868).

(© National Library of Ireland; reproduced by permission)

grafting. We know he obtained seeds and plants from distant parts, from Natal, New Zealand, Western Australia and Jamaica, because he also generously shared them. From Frankfurt he acquired scions, for grafting, of grapes, apples and pears, and split the bundles with David Moore. Seeds from Calcutta Botanic Garden were also passed to Glasnevin. Whately's 1858 donation of seeds collected in Africa by the famous missionary-explorer Dr David Livingstone can be directly connected to Livingstone's visit to Redesdale in 1857 on the occasion of the explorer's visit to Dublin when he lectured at the newly opened Natural History Museum on Merrion Square. Dr Whately surely used other ecclesiastical contacts to facilitate his acquisition of seeds, and both the College Botanic Gardens and Glasnevin benefited when he disposed of any surplus.

But let us return to our subject – 'missleto'. That is how Whately spelled the name when he lambasted the Elizabethan philosopher and politician Francis Bacon in some critical essays published in 1856. Bacon had noted 'the popular belief of his own time, that it is a true plant, propagated by its berries, which are dropped by birds on the boughs of other trees . . . ' But, wrote Whately, Bacon had rejected this 'universally admitted' opinion as 'a vulgar error, and insisted that the missleto is not a true plant, but an excrescence from the tree it grows on'. Whately fumed against Bacon's substitution of 'a random conjecture for careful investigation'. Could this explain the Archbishop's passion for mistletoe – to prove by careful observation the real nature of this oddest of plants?

Archbishop Whately died in 1863. A decade afterwards, on 21 January 1873, David Moore returned to the topic of mistletoe and paid tribute once more to the late Dr Whately, who 'was so enthusiastically fond of everything connected with vegetable physiology'. Conscious that mistletoe was scarce in Ireland, Whatley had 'brought with him from England a quantity of the berries or seeds . . . [and] we both succeeded in getting plants to grow'. Moore noted that 'now there are many plants in various parts of the country', and at Glasnevin 'at

forgotten. He came to the Dublin archdiocese in 1833, and because he did not enjoy having to live in the Archbishop's Palace on St Stephen's Green, he established his family in 'the country' to the south of the city, in Redesdale House, Kilmacud. This villa, demolished in 1998, was situated in a small demesne and there was a walled garden attached. Whately was a very keen gardener with, it is said, a particular passion for grafting trees. Presumably, when episcopal duties permitted, he would potter about at Redesdale, sowing seeds, planting trees and

Mistletoe on an old apple tree growing in the now-dismantled College Botanic Garden, Ballsbridge, Dublin, 1960. (By courtesy of Dr I. K. Ferguson)

Dr Whately's legacy: dense bunches of mistletoe cluster on the branches of lime trees (*Tilia*) in the National Botanic Gardens, Glasnevin. (© E. C. Nelson)

least a couple dozen bunches of mistletoe growing on six different kinds of trees'. Without any sense of concern, Moore proudly announced that mistletoe 'is now beginning to spread in Ireland.'

The Archbishop's mistletoes

To this day you can see fine bunches of mistletoe on quite a few trees in the National Botanic Gardens, Glasnevin – Whately's legacy. There are probably hundreds of flourishing mistletoes elsewhere in the Greater Dublin area – in Terenure, Loughlinstown, Shankill, Dartry, Rathmines, Ranelagh. In County Wicklow, mistletoe is reported at Kilmacurragh, where it was growing in David Moore's day, Mount Usher and Rosannagh. A hot-spot for mistletoe is Bunclody, where Wexford and Carlow merge, on apple trees, poplars and rowans – how it got there we can only speculate. Mistletoe also flourishes at Newtown on the outskirts of Waterford. On the other hand, this alien seems to have become extinct in Cork – during the 1910s there were 'luxurious growths on many trees' in Blackrock. Five old apple trees on the golf course in Adare, County Limerick,

'sport healthy crops' today. Up north, records are quite sparse. You would expect County Armagh, the apple county, to be awash with mistletoe but it isn't, nor is Belfast. 'Oh, mine grows on my gatepost!' which was a living willow tree, quipped the inimitable W. H. Phillips of Lemonfield, Holywood, Count Down, in the 1880s – but there are only a few young mistletoes in that county. The rest of Ireland is virtually a mistletoe-free zone. And that's exactly as it should be.

It is not often one can identify with any certainty the 'forgers of Nature's signature' – the people who introduce, with 'well-meant indiscretion' (to adopt Robert Lloyd Praeger's phrases), and let loose invasive alien plants. In the case of mistletoe, the culprits are known. The Director of the Glasnevin Botanic Gardens in concert with the Archbishop of Dublin did it, *deliberately*, unaided by druids with golden sickles at the new moon.

As a footnote, mistletoe thrives in the garden of the present residence of the Church of Ireland Archbishop of Dublin – a pure coincidence, surely?

2.7
THE EIGHTH JOY OF GARDENING: FERNS

Tanglewood, near Glengarriff, County Cork; white-flowered St Dabeoc's heath with ferns.
(© E. C. Nelson)

Facing page: Another Irish lady fern with a huge crest – this is the type of monstrous, mutant fern that the nineteenth-century fern-hunters sought. The precise origin of this example is not known; engraving from Edward Newman's *A HIstory of British Ferns* (1854).

HOW MANY JOYS are there in gardening? An uncounted number, probably, although one authority on the *Joys of the Garden*, the Reverend Dr Henry Kingsmill Moore, Canon of St Patrick's Cathedral, Dublin, reckoned twelve, one for each month. And, for him the eighth joy was ferns, specifically the native ferns of Ireland: 'when our native ferns are properly grown they are sure of the highest admiration, and can fill in our gardens a decorative place closed against most other plants.'

Moore was a fern enthusiast – a veritable pteridomaniac, a late participant in the fern craze which raged through gardening circles during the mid-nineteenth century and persisted in some quarters (especially in Ireland) well into the twentieth. He was not a lone figure, but one of a 'band of brothers' – there were very few women embroiled it seems – who happily, joyfully, even

ecstatically, went out into the countryside a-hunting ferns and digging up what they thought were unusual and interesting varieties. In 1936, Canon Moore was untroubled to write this: 'In Ireland ferns abound, often in such quantities that no one would miss a few a thoughtful collector might take.' Note the adjective 'thoughtful' – a 'thoughtful collector' is an oxymoron to present-day naturalists and gardeners. Things were different then.

While the Killarney fern is arguably Ireland's most famous fern, and was hunted almost to extinction (as related elsewhere), growing it is not that easy and Moore was not numbering it among those ferns that would be decorative in difficult spots in the garden. From his writings we know that the ferns he grew were much easier subjects, including the hart's-tongue, the royal, the polypody – he had a special 'Polypodery' just for them – and the lady fern. Irish polypody ferns were quite

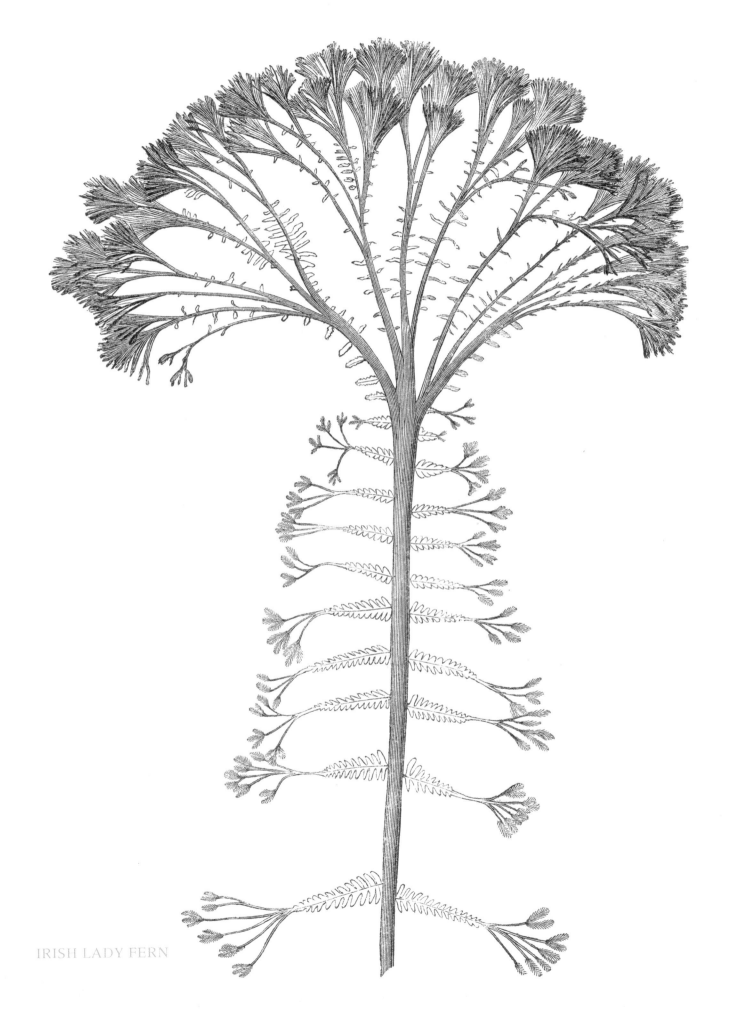

IRISH LADY FERN

James Townsend Mackay's polypody from the Dargle valley, County Wicklow; from Ann Pratt's *Ferns of Great Britain* (1855)

famous to fern enthusiasts: James Townsend Mackay of Trinity College Botanic Garden at Ballsbridge in Dublin had found some fine variants, including one extraordinary feathery one in Dargle Glen, County Wicklow, early in the 1800s, and Canon Moore was to discover others.

The tatting fern from Castlekevin

One of the earliest of the native ferns to gain a permanent place in ordinary gardens, and one that is still readily available, is the tatting fern, found a century and a half ago by a young woman in a glen in County Wicklow. A variant of the lady fern (*Athyrium filix-femina*), the tatting fern bears its discoverer's illustrious surname, 'Frizelliae'.

Mrs Jane Frizell told the story of the tatting fern herself. 'I found it [in 1857] on our own property in a most beautiful reach of the Avonmore river, which runs from Lough Dan', she recalled. The fern was growing 'between two large boulders so fast and with apparently so little soil, that it was with great difficulty my husband removed it.' But the original fern was not dug out immediately: Mrs Frizell 'watched it for two years by the river-side,

and it never had any appearance of seed'– she meant spores which are produced from small capsule-like structures that are produced on the undersides of the fern's leaves (or fronds). Clearly she would have preferred to leave the strange plant alone and try to grow new fernlings from the spores. However, when no spore capsules were obvious, the plant was removed and given to John Bain, Mackay's successor as the curator of Trinity College Botanic Garden. Placed in a greenhouse, Mrs Frizell's fern soon did produce spores and so was propagated and distributed.

The tatting fern is a monstrosity, a freak, but quite a handsome one! The lady fern normally has long fronds made up from numerous deeply divided and elongated segments called pinnules arranged on either side of a central rachis like overblown feathers. In the tatting fern the pinnules are stubby, congested, rounded, and are arranged on the rachis in a way that resembles the tatting work of lace-makers – 'bobbly' might be an apt description of a tatting-fern frond. The fronds are not evergreen as in some ferns, but wither in the late autumn and re-emerge the following spring. The tatting fern, once established, will produce spores and so young fernlings. Sometimes the fronds are not plain and linear, but forked or irregularly branched: plants that produce such fronds are best discarded as they are not true to type. Jane Frizell had noted this: 'I don't think I ever saw any plant of the *Frizelliae* so perfect as the original; there were about eight fronds, none of them with those sports and irregularities one has since seen on it.'

Other Irish native ferns

Nineteenth-century fern-hunters did have a wonderful time finding and removing fern freaks from Irish localities. Some famous names were among the fraternity of trowel-wielding pteridomaniacs. Robert Lloyd Praeger, later famous for his wonderful book *The Way that I Went*, was initiated into pteridomania by a fellow Ulsterman, the inimitable William Henry Phillips of Lemonfield, Holywood, County Down. Phillips was such a maniacal fern enthusiast that his bookplate (I

Welsh poppies are suggested as ideal companions for ferns; they are usually lemon-coloured, but a handsome orange also exists. (© E. C. Nelson)

Henry Kingsmill Moore; the frontispiece to *Joys of the Garden Month by Month* (1936).

treasure an unused original) shows him standing in his fernery among his prize specimens.

In Great Britain the fern craze petered out towards the end of the 1860s but not so in Ireland. Phillips was exceedingly active from August 1855 until his death seven decade later, discovering countless, obscurely distinct ferns throughout the north of Ireland. Phillips' garden at Lemonfield was a 'paradise', with 'an unrivalled collection of hardy ferns . . . with their many and variously tasselled sports'. He enthralled the young Robert Praeger whose youthful pressed specimens (now preserved in the National Botanic Gardens, Glasnevin) attest to an overwhelming concentration on monstrous *Filices* – ferns. Two lady ferns found at Castlerock in County Derry were the teenager's 'open sesame':

Mr Phillips and I became fast friends. I owe a great deal to his teaching, he had a marvellous eye for anything abnormal among the Filices . . . The Irish ferns did more for me than this for they brought me into contact with the best of the English fern men; I explored Devonshire with Col. A. M. Jones . . . and E. J. Lowe . . . and owing to their mistaken belief in my ability I judged British ferns at the Temple Show when I was seventeen . . .

Young Praeger's enthusiasm for ferns soon waned as his fascination for other plants grew, but he certainly maintained a lifelong interest in native ferns even though he learnt to ignore the occasional freak.

The troublesome Crawfordsburn fern

One of the ferns that Phillips and Praeger would have known – or knew, if it still existed! – was the troublesome Crawfordsburn fern. I use 'troublesome' advisedly because, to quote a letter from the late Jimmy Dyce, one of the leading twentieth-century authorities on native ferns, 'The trouble seems to be that any fern collected from [Crawfordsburn] was given the name!' There have been more than a baker's dozen of Crawfordsburn ferns – they still crop up. I was shown one a couple

CRAWFORDSBURN FERN

Belfast
Mr. W. H. Ferguson
1864.

Jane Frizell's tatting fern (© E. C. Nelson)

Facing page: The Crawfordsburn fern. In 1885, twenty-four years after it was discovered, W. H. Phillips and R. L. Praeger, who were then the experts on the ferns of Ulster, wrote:

> This is the celebrated Crawfordsburn fern, one of the most beautiful of a beautiful class, which was found near Crawfordsburn in 1861 by a labourer of Miss Crawford, only a single plant being discovered at the time, and in spite of frequent search it has never been found since. The plants usually sold as Crawfordsburn Ferns in the market are a far commoner form . . . The genuine plant is found in very few collections . . . '

of years ago, said to be authentic. But how can a fern that was probably extinct by the late 1880s still exist in any garden, except by wishful thinking?

The story of this fabulous phantasm of fernery, which was dowered with the Latin name *Polystichum setiferum* 'Divisilobum Crawfordiae', was once straightforward. Phillips and Praeger told it plainly:

> the celebrated Crawfordsburn Fern, one of the most beautiful of a beautiful class . . . was found near Crawfordsburn in 1861 by a labourer of Miss Crawford, only a single plant being discovered at the time, and in spite of frequent

search it has never been found since. . . it is easily recognisable by the very broad and over-lapping character of the pinnae, and the extreme breadth of the fronds.

They added for good measure: 'The plants usually sold as Crawfordsburn Ferns in the market are a far commoner form, viz. – divisilobum Alchinii. The genuine plant is found in very few collections.' No matter, the Crawfordsburn fern makes a reappearance every now and then – yet no one alive can say with absolute certainty what the original looked like. It was celebrated for its beauty and beautiful things can be difficult to grow.

The joy of ferns

Let us return to the Reverend Dr Henry Kingsmill Moore, fern enthusiast and advocate of joy in gardening. As already said, Canon Moore collected ferns in the wild and was candid about this activity although he did write that 'I am not a great hunter, and even if I were I have but scant leisure for the sport.' He had a missionary's zeal for ferns as well as an eye for the freaks – 'true varieties' he called them.

William Phillips potting ferns. (By courtesy of Paul Hackney, Ulster Museum)

William H. Phillips's bookplate. (Author's collection)

What is needed for the discovery of a true variety is experience. Good and novel ferns are not noticed by the untrained eye. One of the most constant that has come my way was growing opposite a cottage. Another had established itself beside a high road scarcely 150 yards from the main street of a busy village.

Once collected, Moore grew his ferns well, no doubt, and passed young plants on to fellow enthusiasts: 'One or two promising collections are coming into existence, formed largely from Cedar Mount ferns.' He devised his own special method of cultivation, growing many prize specimens in logs of elm hollowed out so that they were wooden flower-pots. The polypodies were given special attention and compost of leaf mould and lime rubble. Canon Moore regularly exhibited his ferns at the shows of the Royal Horticultural Society of Ireland, and just as regularly won prizes for them.

Cedar Mount in Dundrum, County Dublin, was Henry Kingsmill Moore's three-acre garden. The ferns were cultivated in those places where few other plants would thrive, and sprinkled among them were wood anemones, bluebells, wood sorrel and Welsh poppies: 'Yellow flowers go well with the green of the ferns.' He advised growing hart's-tongues with the lady ferns: 'If the Lady Ferns are widely intermingled with the Hart's-tongues they will not be missed in the resting time, and the spring birth of their light and feathery fronds will be an annual event of delight.' By choosing some sheltered, dark corner where nothing else would grow, 'there you may plant ferns with confidence'.

'I like ferns, they are always there, flowers pass over quickly,' said the canon's anonymous gardener. There is not a cultivated fern of Irish origin named after Dr Moore who, living until 1943, was perhaps the last pteridomaniac on this island, although Dr Praeger, having given up ferns for houseleeks, outlived him by a decade. It was said that fern-hunting was 'an old man's sport', yet Jane Frizell was only in her early thirties when she found her tatting fern. She lived for another six decades, passing away in November 1917 in her ninety-fifth year. Her fern survives, a joy for anyone's garden: 'How precious in our gardens are these memorials of friends who now are gardening elsewhere!'

3

THE PLANT HUNTERS

3.1
DR BROWNE'S FIRECRACKERS

THERE IS A DELIGHTFUL LITTLE PLANT, grown sometimes as annual bedding although it is naturally a perennial, with tiny, inch-long, tubular red flowers tipped with white and black. It is known by the vaguely descriptive name, the 'cigar flower', and sometimes as the 'firecracker plant'. To my mind it does not look like a cigar, but it does have an Irish connection. The Latin name is *Cuphea ignea*, and *Cuphea* was recorded in print in 1756 by a remarkable, little-known Irishman whose principal relic – apart from a book about Jamaica – is a manuscript about the wild plants of Mayo.

The botanist's name was Patrick Browne, a native of the townland of Woodstock, east of Claremorris, in the southeastern corner of County Mayo. He was born in about 1720 and in 1738, following a year on his family's estates in the West Indies, went to study medicine and botany in France, at Paris and then Rheims. He went on to the famous Dutch university city of Leiden, and thence to work in a London hospital before returning to the West Indies.

Between 1746 and 1754, Dr Browne lived in Jamaica where he treated his patients, collected, named and described hundreds of wild plants and animals, and gathered information for a history of the island. In 1756, in London, he published his notable book, *The Civil and Natural History of Jamaica*, a monumental tome illustrated with engravings of plants and animals. Nowadays, there are very few people who have seen a copy of this handsome volume, and even fewer who have read it, but it is one of the most important natural history books of the epoch. Browne espoused Carl Linnaeus' newly published schemes for naming and classifying plants and was thus the Swedish botanist's first disciple in the English-speaking world.

Patrick Browne returned to the Caribbean in 1757 and thereafter lived on various islands until he retired and returned home to Ireland in 1770, settling in Mayo, at Rushbrook, which is the townland beside Castlemagarret to the southwest of Claremorris. He lived there on and off for the next two decades, although he returned to the West Indies more than once during the same period. Browne died in August 1790 and was buried in the graveyard of the now-derelict Church of Ireland parish church at Crossboyne. No memorial to him was ever erected. He was soon almost forgotten.

But not quite forgotten. His name cannot be expunged from the annals of botany in the West Indies nor in western Ireland. Patrick Browne was a meticulous, careful observer, and I have spent two and more years tramping in his footsteps with some remarkable results. Consider, for example, a little plant, long used as a remedy for toothache, called pellitory-of-the-wall. Browne noted in his manuscript about the wild plants of Mayo that this herb, a relative of the stinging nettles, grew on the walls of Ballintubber Abbey – we do not know the exact date of his note, but it was before 1788. Pellitory-of-the-wall (*Parietaria judaica*) still clings to the mortared crevices of the abbey. It is not a spectacular wild plant, but it has long outlasted its discoverer.

Heartened by this find, I trudged onwards, sometimes accompanied by Wendy Walsh, the botanical artist, who has worked with me on a book about Dr Browne's plants. We took the pilgrim path and began to climb Croagh Patrick but soon set out for the corrie, that wonderful bowl-like amphitheatre of scree and peat on the northern side of the mountain. There on craggy outcroppings, inaccessible to sheep and goats and almost out of our reach, too, was the plant which Browne called *Saxifraga umbrosa*. If there were prizes for silly names, this plant would win hands down! Gardeners know forms of it as London pride, and the English

Top left: The firecracker plant, or cigar plant, *Cuphea ignea*, is a tropical subshrub which can be grown as an annual in Irish gardens. (© E. C. Nelson)

Top: Pellitory-of-the-wall was found by Patrick Browne on the walls of Ballintubber Abbey, and it still grows there. (© E. C. Nelson)

Far left: Pellitory-of-the-wall was used as a diuretic; it is a non-stinging relative of the common nettle. (© E. C. Nelson)

Left: The derelict parish church at Crossboyne where Patrick Browne was buried. (© E. C. Nelson)

name for it in Ireland is St Patrick's cabbage. It is not a cabbage at all, and has as little to do with St Patrick. The Irish name, *cabáiste an mhadra rua*, seems much more apposite if one could imagine a fox tending cabbages on those windswept mountain crags.

In Patrick Browne's manuscript there are many Irish names, and it seems likely that he was fluent in Irish as well as French and English, and he could finely 'turn a phrase' in botanical Latin. The majority of the plants he found in Mayo are described in that language, including the only plant that bears one of his own, original Latin plant names, the great fen-sedge. This belongs to a genus which Browne named *Cladium*, meaning a little branch, a reference to the arrangement of the flowers. The margins of the fen-sedge's sword-shaped leaves are serrated with minuscule teeth which are so sharp the leaf can slice through flesh like a surgeon's knife. Thus, it is fortunate that this sedge grows out of the way in loughs and deep ditches. Browne noted the fen-sedge in his Jamaican book and was surprised, I think, when he found the same rushy plant in the loughs at Rushbrook and Rockfield near Claremorris.

Among the plants that still inhabit the places where they were seen by him two centuries ago are the yellow loosestrife (*Lysimachia vulgaris*), a stately herb that blossoms in August at the same time as meadowsweet (*Filipendula ulmaria*) and purple loosestrife (*Lythrum salicaria*). Browne found the yellow loosestrife on the western shore of Lough Mask, and it can be seen thereabouts today, around Tourmakeady. In the same area he gathered St Dabeoc's heath (*Daboecia cantabrica*), the sumptuous purple-belled heather that is one of the great joys of a Mayo summer.

Left: Cuphea lanceolata is another tropical species, but can be cultivated as an annual in Ireland. (© E. C. Nelson)

Right: Brownea × *crawfordii*: this flower-head was brought from the Royal Botanic Gardens, Kew, to Dublin so that Wendy Walsh could paint its portrait for *An Irish Florilegium II*, because, in the mid-1980s, the only surviving tree of this Irish-raised hybrid was grown in Kew. The flower-head is 'as large as a child's head, as many as seventy flowers being counted in one cluster. Each flower is 3 inches long, about an inch wide at the mouth, and coloured a rich rosy-red.'

    Brownea × *crawfordii* is a hybrid between *Brownea grandiceps* and *Brownea macrophylla* which was created at Lakelands, Cork, under William Horatio Crawford's directions. The original plant was presented to the Royal Botanic Gardens, Kew, after Crawford's death in 1888; a sister plant went to Glasnevin but it did not survive. Crawford made another hybrid, using *Brownea coccinea* and *Brownea latifolia* as parents; William Edward Gumbleton suggested 'B. Lakelandsensis as an appropriate name for it'. Thus Crawford grew at least four different species of *Brownea* in his heated glasshouse at Lakelands, along with the hybrids he had created. (© E. C. Nelson)

Let us reconsider the cigar plant. A little taste of Patrick Browne's Jamaican labours can be appreciated in Irish gardens. While I would not suggest growing great fen-sedge, I can recommend two delightful tropical annuals – the extraordinary cigar (or firecracker) plant and another, quite different *Cuphea* with the richest purple, almost orchid-like flowers, and with two large ear-like upper petals. This is *Cuphea lanceolata*. Both can be sown in spring, in a cool glasshouse, planted out when the frost has finished, and they will blossom through the summer into autumn.

Patrick Browne's home at Rockfield has vanished. His unmarked grave in All Souls' churchyard, Crossboyne, is overshadowed by sycamores. We have no portrait of this Mayo man, only a word-picture: 'The doctor was a tall, comely man, of good address and gentle manners, naturally cheerful, very temperate . . . ' But there is another memorial that should long outlast human generations. In the tropical rainforests of central and South America grows a genus of trees with huge clusters of red flowers – these trees are named after him. *Brownea*, a member of the pea and bean family, is his eternal garland, a brilliant memorial to one of Ireland's, and Mayo's, finest naturalists.

74

3.2
THOMAS DRUMMOND AND THE PRIDE OF TEXAS

OUR GARDENS ARE brim-full of the finest plants from all corners of the globe, but how often do we think about the people – the plant hunters – who first went out to collect them for our enjoyment? What was the cost to them, not in shillings and pence, but in discomfort and hardship? Indeed, what was the cost in terms of human lives?

A lovely yellow-flowered mountain avens, a relative of the white-blossomed one that abounds in the Burren, arrived in our gardens following a bitter, lonely winter endured in a flimsy wooden hut in the back of beyond. Its cost included a nasty encounter with a mother grizzly bear and her cubs, and a frightening journey in an open boat on a very stormy Hudson Bay. Innumerable mosquito bites and short rations were also part of the uncounted price. In short, the man who found it and gathered its seeds for the first time was not on an all-inclusive package holiday in a comfortable luxury hotel, and he had not travelled by jumbo-jet. No! He had trudged hundreds of miles through the remotest parts of Canada, endured cold and utter isolation, living on his wits most of the time, just to discover some new plants.

Who was he? A 32-year old Scot named Thomas Drummond who was born at Inverarity in Forfarshire. His father, also Thomas, was a gardener on the local estate. Thomas had an older brother, James, and both lads were to follow in their father's footsteps, and then go much farther to unheard-of places. They both trained as gardeners, probably beginning as garden boys on the same estate where their father worked. James Drummond became the first and only curator of the short-lived Cork Botanic Garden, and Thomas became the first curator of the Botanic Gardens in Belfast. James was destined for the Swan River Colony (now Western Australia) and Thomas for North America.

Thomas Drummond; coloured crayon drawing by Daniel Macnee (reproduced by courtesy of the Royal Botanic Gardens, Kew ©)

By the time he was twenty-one, Thomas was working as manager of a Forfar nursery, but when he was offered an appointment on one of the great expeditions of exploration he accepted with alacrity. Thus Thomas Drummond became assistant naturalist on Sir John Franklin's second expedition (1825–1827) to the polar regions of North America. This expedition was not a holiday trip! It was entering one of the world's most inhospitable places – the Canadian Arctic.

Evidently Drummond was considered capable of undertaking exploration of uncharted country by himself and so was assigned a trip of his own, to explore the Rockies. He bade farewell to his colleagues in August 1825, and headed west with the Hudson Bay Brigade. Soon he decided to part company with the brigade and to continue by himself, with only an Indian guide for company. Bad weather and problems with the guide, who quit

The yellow-flowered mountain avens which was named after Thomas Drummond; photographed in the Washington Cascades, northeast of Seattle, USA. (reproduced by courtesy of Richard Ramsden).

and went home, eventually compelled Drummond, on New Year's Day 1826, to give up. He built himself a brushwood hut near the Baptiste River and for the next two months, during extremely severe weather, lived there all alone without food, except whatever he could shoot. Drummond later admitted he had been lonely. The wonder is that he survived to tell the tale.

More adventures and narrow escapes followed, and another winter. The next spring, Drummond continued his trudging and finally returned to the expedition's base on Hudson Bay. There he met David Douglas who had travelled across from the Pacific Ocean. Douglas was also on the same quest – new plants for insatiable gardeners. Like Drummond, he was Scottish, but while Douglas' life-history is well known, Drummond's is not. Perhaps this lapse of memory has sometime to do with the plants that these two intrepid explorers found, or perhaps it has to do with the sizes of their living memorials. There was nothing in Drummond's knack-sack to compare with Douglas's fir!

Thomas Drummond's discoveries in the Canadian wilderness were modest plants, but the important point is that he collected seeds (for gardeners) as well as pressed specimens (for botanists). That is not an easy undertaking, requiring either a long period camped in the field waiting for the flowers to produce ripe seed, or two visits to the same place, once in flowering season and again later when the plants have seed.

The lovely yellow-blossomed mountain avens was named after him: *Dryas drummondii*. Like the Burren species it forms a dense mat of dark green leaves but bears nodding, yellow flowers on short stalks. As might be expected it is very hardy, but not at all common in our gardens. Drummond also found and introduced the elegant old man's whiskers (*Geum triflorum*) which looks very like our native water avens (*Geum rivale*) but is not so tall and has wonderful grey-green foliage and pink flowers. Again, it is hardy, but not often seen, although tolerant of lime and amenable to neglect.

Drummond's other plants are less easy to grow successfully. He introduced, for example, the white rhododendron (*Rhododendron albiflorum*).

Drummond's seeds were distributed to various gardens and when the seedlings bloomed a number of the plants were painted and then figured in *Curtis's Botanical Magazine*. Those illustrated include two blue-flowered Jacob's-ladders, *Polemonium boreale* and *Polemonium pulcherrimum*, and a couple

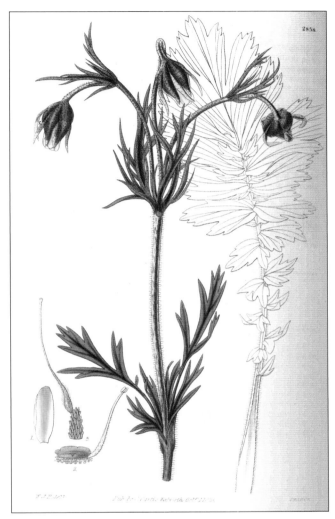

Old man's whiskers, *Geum triflorum*; from *Curtis's Botanical Magazine* plate 2858 (as *Sieversia triflorum*).
(Reproduced by courtesy of the National Botanic Gardens, Glasnevin)

The Belfast Botanic and Horticultural Society met on 5 January 1828 to form a public botanical garden. The Society was obliged to look to Scotland for a man suitably qualified for the job of curator. Thomas Drummond was offered the post and arrived in Belfast in the summer of 1828 bringing with him some packets of his seeds. Over the next few years, many of these seeds germinated in the new botanic garden at Stranmillis. Within a year the garden was taking shape, but only slowly, to Drummond's frustration. The workmen employed were not up to the task, and needed constant supervision. Even so, the curator managed to raise more than 500 species from seed in 1830 alone. However, by the late summer of 1830 Drummond had had enough and told Hooker he wanted to leave, and undertake another foreign trip to collect seeds – Nepal, South Africa, South America, anywhere as long as it was not Belfast.

Thomas Drummond had endured loneliness in the Arctic. Perhaps there lies a clue to his behaviour in Belfast. He could cope with isolation, but he needed to be his own master. He was, without doubt, neither a quiet man nor as respectful to his superiors as they thought he should be. Also, Drummond had, according to one of his friends, 'a fatal propensity for strong drink', to such an extent that the Society requested an assurance from him that he would abstain from 'fermented Liquors' for one year. In late November 1830, Drummond's career took a not unexpected turn. He was sacked by the Society because he had used 'hasty words' when reprimanding one of the Society's committee members who interfered with Drummond's instructions to the labourers. He 'cheerfully acquiesced', and set his sights on the southeastern United States as a suitable, profitable hunting-ground. Early in 1831 Drummond left Belfast, and, one suspects, the Society was relieved to be rid of him: the parting was evidently acrimonious.

Promising Professor Hooker that he would continue abstaining from intoxicating drink, Thomas Drummond set off for North America, again to collect seeds for a syndicate of gardeners, as well as dried specimens for Hooker. He reached New

of penstemons, *Penstemon gracilis* which bears pale violet flowers, and the blue-purple blossomed *Penstemon procerus.*

Both Drummond and Douglas were protégés of the professor of botany in the University of Glasgow, Dr William Hooker, later director of the Royal Botanic Gardens, Kew. Douglas, who was six years younger than Drummond, spent most of his short adult life travelling and collecting plants – he had no time to get married and settle down and raise a family. Drummond, on the other hand, did get married and at one time it looked as if he would settle down as curator of the Belfast Botanic Garden.

York on 25 April 1831 and began collecting with moderate success. However, when Drummond reached St Louis late that summer, he was ill with a fever that reduced him to 'skin and bones'. He abandoned collecting and went south by Mississippi steamer to New Orleans which served as his base for 1832. That year he found, among other plants, two insect-eating plants: *Sarracenia drummondii*, the white-topped pitcher-plant (now called *S. leucophylla*) and the low-growing parrot pitcher-plant (*Sarracenia psittacina*) which produces strange lobster-shaped pitchers. The following year Drummond headed for Texas. It was a disastrous year, with devastating floods, a cholera epidemic and political unrest. Drummond reached the tiny settlement of Galveston Bay but soon he and the other inhabitants contracted cholera. Thomas dosed himself with opium and eventually pulled through, but most of the residents died and the few survivors were starving because they were too weak to get food. All the same, in 1833 Drummond discovered the lovely yellow-blossomed beach evening primrose which now bears his name, *Oenothera drummondii*.

1834 was not much better. In the autumn he contracted a fever again, with severe diarrhoea, followed by an attack of boils that meant he could not lie down. That Christmas, poor Thomas Drummond was miserable, homesick, missing his wife and family, and not in the best of health. Even so, he was planning to return home to Scotland and fetch his family, and then return to Texas where he had applied for a land grant.

Drummond left Texas by sea and headed for Florida. 'I sail this evening for Havanna' were the last words he wrote to Hooker early in February 1835. By the end of March, Thomas Drummond was dead. Mystery surrounds his death in Cuba although with none of the gruesomeness that is associated with David Douglas's death in a bull-pit in Hawaii a few months later. In the space of just four months, William Hooker lost both his protégés in unexplained circumstances.

Thomas Drummond and David Douglas were both eulogised as 'martyrs' for botany and gardening. A handsome little annual phlox, the Pride of Texas,

Phlox drummondii, the Pride of Texas. (© E. C. Nelson)

that Thomas had gathered in Texas was to be his final memorial – *Phlox drummondii* blossomed in Belfast, in the botanic garden he had established, in the summer of 1835.

Among Thomas Drummond's contributions to the beauty of our gardens was the Texan bluebell (*Eustoma grandiflora*), an annual relative of the gentians, with satiny flowers in many shades of purple and pink. And a hundred-odd American plants carry Thomas' name. *Acer rubrum* var. *drummondii* is a variety of the red maple with pale green leaves veined red. Drummond's onion (*Allium drummondii*) has white, pink or red bell-shaped flowers. His wood sorrel (*Oxalis drummondii*) bears purple flowers and has deeply notched shamrock-like leaves, while the lovely white-flowered giant prairie lily (*Zephyranthes drummondii*) produces fragrant trumpets which open only at night.

Calculating the cost of the phlox, mountain avens and evening primrose is impossible. The tally includes a widow left in straitened circumstances, and a young family. It also includes the privations and unthinkable pain endured by Thomas Drummond, surely one of the most tragic of all plant-hunters. Perhaps in the end it was all too much for him, and his promise to Professor Hooker to abstain from intoxicating liquor was abandoned for the last time in Havana – but we will probably never know how he really met his end.

A pinch of seed of the simplest, loveliest garden flower can be tragically expensive.

3361.

Pub. by S. Curtis Glazenwood Essex Nov.ʳ 1 1834.

Swan Sc.

1

Beach evening primrose from Texas; *Oenothera drummondii* was illustrated in 1834 in *Curtis's Botanical Magazine* (plate 3361) having been raised from seeds sent by Thomas Drummond. (Reproduced by courtesy of the National Botanic Gardens, Glasnevin)

3.3
ON THE TRAIL OF THE BIG-CONE PINE

Big-cone pine cone: drawn in Chinese ink by Wendy F. Walsh. The cones can be twice the size of this example.

(© Wendy F. Walsh; reproduced by permission) (Author's collection)

CALIFORNIA IS A PLACE of excess and extravagance. The biggest trees in the world – the giant redwoods – grow there. One of the most extrovert of all poppies is a Californian native. The pine with the biggest pine cones inhabits the mountain ranges that lie inland from the coast between San Francisco and San Diego. And if you follow the trail of the big-cone pine, you will tread in the steps of a man from County Louth.

In 1831 a six-foot tall, red-haired Irish doctor stepped ashore at the tiny military post called Monterey on the California coast – at that time California was a province of Mexico and English-speaking visitors were infrequent. The Irish visitor had spent the previous few years in Mexico, but now he was about to embark on his long dreamed-of great plant-hunting adventure. By coincidence, another plant-hunter was in Monterey at the same time, the Scot, David Douglas. Nowadays Douglas – of the Douglas fir – is much more famous than the tall Irishman, mainly because he met a gruesome death in a bull-pit that ensured him a place in the martyrology of botany and gardening. The Irishman lived to tell his own stories, and by all accounts enthralled many in Dublin and Dundalk with tales of Mexican revolutions and Californian deserts.

Douglas was delighted to fall in with a fellow plantsman, and one who was also a superb shot and addicted to fly-fishing – plant-hunters in those days had to live off the land. Douglas even wrote to his patron in Glasgow, Professor William Hooker, exclaiming that 'it is a terrible pleasure to me to find a good man and a man who can speak of plants'. So, who was this lanky, Irish traveller?

Dr Thomas Coulter was his name, of Carnbeg, Dundalk, County Louth. Nowadays Thomas Coulter is familiar to all lovers of beautiful flowers, for his family name is immortalised in the second part of *Romneya coulteri*, bestowed by Dr William Harvey on the sumptuous white poppy that we all admire and hanker to grow. It is a wilful plant, stubborn about becoming established, yet when it is happy, the roots are capable of creeping under walls and burrowing below concrete paths. But beyond

The gold lace cactus, *Mammillaria elongata*, from the hinterland of Zimapan, was another of the species Coulter sent from Mexico.
(*Curtis's Botanical Magazine* plate 3646; reproduced by courtesy of the National Botanic Gardens, Glasnevin.)

Big-cone pine: young shoot (© E. C. Nelson)

price! Those white flowers with petals of crumpled silk are so evocative of the Californian sun that this poppy deserves to be in every garden from Dundalk to Dunquin. Plant it in the most awful gravelly builder's rubble, and it will thrive because it is a plant of the parched, rocky hill sides of southern California. Undoubtedly, from our point of view, the wonderful *Romneya coulteri* – called *matilija* by the Spanish-speaking Californians – was Thomas Coulter's most exciting discovery.

Thomas Coulter. Detail from portrait in oils (reproduced by courtesy of Trinity College, Dublin)

The big-cone pine cone which Thomas Coulter brought home from California; this cone is in the collections of the School of Botany, Trinity College, Dublin. (© E. C. Nelson)

Dr Thomas Romney Robinson, astronomer and friend of Thomas Coulter.

(Detail from portrait in oils; reproduced by courtesy of the Royal Irish Academy, Dublin.)

Years before he set foot in California, Dr Coulter was managing silver and lead mines in central Mexico. Their hinterland was a desolate, parched terrain on which little but cacti grew. In the early 1830s, Thomas Coulter sent collections of Mexican cacti to the botanic gardens in Geneva and to his friend James Townsend Mackay at the Trinity College Botanic Garden in Ballsbridge, Dublin. Coulter's cacti were among the first noteworthy consignments of these spiny plants to reach Europe, and a number of new species were named by botanists in Geneva, based on Coulter's plants.

However, it was California that was Coulter's most fruitful territory. At Monterey, David Douglas and Thomas Coulter wandered into the pine forests and amongst the cypress trees. They may have gone together to see the cathedral-like redwood groves in the Sur valley. Coulter collected cones of the pines, including one huge cone that is still in Trinity College, Dublin, today. Using Coulter's pine cones, the English botanist David Don named and described several important new species. The most significant was *Pinus radiata*, which is today extremely rare in its native habitats at Monterey, but is, of course, universally used as a forest tree and for shelter-belt timber. But the most stunning of the pine cones was unlike anything seen before, a heavy, clawed monster, more than a foot long. Don named the tree from which the cone had come *Pinus coulteri*, and thus its common name is Coulter's pine or big-cone pine.

Thomas Coulter's time in California was well spent, but arduous. He rode along the narrow, rough trail called *El Camino Real* – the King's Highway – that linked the Franciscan missions which were the only European-style settlements in California in the early 1830s. From Monterey, Coulter went to Santa Barbara and back and then, the big trek, southeastwards again through Santa Barbara and San Gabriel into the Colorado desert to the banks of the Rio Colorado where the sun was so hot that Coulter recorded a daytime temperature of 140 ℉. On his return trek, he visited a little port called San Pedro and the nearby Pueblo de Nuestra Senora Reina de los Angeles de Porciuncula lying southwest of San Gabriel. Later, Coulter wrote that thereabouts was the only fertile spot in California south of San Francisco, and the only place capable of supporting a large population. 'It is in many points fertile', he noted; 'wheat where it can be irrigated yields better here than in any other part of the Mexican territories I have seen. The vine also thrives better and is beginning to be extensively cultivated.'

Dr Thomas Coulter from Dundalk suggested with uncanny accuracy that this place would 'rise rapidly to the rank of a considerable town' – the vast city of Los Angeles cloaks that plain today, taking its name from Pueblo de Nuestra Senora Reina de los Angeles de Porciuncula. Thus, an Irish traveller was the prophet of the City of Angels, as well as the discoverer of the pure white, silky-flowered *matilija* poppy which has been described by William Robinson as the 'fairest plant that ever came to our land from the country of flowers, California.'

The California tree-poppy, *Romneya coulteri*, the 'fairest plant that ever came to our land from the country of flowers, California'. (© E. C. Nelson)

3.4
THE MOST SPLENDID VICTORIAN VEGETABLE AND A FEATHER-FLOWER BED

THIS STORY BEGINS 160 years ago with the germination of seeds in a glasshouse at the Royal Dublin Society's Botanic Gardens in Glasnevin during autumn 1847. That was not the happiest time in Ireland; the Great Famine was at its worst and the potato crop had been a total failure for the third year running. In one pan, four seedlings came up – they probably did not look especially exciting but they were, all the same, quite remarkable. This was certainly realised by Dr William Harvey, who kept a close eye on happenings in Glasnevin. The Gardens' Curator, David Moore, was undoubtedly distracted at the time because his wife, Isabella, was dangerously ill and she died that November. Yet he is sure to have known that these seedlings were no ordinary ones because the seeds had come from a little-known part of the world that was proving a rich source of unusual plants – Swan River Colony, or Western Australia. They were also likely to have been treated with special care because Moore had received them from the Archbishop of Dublin, The Most Reverend Dr Richard Whately.

Alas, what subsequently happened to these four seedlings is not recorded, and we only know about them because Dr Harvey mentioned their existence in a letter to his good friend Sir William Hooker, Director of the Royal Botanic Gardens, Kew. They were unique at that exact time: one up for Glasnevin over Kew. However, if they grew into sturdy shrubs, they probably looked undistinguished with grey-green, leathery leaves. We have no reason to suppose that they did not flourish for Moore, who was keen on Australian plants and skilful in cultivating them.

Harvey liked to keep Hooker informed about matters botanical and in a letter written early in January 1848, he announced the existence of the quartet of 'Drummond's Hakea victoria'. We don't know Hooker's reaction to this news – he can't have been delighted, however, hearing that Glasnevin had pipped Kew to the post and was the first to grow this new exotic, one that was hailed by its finder as the 'most splendid vegetable production which I have ever seen, in a wild or cultivated state'.

Archbishops are not often insatiable plantsmen, enthusiastic about raising new plants from seeds, but Dublin's Dr Whately was – Dublin gardens owe the mistletoe to him. He procured numerous packets of seeds from the Swan River Colony, and at least one handsome illustration confirms that their progeny flourished and bloomed at Glasnevin. While not perhaps as strange as the parent of the four 1847 seedlings, a shrub of *Banksia occidentalis* flowered in Glasnevin a couple of years after the *Hakea victoria* seedlings had germinated, and was illustrated in Sir Joseph Paxton's *Magazine of Botany* during 1850. The *Banksia* seeds had come through the archbishop. Dr Whately also provided seeds to Trinity College Botanic Garden. An unusual relative of the myrtle and Australia's gum-trees, raised from the archbishop's donation, was to be named by Dr Harvey and thereby gives us a clue to the archiepiscopal source. *Hypocalymma phillipsii* honours John Randall Phillips, the Administrator and Resident Magistrate at King George Sound. While he supplied Dr Whately with seeds, he was not necessarily their collector.

To continue the tale of the *Hakea* seedlings, we must skip ahead a few years to 1854. Imagine, if you will, a low wooden house, roofed with shingles and encircled by a broad verandah. The evening is mellow; a breeze stirs the leaves on the gum trees all around. There are two men sitting at ease on the verandah, the older, bearded gentleman is speaking with a Scottish accent that might tell you he came

Banksia occidentalis, the red swamp banksia, from southern West Australia was grown at the Glasnevin Botanic Gardens having been raised from seed donated by the Archbishop of Dublin, Dr Richard Whately (from Joseph Paxton's *Magazine of botany*; reproduced by courtesy of Stephen Besley, Besleys Books, Beccles, Suffolk).

plant-collecting journey and had recently arrived in the Colony from Ceylon. Drummond and Harvey had much to talk about, information to exchange about mutual friends, and reminiscences of Irish gardens to review. James Drummond had left Cork, with his family, and sailed early in 1829 for the Swan River Colony where he was Government Botanist. He probably maintained contact with Irish friends – both Moore of Glasnevin and James Mackay, curator of the College Botanic Garden, were fellow Scots.

As one of the first settlers in new colony, Drummond was a veritable pioneer, acquiring land in the area to the northeast of Perth, and there establishing his farm. As well as farming, he was part of Sir William Hooker's worldwide network of plant collectors. James happened to have landed in one of the world's botanical 'hot spots', for the bush in the southwestern part of Australia contains thousands of unique plants, his *Hakea victoria* among them.

Harvey had reached the tiny settlement of Albany on the shore of King George Sound in the south of the Colony early in 1854. It was too late for flowers but Harvey's main interest was seaweeds and he was able to enjoy himself collecting these in the sheltered waters of the Sound. At Albany he became friendly with George Maxwell, a carter who had worked for Drummond on plant-hunting expeditions. Early in April, Harvey set off in Maxwell's mail-cart on the long, rough ride, which took eleven days, to Perth. No doubt Harvey had alerted Drummond – no sooner had Harvey reached his lodgings with the Colonial Secretary, William Sanford, than who should arrive but Drummond.

James Drummond was then in his late sixties, 'a venerable looking man with snow-white Hair & long beard, square built frame, ruddy features, & an intelligent eye that lights up with enthusiasm'. He reminded Harvey of Mackay of the College Botanic Garden. The botanical collector was bursting with news of new plants and took full advantage of the visitor – he probably hardly stopped for breath as he told his tales. Harvey's letters brim over with the excitement.

from the county of Angus. The younger man, listening attentively, speaks with a Irish lilt – he is from Limerick. It's April, the end of summer – the house is half a world away, just outside the small, but growing town of Perth, one of the most isolated places on earth, the young capital of the Swan River Colony.

The Scot is James Drummond, a famous plant collector, who had lived a third of his life in Cork, the one and only curator of the city's short-lived botanic garden. The Limerick man is Harvey, by now Professor of Botany to the Royal Dublin Society. The professor is on a round-the-world

James Drummond: 'the botanic explorer of this colony had arrived, having come upwards of 40 miles to have a botanical chat with me'. (Reproduced by courtesy of Dr Philip Short.)

Professor William Henry Harvey. (Frontispiece from *A Manual of British Marine Algae*: author's collection).

Drummond chatted about his explorations, how he would set off into the bush with three ponies, a bullock-drawn waggon, and a few native guides. They camped out under the stars for several months when the flowering season was at its peak. Quite recently, about 300 miles to the north, he had found an amazing new feather-flower with bright crimson flowers the size of a half-crown, huge compared to the known species of the genus. The shrubs formed a sheet of blossom, so beautiful that the waggon-driver actually turned his bullocks off the track to avoid trampling on, and destroying, the plants. Drummond gathered armfuls of the new feather-flower, which he called *Verticordia grandis*, and set about pressing the specimens so he could add them to his next collection for Sir William. Harvey must have listened in amazement as the old Scot admitted that he had collected so much material that he made his bed that night from the twigs he could not get into his bulging plant-press.

As the sun set that evening, I imagine that Harvey turned the conversation to those four seedlings that had sprouted at Glasnevin six years earlier, and prompted Drummond to tell the tale of that journey, far to the southeast into the Barren Range.

Drummond had travelled from Perth towards Albany, 250 miles away, and had branched off a little north of Albany into the Stirling Range. George Maxwell was with him but had business somewhere nearby and left Drummond alone in camp. Not wanting to be idle, Drummond climbed a nearby hill and was rewarded with a charming new species of *Darwinia* (named after Charles' grandfather, Dr Erasmus Darwin) with tulip-like, drooping flowers, the Mondurup bell. When Maxwell rejoined him, they headed further southeast, aiming for the coast and the Barren Range where an even more exciting plant awaited discovery. This was the astonishing *Hakea victoria*, parent of the Glasnevin seeds, which resembles a towering, elongated cabbage. The shrubs usually have an unbranched stem, and can reach four metres in height. The extremely tough, leathery leaves encircle the shoots and are naturally variegated – red, gold, orange, yellow, green.

Drummond collected sixteen of these extraordinary plants, but he could not press them – they were too bulky and the pressure of the plant-press broke the leaves. So he made up two bundles, loosely tied with the stems of a local creeper, and slung one bundle each side of his old grey pony.

Left: Royal hakea plants in the Fitzgerald River National Park, Western Australia. (© E. C. Nelson)

Centre: The scarlet feather-flower, *Verticordia grandis*, which provided Drummond's bed. (© E. C. Nelson)

Right: Royal hakea, *Hakea victoria*, has naturally variegated foliage. (© E. C. Nelson)

Sprigs of another Western Australian shrub which William Harvey named *Hypocalymma phillipsii* after John Randall Phillips (1791–1852). This was raised in the College Botanic Garden, Ballsbridge, Dublin, the seed donated by the Archbishop of Dublin.

The best specimen, a fourteen-footer, Drummond carried all the way along the coast to Albany, to ensure it stayed in prime condition. Alas, the sun soon bleached the leaves and the variegation was no longer luminous. It must have been a bizarre sight – a plodding pony with orange, green and gold bundles, and a white-bearded Scot holding the best stem aloft like a giant spear.

I had the great privilege in the early 1970s to spend time in the Barren Range and to walk among these unique plants, to tread, so to speak, in Drummond's footsteps. For Drummond, the discoverer, the sight must have been amazing. Nothing could have prepared him for this vegetable wonder. He named it after Queen Victoria. Believing that the plant 'will soon be in cultivation in every garden of note in Europe, and in many other countries', Drummond made sure to collect good quantities of seed.

At Albany, Drummond started sorting, labelling and packing his plant collection ready to send to Sir William Hooker who would arrange for the fourteen sets of pressed specimens to reach the people who were paying for them. This was Drummond's wage for his work. It took Drummond until July 1848 to get all the material ready. He also had seeds: 10 lots,

each containing 200 species (including *Hakea victoria*), for which a subscriber was asked to pay £10 (about €800, in today's money). None of the specimens left the Colony before July – none?

Except – and this is a mystery – somehow some seeds of *Hakea victoria* left Albany *before* Drummond set off home. Otherwise, how could the seeds have sprouted in Glasnevin by the end of that same year? Certainly, the *Hakea* seeds did not reach Ireland through the usual channels: Hooker at Kew.

I suspect John Randall Phillips. He would have been in Albany when James Drummond, leading his pony laden with the specimens, arrived from the Barren Range, and he is known to have sent other seeds to Archbishop Whately – *Hypocalymma phillipsii* proves that.

Hakea victoria is outlandish and contrary – in cultivation it never grows like a columnar, variegated cabbage. That it first grew outside its native habitats in one of Ireland's botanic gardens reflects the insatiable curiosity that keen plantsmen possess for novel plants. They stop at nothing to get them; even an archbishop will circumvent the system to obtain 'botanical gems'!

3.5
WILLIAM ROBINSON'S LITTLE TOUR IN THE ALPS, 1868

A FEW WEEKS BEFORE he turned thirty, in mid-June 1868, William Robinson went plant-hunting in the Alps. It was to be a short excursion, a chance to explore and collect, and one of the results was a series of articles about the trip in *The Field*, the weekly paper for which he then wrote regularly. He was yet to publish his best-known works, and acquire the sobriquet 'Father of the English flower garden'.

This 'little tour' of the Alps began at Geneva, and the first day 'was devoted to the ascent of the Grande Salève, which, though not a great mountain . . . is nearly 5000 feet high, and affords a good opportunity of commencing training for more serious work.' Starting before six o'clock in the morning, Robinson and his guide set off up the mountain through meadows full of pinks, harebells and sages. Leaving the flowery meadows, they reached hazel woodland carpeted with lily-of-the-valley. Robinson becomes quite lyrical, and quoted Byron's *Childe Harold*: 'the scene is one of unalloyed beauty and abounding life' –

A populous solitude of bees, and birds,
And fairy-formed and many-coloured things.

There are many 'fine rock-plants' on these scrubby slopes. 'Soon I gather my first truly wild Cyclamen.' Three hours of climbing gets the walkers to the top. Robinson had expected a barren, stony summit, but he found instead 'an immense plateau, stretching miles in length, and covered with the greenest and freshest verdure', better, he thought, than any in 'the Green Isle'. He was, however, 'very glad to meet with my first silvery saxifrage in a wild state.' There were 'brilliant' spring gentians everywhere: 'it is . . . a hardy little gem-like triumph of life in the midst of death, buried under the deep all-shrouding snow . . . near the margin of the wide glaciers.' He remembered that 'it also ventures into non-alpine countries, being found in Teesdale and Galway'.

Robinson had planned his trip with some care it seems. He intended to base himself at 'the little earthquake-shaken town' of Visp, in the Rhône valley to the east of Geneva, and then to walk south up the Saas valley. 'Provided only with an alpenstock', he would explore alpine meadows and return to Visp in a day or two. It was about fifteen miles from Visp to Saas. The landlord of the Visp hotel pointed out the route, and Robinson left at around ten o'clock on a dull morning. Soon he overtook a man who told him he was a chamois-hunter and guide. 'It was lucky that I met him', quipped the plant-hunter. On this rather gloomy day, with gloomy rocks towering overhead, Robinson could enjoy the plants – there was no distraction from the scenery. Cushions of the cobweb houseleek grew in almost every chink: 'I could have gathered thousands of plants of it. Next our pretty old friend, the Hepatica, came in sight, peeping here and there under the brushwood.' After a walk of almost two hours, the pair reached a village, with a very poor inn, where they had some black bread and wine. By this time it was raining, but they set out again. Another hour's trudge in the rain brought them to a chalet and they debated whether to stay, but Robinson was to meet a friend at the head of the valley, so they continued through the sleet. Crossing torrents by means of precarious, rickety pine-log 'bridges', they walked on. Not everything was gloomy. Little caves by the path were 'literally lined with the pretty little yellow Viola biflora. Every cranny was golden with its flowers; every seam between the rocks and stones enlivened by it.' Alpenrose (*Rhododendron ferrugineum*) was also in bloom.

William Robinson as a young man; this photograph probably was taken about the same time as his trip to the Alps.

(Reproduced by courtesy of Lieutenant-Colonel Philip Haslett)

Common hepatica, *Hepatica triloba*: 'There is a cheerfulness and a courage about . . . this exquisite little flower'. A cultivated plant, growing with red-veined foliage of a Chinese fumitory. (© E. C. Nelson)

'In the hotel'; the beared, hunched-over, miserable man looks remarkably like the young William Robinson!

'Excelsior!'

'A disputed passage': is the man confronting the goat Robinson's friend Mr A. Wheeler?

Glacier crowfoot, *Ranunculus glacialis*: 'I have scraped away the snow in quantity to get at it'. (© E. C. Nelson)

Alpenrose, *Rhododendron ferrugineum*: 'I shall remember the shallow caves . . . crested by the Alpine Rose longer than many sunnier scenes.' (© E. C. Nelson)

Several hours later they reached Saas, only to find the hotel closed. Soaked through, without a change of clothes – he had left his luggage in Visp – Robinson was thoroughly miserable. He stood on the threshold of the hotel until the local curé took pity on him, instructed a maid to make a fire 'with all haste' and ordered dinner. The curé borrowed a pair of breeches 'from the wardrobe of a native' and Robinson put these on, and a pair of stockings. 'I seized the duvet, or bag of down a foot thick, which frequently lies on the beds in continental houses, and, wrapping it round my shoulders, sat down to extract as much heat as possible out of the fire – not a good one, despite my passionate entreaties for more wood. I felt horribly lonely, and was, I should say, not very ornamental, crouched over the fire in this attire.' Dinner was bacon 'swimming in an inch of oil, accompanied by almost unbearable fried potatoes'.

The snow now lay at least a foot deep, so searching for plants was not going to be easy. Robinson's friend had already left for the pass of Monte Moro but the curé sent men to fetch him back to Saas. Robinson now changed his plans:

'rather than return by the same long and dreary valley, I determined to cross the Alps and descend into the sunny valleys of Piedmont, where we should, at all events, probably see some traces of vegetable life.'

The following day, Robinson and friend set out for Mattmark, nearly nine miles from Saas, and more than 7,000 feet higher up. Under ledges where the ground was not covered with snow they 'found many ordinary and well-known plants.' One prize was *Ranunculus glacialis*. By scraping away the snow they found saxifrages and a few sempervivums, spring gentians, a pink-flowered flax, and the beautiful *Eritrichium nanum*, 'from half an inch to an inch high, and with cushions of sky-blue flowers.' They explored the pass, where there was a great glacier, and the Belvedere between two branches of that glacier, but these places were 'a desert, so far as rare alpine plants were concerned.' Lower, below the snow-line, the 'great bearded seed-heads' of alpine pasque-flowers cloaked the alpine meadows. The beautiful white-flowered buttercup called fair-maids-of-France (*Ranunculus aconitifolius*) was common here too, and there were campanulas and

Yellow wood-violet, *Viola biflora*; 'a lovely little ornament . . . on the Alps'. (© E. C. Nelson)

Spring gentians, *Gentiana verna*: 'its vivid colour and peerless beauty stamp themselves on the mind of the dullest traveller that crosses the Alps'. The gentians reminded Robinson of western Ireland, too. (© E. C. Nelson)

lily-of-the-valley and carpets of mountain azalea (*Loiseleuria procumbens*). A few days later the pair continued over the pass of Monte Moro into Italy, and walked several miles through the snow 'before a trace of vegetation could be seen.'

Forsaking the Alps, Robinson now decided to head for Lecco on Lake Como, 'ascend Monte Campione, and find Silene Elisabethae'. The following day they set off at half-past three in the morning and covered twelve miles before breakfast: 'every step revealed a new charm.' In the valley, they found 'well-built and clean-looking houses'. The terraced hills were cultivated, and there were vines 'trained on a high loose trellis from five to seven feet above the surface of the ground, so as to permit of the cultivation of a crop underneath'. All along the valley, nearly every rock and cliff was covered with great silvery saxifrages.

They came to Lake Maggiore, with its famous garden-covered islands, and stopped for a while, but William Robinson was not excited: 'the isles look pretty, but not beautiful, because of the rather extensive and decidedly ugly buildings and terraces upon them.'

Reaching Lecco on Lake Como, the pair prepared 'to hunt for the handsome Catchfly on the crest of Monte Campione.' Again, they started early, at three o'clock in the morning. 'Soon we find ourselves on the spur of a mountain, on which Cyclamens peep forth here and there.' Bloody cranesbill was everywhere, with aconites and lilies. A dwarf, very floriferous privet also impressed Robinson. 'The orange Lily is a great ornament hereabouts. I saw on one of the topmost and most inaccessible cliffs of the mountain one of its bold flowers like a ball of fire in the starved wiry grass.' There were dwarf brooms with mingled groups of hepaticas and cyclamens. 'The Cyclamens are deliciously sweet, and the great spread of Erica carnea, seen in all parts, must afford a lovely show of colour in spring.' In the small meadows on the mountain slopes orchids, harebells, 'and a host of meadow plants, struggle for . . . mastery. Conspicuously beautiful was the St. Bruno's Lily, growing'. Edelweiss – Robinson called it 'The Lion's-paw Cudweed' – abounded on Monte Campione, and so did *Gentiana acaulis*. Mountain avens were in full bloom. But, there was no sign of *Silene elisabethae* until, descending, they spotted a plant

Wild *Ranunculus aconitifolius* was very common in the grassy fields: the 'double' variant of this is called Fair-maids-of-France. (© E. C. Nelson)

St Bruno lily, *Anthericum lilago*: 'just high enough to show its long and snow-white bells above the grass. ' (© E. C. Nelson)

growing from a chink on a low mass of rock. By carefully breaking away portions of this we succeeded in getting the plant, roots and all, out intact, and by very diligent searching, found a few more specimens of it . . . Then a long trudge down mountain, valley, and hilly road brought us home to our quarters at half-past nine, after a long and interesting day of nearly twenty hours' walking.

Having 'had the pleasure of gathering' Elisabeth's elusive catchfly, which has large flowers 'of a bright rose colour', Robinson headed home, crossing back to the Rhône valley by the Simplon Pass. Most probably he used the diligences that linked the towns and cities, to retrace his way to Visp to collect the luggage he had left there.

Two years after this alpine adventure, William Robinson published *Alpine Flowers for English Gardens*, reprinting in the chapter entitled 'A little tour in the Alps' four cartoons that had enlivened his articles in *The Field*. The one captioned 'A disputed passage' is not explained, except by a

sentence below it: 'Happily, in crossing we did not encounter any unexpostulating but stubborn denizens of the mountains hurrying down from the snow-clad pastures.' 'In the hotel' needs no explanation; it is a good representation of a cold, hungry, tied, lonely, miserable plant hunter.

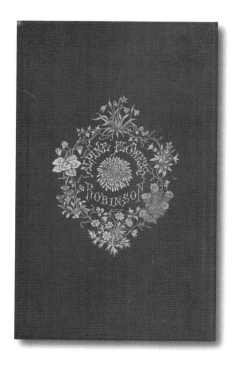

3.6
'FROM SEA TO SHINING SEA': WILLIAM ROBINSON CROSSES NORTH AMERICA, 1870

RMS *RUSSIA* was not an immigrant ship carrying the displaced and dispossessed heading for the New World; she was a liner with first and second class berths and carried only travellers and well-to-do migrants. When she left Liverpool on 23 July 1870, one such traveller, describing himself as an author, was the Irish-born horticulturist William Robinson – not yet at the height of his fame but renowned none the less for his acerbic commentaries about the state of gardening in England.

Cobra lily, *Darlingtonia californica*, in the wild in the northwest United States. Robinson went to North America to find this insectivorous plant and brought living specimens home with him.
(© E. C. Nelson)

It was almost ten years since William had left Ireland to further his career, to work as a gardener in the Royal Botanic Society of London's garden in Regent's Park. He stayed there about five years before resigning to take up journalism full time. Robinson had spent most of 1867 in France studying horticulture, and writing up his observations for *The Times* of London. These articles catapulted him into the public eye for he dared to compare English gardens most unfavourably with those of France. Consequently, his books about the gardens of Paris were best-sellers! He had also been to the Alps and out of that trip, along with his knowledge of rock gardens in Britain and Ireland, he had composed *Alpine Flowers for English Garden*s. This book was published just before he left for North America.

Russia docked in New York on 3 August and William disembarked to begin his stay of eighteen weeks. Very soon afterwards he set off for London in Ontario, Canada, then a small town. This gave him a chance to start looking at the native flora, and he noted particularly the tall phloxes that grew luxuriantly on the shore of Lake Erie. Like any tourist, Robinson went to the Niagara Falls, walking for a mile or so along the river on the Canadian side. He was overwhelmed by the place:

the noblest of Nature's gardens I have yet seen is that of the surroundings and neighbourhood of the Falls of Niagara, and very suggestive it is to those interested in forming artificial or improving natural cascades and the like. Grand as are the colossal falls, the rapids and the course of the river for a considerable distance above and below possess more interest and beauty . . . The high cliffs are crested with woods, the ruins of the great rock-walls, forming wide irregular banks between them and the

water, are also beautifully clothed with wood to the river's edge, often so far below that you sometimes look from the upper brink down on the top of tall pines that seem diminished in size. The wild vines scramble among the trees, many shrubs and flowers seam the high rocks, in moist spots here and there a sharp eye may detect many flowered tufts of the beautiful fringed Gentian, strange to European eyes, and beyond all, and at the upper end of the wood-embowered deep river-bed, a portion of the crowning glory of the scene – the falls – a vast cliff of illuminated foam, with a zone towards its upper edge as of green molten glass.

Robinson returned to the United States, visiting nurseries in Buffalo and New Jersey, horticultural shows in Boston, and famous parks, private gardens and great garden-like cemeteries. He called at the US Department of Agriculture in Washington DC, and spent time learning about the ways and means used to preserve fruit and vegetables. Tomatoes, eggplants, watermelons, pears, peaches, vines and apples all impressed him. 'The egg plant is an excellent vegetable, though in the hotels it resembles small leathery pancakes boiled in grease till black and tough. It is very good when properly fried, and also when baked or in pies.' Clearly he enjoyed his food, and often wrote about the fare available in hotels, but he was far from pleased by the bread:

> The varieties of bread placed before you at a good hotel you find so hot and soft and sickly-sweet that you appeal to the waiter for some brown bread, which you find included in the breakfast *carte*. He brings some, apparently quite sound, and you fall upon it with desperate satisfaction; but to your horror you find that, previous to the baking, it has been thoroughly saturated with treacle!

Relating that one of his fellow passengers on the *Russia* had expressed disappointment on learning there were no tomatoes available on board, Robinson launched into these instructions on eating them.

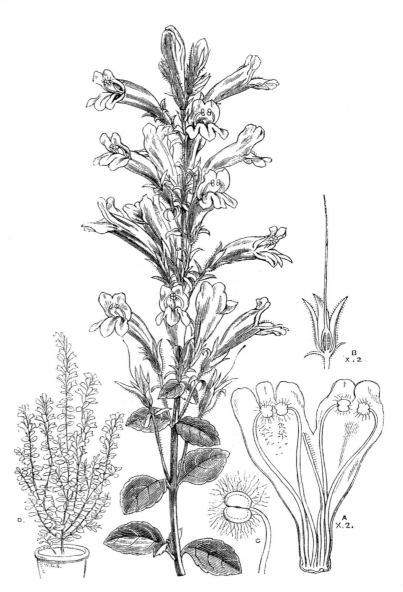

PENSTEMON ROBINSONII

'Robinson's pentstemon' was illustrated in *The Gardeners' Chronicle* on 20 July 1872. Robinson had brought plants from the Sierra Nevada and they bloomed in cultivation. This is now thought to be a variant of *Penstemon newberryii*.

Facing page: Purple mountainheath, *Phyllodoce breweri*.
(© Neal Kramer)

Stewed, baked, as sauce or in soup, eaten raw as a salad or with sugar, in all these ways it is good; but during the heats of summer in no way is the tomato more agreeable to those who know its merits than eaten 'from the bush.' The process is simple. 'Select a good ripe fruit, place the lips against its glossy sides, bite a piece clean off without fear, and then suck with all your

The cobra lily grows in the same habitats as the California lady's-slipper orchid, which has elegant spikes of white-pouched flowers. (© E. C. Nelson)

I came upon the Darlingtonia, greatly to my satisfaction, on the north side of a hill, at an elevation of about 4000ft., growing among *Ledum* bushes, and here and there in sphagnum, and presenting the appearance at a little distance of a great number of Jargonelle pears, holding their larger ends uppermost, at a distance of from 10in. to 24in. above the ground.

Darlingtonia californica, the Californian cobra lily, is a relative of the eastern American pitcher-plants (*Sarracenia*), differing in having a strange hooded pitcher, but having the same habit – they trap insects in their hollow leaves. Robinson was delighted with himself: 'I shall bring home some plants, and have no doubt that I shall easily cultivate this plant, hitherto considered almost uncultivable on both sides of the Atlantic.'

In San Francisco, again the vegetables and fruits amazed him: lettuces, tomatoes, globe artichokes and Chinese radishes grown in neat vegetable gardens. As for the vine, here he found European varieties flourishing, in contrast to the native ones on the eastern coast. As for the Muscat grapes,

judicious selection of locality will in time produce as good Muscats in the open air here as ever grew in an English hothouse. Those in the market now are far better than many specimens of Muscats grown with us. It is calculated that there are now considerably over thirty millions of grape vines planted in the State of California; and wine making is turning out so satisfactorily that vine culture is likely to be carried out to a very much larger extent. It is probable that more gold will be got out of the earth in this way than ever it yielded to the miner . . .

might. At first certain succulent leathery coats may offer some resistance; but soon the red heart's juice, kept cool in the hottest days by the outer coats, will begin to flow, and victory will be yours.

Leaving the east coast in early October, Robinson took the train westwards via Chicago towards California. It was a long and often dreary journey on a railroad system that had only been completed the previous year, and he must have been one of the earliest travellers to cross the continent coast to coast, and return. Once he reached California, he headed into the foothills of the Sierra Nevada for a particular purpose. Staying in 'a city of two houses and two stables' where people grumbled about the smallness of the trees, he set off in search of a unique plant.

Time would tell, he concluded, 'and then we shall hear much more of Californian wines that an present.'

There was no time to linger – Robinson was a young man in a hurry. Early November saw him back on the train heading east, but there were two more stops to be made. Again in the mountains, William stayed at Summit House, an hotel near the railway run by a fellow Irishman, from which the Sierra Nevada's summits were accessible. There was a foot or two of snow on 15 November, but Robinson was able to find another plant he wanted to see: *Phyllodoce breweri*, a relative of the European heathers. 'After trudging for hours over snow and rock in quest of this, I had given it up, when a spray, with a withered truss of bloom, was seen, and soon I had dug a few score plants of it from beneath a couple of feet of snow. Another fall, and I should have been too late.' So he had more plants in his luggage! The locals wondered why he bothered to try to look for plants at this season instead of summer when 'every yard of the ground is a brilliant garden'.

From the snow-capped mountains, he re-entered the dreary deserts, and, leaving the main transcontinental line, Robinson made an interesting diversion, by a branch line, to Salt Lake City to see how gardening fared among the Mormons.

> The idea originally was that the capital should be a city of gardens as well as a city of saints; that every man was to sit under his own vine and fig tree; and that each house was to stand isolated in a garden. But in the chief streets the demon of trade has already defeated Mr Brigham Young in this. He – the demon – destroyed all the little gardens before and between the houses, and piled store against store, and against the footways, precisely as he has done in the Gentile thoroughfare known as the Marylebone Road, London, N. W. However, in all but the main streets the original idea is carried out, and all the streets are wide and planted with trees.

Once more, vegetables excited his attention, especially the gourds, maize, potatoes and tomatoes.

By the end of November, Robinson was back in New York, collecting examples of garden tools, buying tinned tomatoes, bottled fruit and pop-corn. No doubt he also checked his plants, the cobra lilies, the lily bulbs and precious alpine plants that he had gathered in the Sierra Nevada. The Cunard liner *China*, a sister ship of the *Russia*, sailed for Europe on 8 December, and William landed at Queenstown (Cobh) a week or so later.

No book resulted from his adventures in North America, probably because there simply was not enough to tell. While the wild plants and the vegetables impressed him, the gardens he had seen did not. Early on he had reached this opinion: 'I have traversed about a thousand miles of the United States, and, as regards horticulture, have found about as much interest and novelty as a student of snakes could collect during a like period in the land of St. Patrick. Around the houses generally there is about as much garden as on the parched wooden roof.'

Most of the plants he had purloined from the North American wilderness seem to have survived the transatlantic journey. Robinson's *Darlingtonia* plants, most of which were destined for Messrs Veitch's Chelsea Nursery, provided the model for a illustration published in *Curtis's Botanical Magazine* during August 1871. He introduced a tall variety of the panther lily: *Lilium pardalinum* var. *robinsonii* had stout stems, massive foliage and bright vermilion flowers, with petals shading to yellow and freely spotted. Hidden in the pages of The *Gardeners' Chronicle* is an engraving of a magenta-flowered variety of penstemon also named after him: *Penstemon menziesii* var. *robinsonii*.

'Panoramic View Arsenal Hill', looking along Main Street, Salt Lake City, in about 1873, much as Robinson would have seen it. The large domed building is the newly constructed Church of the Latter Day Saints' tabernacle at Temple Square.

3.7
'PAINTING PICTURES' IN 'BEAUTIFUL, LAUGHING BURMA'

TOWARDS THE CLOSE of the nineteenth century, a somewhat nervous bride arrived in Rangoon. When she left twenty-five years later, she had added three new species to the catalogue of native plants, painted watercolours of Burmese orchids, and fallen in love with 'beautiful, laughing Burma'.

Charlotte Isabel Wheeler Cuffe's story is a rare one, and her achievements perhaps rank above those of her male contemporaries in one particular regard – at the request of the Government of Burma she was responsible for the formation, design and planting of the Botanic Garden at Maymyo, a hill town established by the British as a 'Hot Weather' retreat, forty-three miles by road northeast of Mandalay.

Charlotte was brought up in Wimbledon and in County Kilkenny, her mother's home. She was taught to paint and trained as a nurse. On 3 June 1897, aged thirty-one, Charlotte married Otway Wheeler Cuffe, who also had Kilkenny connections, and a fortnight later they embarked for Burma where he was employed by the Public Works Department as an engineer. Charlotte was not content, like many wives of British civilian officials and military officers posted to the Indian subcontinent, to remain as a house-bound *memsahib*, and as Otway frequently was required to travel around Burma on survey and inspection trips, she took the opportunities these presented to explore, and to collect and paint native flowers, especially orchids. She loved gardening too, and as she learned to speak Burmese and Hindustani, she was able to discover the local names for the plants that she gathered.

The first decade of the twentieth century saw a burgeoning of botanical exploration of temperate eastern Asia. Ernest Wilson went to China for the first time in 1899, in the footsteps of Dr Augustine

Charlotte Isabel Wheeler Cuffe.
(Reproduced by courtesy of Hugh Langrishe; © E. C. Nelson)

Henry – his secret quarry was the dove tree, *Davidia involucrata*. George Forrest began his career in 1904, travelling through Burma into western China – Charlotte Cuffe met Forrest, *en route* for Yunnan, at Rangoon in 1912. Frank Kingdon Ward started work a schoolmaster in Shanghai during 1907, and later became a plant hunter; he also used routes through Burma into western China. During the autumn of 1915, Ward stayed in Maymyo where Charlotte Cuffe got to know him quite well – 'a curious boy', she recorded, 'but I get on with him.'

In 1917, Ward commissioned a watercolour of a blue poppy (*Meconopsis speciosa*) from her. Reginald Farrer also passed through 'haughty' Maymyo in the winter of 1920 and met the Cuffes there.

Remembering that Forrest, Ward and Farrer were active in this region, what was Charlotte Cuffe's contribution to botanical exploration in Burma?

In 1911, she was invited by Mrs Winifred Macnabb 'to contemplate a rather sporting expedition' to Mount Victoria, at over 3,000 metres the highest peak in western Burma, 'to enjoy ourselves together, sketching & prowling'. With just a little hesitation, Charlotte accepted. Accompanied by Nicholas Nepean, Assistant Superintendent of the Pakokku Hill Tracts, they explored the mountain to its summit. Charlotte was ecstatic. There were orchids everywhere, and a 'wee skyblue' gentian. An extraordinary white-blossomed, scented rhododendron which grew only piggyback on pines, and red-flowered tree rhododendrons (*Rhododendron arboreum*) were in full bloom at an altitude of about 2,500 metres. Higher up the pines disappeared and shrubs of a daphne and a yellow-fruited raspberry abounded. Then they found a yellow-flowered rhododendron, and great patches of what Charlotte thought was a blue-flowered buttercup. On the summit was a solitary red rhododendron 'brandishing defiance to the four winds of heaven'. Winifred and Charlotte prowled and sketched, and after three glorious weeks reluctantly wended their ways home.

One year later the pair returned, and on this occasion Charlotte Cuffe collected plants to send home. Some of these reached Glasnevin Botanic Gardens in Dublin. Sir Frederick Moore, the Keeper, was delighted, and when the blue buttercup, an orchid and two rhododendrons flowered he sent them to Kew to be identified – they were 'new to science'. The yellow rhododendron was named *Rhododendron burmanicum*, while the white one became *Rhododendron cuffeanum*. The blue buttercup was *Anemone obtusiloba* f. *patula*. An epiphytic orchid, *Ione flavescens*, was the fourth of Charlotte Cuffe's discoveries.

The crimson tree rhododendron, *Rhododendron arboreum* subsp. *albotomentosum*, on Natmataung (Mount Victoria). (© E. C. Nelson)

The author and friends on the summit of Natmataung (Mount Victoria) in November 1998. (© E. C. Nelson)

'. . . & on the actual summit was a crimson rhododendron brandishing defiance to the four winds of . . . & such a view!': Charlotte Cuffe's watercolour sketch of the summit of Mount Victoria in May 1914.

99

Spurred on by the exciting finds on Mount Victoria, Charlotte Cuffe gathered plants elsewhere in Burma, transplanting many to her own garden in Maymyo. She was perhaps the first European with a 'botanical bent' to visit the remotest regions of the Chinese frontier, while accompanying Public Works Department parties, led by her husband. She was in Hpimaw a few months before Frank Kingdon Ward. None of her later travels resulted in new species, although undoubtedly she saw and gathered many plants that had not yet been described, because she was not, like Forrest or Ward, collecting systematically for horticultural or scientific reasons. Charlotte Cuffe was simply a lady who loved plants and when she could she brought home bits and pieces, and sometimes she painted them.

By 1917 Charlotte Cuffe had known Burma for twenty years. A war was raging and most of the younger men were on active service. Government departments were short of experts. She felt useless although she did engage in charitable works. In mid-November that year, the British administration approached her to undertake the supervision of a major new project – a botanical garden for Burma in Maymyo. She was highly flattered and accepted the commission, and immediately wrote a most excited letter to Otway Wheeler Cuffe's cousin, Baroness Pauline Prochazka.

. . . Can you imagine a more charming piece of work? The idea is to have a garden of all the beautiful indigenous flowers trees & shrubs, with just a few imported things, but very few. There are a lot of beautiful wild things in the area now, including a small patch of primeval forest, a marsh, some rocks, a little lake, & a wide stretch of open valley covered with bracken fern, wild raspberries – & weeds! The first job will be to clear out the rubbish & make a few paths, & then I can see my way by degrees – but I have visions of a sort of earthly paradise in that valley! A rock garden & a fernery & a marsh & a lake, & clumps of bamboo & flowering trees & shrubs & wild flowers – primulas & ground orchids &

hedychium & a thousand other lovely things – & a little shady pools & wide open stretches of grass with beautiful specimen trees! I couldn't sleep last night with excitement over it (which was very silly of me) after talking it over with Mr [Charles] Rogers, the head of the Forest Dept.

Charlotte Cuffe was allowed 'a free hand & as many labourers as I want'. For the next three years, with native workers to do the heavy work, she worked closely with Charles Rogers, putting heart and soul into formation of her 'earthly paradise'. They walked the ground and decided what plants should be planted, and where. Separate areas were earmarked for separate families, a willow brook, a rose – Rosaceae – garden, a bamboo grove and a glade of palms. A perennial spring was discovered and then enclosed with a traditional, carved Burmese well-head ornamented 'with curvy dragons'. Rambling roses were planted beside it. 'The whole thing is like painting a picture to me – only working with earth & rocks & water & lovely live growing things instead of paint & paper.'

Charlotte spent all day, every day, on the site. 'My life is a daily pic-nic!' she told Polly Prochazka.

I ride up to the garden every morning starting about 7 or 7.30, go round the various gangs of coolies, some jungle clearing, some at earth works, some building bridges, gravelling paths or so forth – I have about 70 at work – & see what they are all to do for the day & make up my mind which part needs my presence most (the garden is nearly a mile long, & ½ wide so the pony comes in useful!) – get holes dug for plants . . .

She had a picnic breakfast at 10 o'clock, and then 'I generally potter round my special pet plants, rock garden etc. While the men eat [at midday], I think out plans and schemes meanwhile, & then supervise whatever job is most important till 4, & so home to tea.'

Detail of Charlotte Cuffe's watercolour portrait of *Rhododendron burmanicum*.

Maymyo Botanic Garden in the early 1920s.

Detail of Charlotte Cuffe's watercolour portrait of *Rhododendron cuffeanum*.

Maymyo Botanic Garden in November 1998. (© E. C. Nelson)

'The back view of me was something like this!!': Charlotte Cuffe on her pony during a plant hunting trip in September 1917. (Pen-and-ink sketch.) (© E. C. Nelson)

After the war ended, Sir Otway and Lady Cuffe returned on furlough to Europe, and she took the chance to the botanic gardens at Peradeniya in Ceylon, Kew and Glasnevin, seeking advice.

I introduced myself as an ignorant amateur charged with the creation of a garden and threw myself on their mercies. (My actual words to them were 'an ignorant small woman with a job six times too big for her.') Without exception I found them most helpful with advice and practical instruction, and I must freely acknowledge their courtesy.

One lesson she learned was the importance of maintaining vistas, and she was most careful to preserve views in her garden. When Reginald Farrer was in Maymyo late in 1920, he visited the young garden and was fulsome in its praise: 'I have no doubt that the Maymyo Botanical Garden will be a paradise . . . all the natural advantages are being made the very best of by Lady Cuffe and Mr. [Alex] Rodger, who bit by bit, are laying out the garden with a special eye to aesthetic, as well as cultural, effects.'

In 1922, the Cuffes left Burma for good and retired to County Kilkenny. Roland Cooper, who had trained at the Royal Botanic Garden, Edinburgh, came out as the superintendent of the Maymyo Botanic Garden. The garden still survives, despite the many vicissitudes that Burma (now named Myanmar) has endured since the 1920s. Its continuance fulfils Charlotte's excited hope, expressed the night she was asked to undertake the task, that the plants she had collected all over Burma, would not perish when she left. 'The joy of it is that now I feel . . . every treasure I have collected will be valued & cared for & be of scientific interest.'

Charlotte Isabel Wheeler Cuffe lived at Leyrath, outside Kilkenny, into her 100th year. She was an exceptional lady. While her botanical discoveries are modest when compared with the hordes of plants collected by her male contemporaries, her contribution to the history of Burmese botany is worth more than a footnote. Her splendid paintings of Burmese orchids and of her rhododendrons from Mount Victoria are now among the treasures of the National Botanic Gardens, Glasnevin.

Rhododendron cuffeanum is in cultivation, although exceedingly rare, and it continues to blossom on the higher slopes of Mount Victoria. *Rhododendron burmanicum*, which she also introduced, graces gardens in the milder parts of Ireland and Britain. *Anemone obtusiloba* is a somewhat miffy plant yet often I have admired it in full flower in Irish gardens. At Glasnevin there is a handsome Indian chestnut which was raised from seed she gathered at Simla in India, and in Pyin-U-Lwin, Myanmar (otherwise Maymyo, Burma), her 'earthly paradise' endures.

This Indian chestnut, *Aesculus indica*, in the National Botanic Gardens, Glasnevin, was raised from 'conkers' collected at Simla in India by Charlotte Cuffe. (Grace Pasley ©)

3.8
FLORAL GEMS FROM THE CELESTIAL EMPIRE

IN RECENT YEARS we have come to appreciate the personal links that Ireland and her gardens have with China, the Celestial Empire, fabled Cathay. Of those links, the one that always comes to the fore is that involving Dr Augustine Henry, and he is paramount among the Irish men and women who contributed to European knowledge of the riches of the flora of China. In terms of the number of preserved specimens, Henry far exceeds everyone else but while he gathered, pressed and dried countless plants, he did not introduce many species into cultivation. We have explicit records of only around thirty plants raised from seeds sent by Henry from China including a variant of the butterfly bush (*Buddleja davidii*) and the single-flowered form of Lady Banks' rose, the lovely pale yellow *Rosa banksiae*. Henry also found the wild progenitor of the China roses, the true *Rosa chinensis*.

Henry was not the first, nor has he been the last Irish collector to pocket a few seeds while visiting China. The first known Irish visitor to the Celestial Empire was one Brother James who accompanied an Italian Franciscan monk there in 1322, but Irish adventurers were very few and far between for the next four centuries. The two diplomats who headed an extraordinary mission despatched in 1792 by King George III to the Qianlong Emperor were Irish. Lord Macartney from Lisanoure, County Antrim, and Sir George Staunton from Cargin, County Galway, reached Beijing in the late summer of 1793 and were eventually admitted to an audience with the Emperor. This important audience was delayed because the ambassador, Lord Macartney, declined to perform the ceremonial *kowtow*, the traditional act of deepest respect, kneeling and bowing one's head to touch the ground in front of the Emperor. The two diplomats were sent home without achieving their main goals. Both Macartney and Staunton had botanical interests and a gardener was attached to

Macartney's rose, *Rosa bracteata*, is an invaluable late-flowering, semi-evergreen species; it has also been called Staunton's rose.
(© E. C. Nelson)

the embassy so evidently they intended to acquire some Chinese plants. Indeed, they returned to London with quite a few nice ones. They had the seeds of a rose that is known as Macartney's rose, the superb autumn-blooming, thorny, white-flowered *Rosa bracteata*: it was once named *Rosa macartnea* and even 'Staunton's rose'.

In the two centuries that have elapsed since their return, Staunton's name has fared better than Macartney's. Among cultivated plants are *Elsholtzia stauntonii* (and its white-flowered cultivar), the privet *Ligustrum sinense* var. *stauntonii* and the evergreen climber *Stauntonia*. Thus Sir George was the first Irish person to have an entire Chinese genus named after him. Undoubtedly the best known of the embassy's haul of plants was the lovely plume poppy with its subtle colouring and wonderful foliage. *Macleaya cordata* is a worthy denizen of Irish gardens although the plant most frequently seen is a hybrid – each flower of the true species have at least two dozen stamens whereas the hybrid has half that number.

In the second half of the nineteenth century, quite a few Irish people resided in China, especially the men employed in the British-run Imperial Maritime Customs Service, including, of course, Dr Augustine Henry. The person who recruited Henry, Sir Robert Hart, may also have been instrumental in recruiting William Hancock of Lurgan, County Antrim, who spent some of his time collecting and

The Chinese plume poppy, *Macleaya cordata*, was introduced into European gardens as a consequence of Lord Macartney and Sir George Staunton's visit to China. (© E. C. Nelson)

Viburnum utile, the useful Guelder-rose: seeds were sent to Europe by Newtownards man Thomas Watters. The Chinese made tobacco-pipe stems from the twigs. (© E. C. Nelson)

pressing plants for scientific study. Hancock took a special interest in ferns, in seems, for quite a number of Chinese species bear the epithet *hancockii*. His sumptuous white rhododendron, *Rhododendron hancockii*, is apparently not cultivated in Ireland but may be grown elsewhere. Orchids also attracted him – a whole genus was named *Hancockia* in his honour, as was *Dendrobium hancockii*, a species with the striking, lemon-yellow blossoms. There is also a handsome clematis: *Clematis hancockiana* is not in cultivation as far as I can tell, but the *Flora of China* describes it as having red- to blue-purple flowers in spring.

Two other men, both of whom served as British consuls in China, 'left' their names on Chinese plants. George MacDonald Home Playfair, a graduate of Trinity College, Dublin, is commemorated in a bramble, *Rubus playfairii*, and in a member of the laurel family, *Neolitsea playfairii*. Thomas Watters, of Newtownards, County Down, whose sister Martha was a friend of Augustine Henry, has a milkwort and a nettle-relative named after him: *Polygala wattersii* and *Boehmeria wattersii* respectively. Watters it was who discovered the splendid, highly scented *Viburnum utile* near Yichang.

Among the litany of the Chinese flora there is only one Irish woman, Edith Osborne, Lady Blake. She came from Clonmel, County Tipperary. Her husband, Sir Henry Blake, was a Limerick man. He was appointed Governor of Hong Kong in 1897 and while the couple were resident there they collected plants. Two evergreen oaks bear their names – *Quercus blakei* and *Quercus edithiae* – but they are now placed in a different genus: *Cyclobalanopsis*. Most notable is the splendid orchid-tree *Bauhinia* × *blakeana*, a sterile plant known only in cultivation, which also commemorates the couple who took a 'kindly interest' in the Hong Kong Botanic Gardens while living in the colony. Its five-petalled purple flower had been the floral emblem of Hong Kong since 1965, and in 1997 it was incorporated into the flag of this Special Administrative Region of China.

The final person in my present litany of the Irish who explored China's flora is that of Hugh Scallan whose name is familiar in *Rosa hugonis*, described by Graham Stuart Thomas as one of the two roses that 'revolutionized the horticultural appraisal of wild roses'. Thomas also applied the adjective 'exquisite' to it. *Rosa hugonis*, Father Hugo's rose, has small yellow blossoms and was first raised in the Royal Botanic Gardens, Kew, from seeds that had been sent from China to the Keeper of Botany at the British Museum (Natural History), London. The sender was an Italian missionary, Padre Giuseppe Giraldi. In a letter, written in Latin, Giraldi merely stated that '*Pater Hugo Scallan Anglus*' had asked him to send to London some plant specimens that he had collected in the mountains of Shang Xian.

For many years I was puzzled why a man with a distinctively Irish surname should have been described as '*Anglus*' – English! As he might have been a Jesuit missionary, I contacted the Reverend Harold Naylor SJ, of the Irish Province and a graduate in natural history of University College, Dublin. Soon Father Naylor was able to reply that Pater Hugo Scallan had been a Franciscan missionary and that my hunch about his Irish origins was correct.

John Aloysius Scallan was born on 6 September 1851 in Rathmines, Dublin; his parents' names were Aloysius Scallan and Catherine Hart. Hugh was granted a Franciscan bursary to study at St Gregory's School in Douai, France, and joined the Franciscan Order on 30 May 1874 at Thielt in Belgium, making his temporary profession on 31 May 1875 and his final profession on 2 June 1878. John Scallan was given the religious name Hugh. On 10 April 1882, at Liege, Hugh Scallan was ordained and for the next four years he taught in a school near Manchester. Early in 1886, Pater Hugo (the Latin form of his name) departed for China, arriving in Shaanxi

The Blakes' orchid-tree, *Bauhinia × blakeana*, was named after Sir Henry Blake and his wife, Edith; this tree is known only in cultivation. (© E. C. Nelson)

Since 1965 the flower of *Bauhinia × blakeana* has been the floral emblem of Hong Kong, and it is incorporated in the flag of the Special Administrative Region of Hong Kong.

(Shensi) Province on 10 April 1886. He never left China, dying there forty-two years later, at the age of seventy-six, on 6 May 1928.

Little is recorded about Pater Hugo's work as a missionary, but a short obituary hints at tribulations and dangers: 'once he was almost stoned to death by pagans, once imprisoned, and frequently he was robbed', it reported. He worked in China during a time of considerable turmoil for the Chinese people. Foreigners were in great danger too, facing anti-foreign feelings, and it is not surprising that he was so treated. The Boxer Rebellion took place in the closing years of the nineteenth century, and the Tai Peng Revolution followed. Many foreigners perished, and famines and floods added to the hardships suffered. Of one violent incident involving Father Hugh there is a record. Late in 1893 Monsignor Pagnueci reported that 'an English Franciscan' had faced a mob of 'fanatic pagans' who attacked the mission residence, scattering the

Father Hugh Scallan's rose, *Rosa hugonis*. (© E. C. Nelson)

The original shrub of *Rosa hugonis* growing in the Royal Botanic Gardens, Kew. (© E. C. Nelson)

school-children. The mob tried to force the catechists to apostasy by torturing them, tying their hands so tightly that the cords cut their wrists. But the young men refused to submit and eventually the attackers let them go, but Father Hugh 'having been to the mandarin to ask protection they all fell upon him, and left him for dead in the street, together with two neophytes. Fortunately they were rescued and after a long and cruel illness, Father Hugo is once more quite recovered.'

Missionaries living in China were frequently approached to collect plants. In 1893, Dr Henry had deliberately addressed *Notes on Economic Botany of China* to them. Henry had contacts with the missions, and so had Arthur Bulley, the founder of the famous Bees Nursery in Chester, who once complained that the missionaries were unsatisfactory as sources of good garden plants – thanks to the missionary-botanists his garden contained the 'best international collection of dandelions to be seen anywhere'. The Swiss horticulturist Henri Correvon even assumed, mistakenly, that Henry was a missionary and had enquired of Bulley: 'Is your friend Henry the abbé Henry?' It would be pleasant to suppose that Dr Henry's book stimulated Father Hugh to collect plants.

The original plant of *Rosa hugonis* flourishes in the Royal Botanic Gardens, Kew. It is now a large

shrub having long since passed its hundredth birthday. This rose remains one of the best garden shrubs – it is vigorous, can reach four metres in height, and has delicate, fern-like foliage. Its yellow flowers open as early as May. Strangely, it blossoms best when planted in poor soil; this rose flourishes on benign neglect!

Pater Hugo's 'very beautiful yellow wild rose, tall and free' was not his only discovery. I now know that he also found an onion and a groundsel – *Allium hugonianum* (which is actually the same as the starry, blue-flowered *Allium cyaneum*) and *Senecio hugonis* respectively – and three grasses, *Agrostis hugoniana*, *Deyeuxia hugoniana* and *Eragrostis hugoniana*, as well as a stonecrop, a St John's-wort and a fern: *Sedum scallanii*, *Hypericum scallanii* and *Dryopteris scallanii*, respectively. That is not all: he was the discoverer of the willow called *Salix biondiana*, and the dusky aroid named *Arisaema brevipes* which is a very desirable and rare garden plant.

It is also clear now that Hugh Scallan was one of the earliest westerners, but not the first, to botanise on the sacred Buddhist mountain called Emeishan (Mount Omei), perhaps the most famous 'botanical' locality in China where more than 3,000 different species are native. Pater Hugo must have thought he was in heaven!

3.9
'THE WAY THAT I WENT': PRAEGER'S FOOTSTEPS IN THE CANARY ISLANDS

ROBERT LLOYD PRAEGER'S most enduring work is his evocative book about Ireland, *The Way that I Went*, published in 1937. He was Ireland's foremost field-botanist during the late 1800s and early 1900s, publishing numerous articles and another brilliant book, *The Botanist in Ireland* (1934). In the 1920s, shortly after he retired as Director of the National Library of Ireland, Praeger undertook a less-well-known project which resulted in the publication of two monographs about plants that are found mainly outside Ireland – the stonecrops (*Sedum*) and the houseleeks (*Sempervivum* and related genera).

Thus it was that in 1924 Praeger accompanied by his wife, Hedi, sailed to the Canary Islands in search of new houseleeks. He wrote of Lanzarote, the most easterly of the islands:

> When we first saw Haria from the corkscrew high road that twists to and fro down the precipitous slope that overhangs the town to the southward it seemed to us a very Garden of Eden. It lay in a hollow among high hills, its white and buff flat-topped houses embowered in tall palms, and embosomed in green field – actually green fields.

I know the place too. Haria has not altered much in appearance since the Praegers visited in 1924. The enveloping landscape is too resilient and unyielding, nor has the climate changed. There is a new road, hewn mightily into the solid lava that composes the volcanic hills of the northern extremity of Lanzarote, and it also 'twists to and fro'. There are new buildings but all in scale and all painted white. So we can still take Praeger's brief reports of his visit as our guidebook.

Haria, in the north of Lanzarote, seen from the ancient pilgrim track which the Praegers must have used. (© E. C. Nelson)

The pilgrim path winds up a steep slope, through hummocks of native plants including Praeger's quarry, *Aeonium lancerottense* (© E. C. Nelson)

We will stick to the now almost invisible old road, the pilgrim path, worn smooth by centuries of treading feet, which links Ermita de La Virgen de las Niéves with Haria and experience some of the excitement that Praeger must have had. The path is cobbled with large slabs, and meanders down the slope in gentle switchbacks that leave the modern

107

The sand crocus, *Romulea columnae*. (© E. C. Nelson)

Facing page: Robert Lloyd Praeger 'with his best find'. This must have been taken sometime after his trip to the Canary Islands; the flowering plant in the pot is *Aeonium nobile* which he gathered on La Palma.
(Reproduced by courtesy of the Royal Horticultural Society of Ireland)

tarmac highway well alone in its hasty contortions. You are treading a path that owes nothing to modern machines, that derives all its beauty from that innate sense of landscape that led someone to establish this town in its palm-embowered valley. You are walking through knee-high shrubs among rocks encrusted with ancient lichens.

In late winter, mists and clouds from the ocean stir the herbs into blossom. As our guide observed, buttercups run riot. *Ranunculus cortusifolius*, with velvety foliage and large, glossy, bright yellow flowers, covers all the north-facing slopes. Friar's cowls (*Arisarum vulgaris*) keep the buttercups company; these diminutive relatives of lords-and-ladies have arrow-head-shaped leaves and a green, striped spathe that resemble a friar's cowl. Sand crocuses (*Romulea columnae*) speckle the slopes with miniature purple goblets, golden in the centre. Rosy white onions also throng this natural rock garden, mingled with the purple-, blue- and red-flowered viper's bugloss: 'loveliest of all the lovely Canarian weeds' was Praeger's high praise for this humble herb.

The path zigzags downwards through hummocks of *Aeonium*, one of the relatives of the houseleek, Praeger's beloved 'Sempervivums', that were his particular interest at that time. He came to the Canary Islands twice especially to study them in

their native habitats and to see living examples. The one that throngs the uppermost slopes of the Haria valley is *Aeonium lancerottense*, with red-rimmed leaves and sugar-pink flowers in pyramidal plumes. Oddly, these blossom in the hot midsummer, not in the damper and cooler spring. *Aeonium lancerottense* forms a 'rather glaucous round bush', but in 'our climate the red leaf-margin disappears'.

Haria, to quote Prager, 'lies among high hills, which to the west drop into the ocean in a long line of magnificent 2,000ft. cliffs'. There is a rough track leading westwards from the town along a barranco. It is an easy, gentle dander after a pause for some thirst-quenching water in the shady square. This road wanders along, rising steadily, through cultivated ground in which maize is newly sprung and the wizened vines are protected – embowered, to use Praeger's word – in enclosures built of lava rocks, marvels of masonry as remarkable as any drystone wall in the Burren – simple walls that filter the gales, deflating not exacerbating the wind.

This track does not twist to and fro; its path is a sinuous climb. Wild chrysanthemums and stork's-bills crowd the sides, while stately Canary date palms march along the barranco. The well-made track eventually peters out and we climb the slope by a dusty path, made no doubt by goats, until we reach the crest. *Caramba*! What a view! Twelve hundred

Ranunculus cortusifolia occurs in shaded places beside the pilgrim path. (© E. C. Nelson)

The native lavender on the Famara cliffs, *Lavandula pinnata*. (© E. C. Nelson)

feet below is the boiling Atlantic Ocean, waves crashing on the crescent-shaped beach at Famara. There is a very strong, warm, westerly wind hitting these cliffs and the two Egyptian vultures circling overhead take full advantage of the updraught to wheel and glide and inspect the place for likely banquets.

This was our best ground, but its exploration was rendered difficult by a persistent gale of wind that made cliff-climbing a dangerous form of exercise. However, I crawled along ledge after ledge, and had the satisfaction of finding *Æ. Balsamifera* unquestionably native, [and] another *Æonium* not yet determined.

The 'not-yet-determined' *Aeonium* from the Lanzarote cliffs is *Aeonium lancerottense* which Praeger named in his 1925 paper about Canarian and Madeiran 'Semperviva', read to, and published by, the Botanical Society of Edinburgh. He recorded then that this was locally abundant, as indeed it still is, around Haria. Praeger also reported that it grew on roofs in Haria – I have to say that I did not see any growing on roofs, perhaps an indication only of modern fastidiousness. *Aeonium balsamifera* is only native to the cliffs of Lanzarote, but because it yields a balsam that was used to harden and preserve fishing lines, it was transplanted to the neighbouring island of Fuerteventura, and was known to Praeger from botanical gardens elsewhere in Europe. This second species has yellow flowers and much smaller rosettes than *Aeonium lancerottense*.

The viper's bugloss, 'loveliest of all the lovely Canarian weeds'. (© E. C. Nelson)

Praeger must have been as agile as a mountain goat. Even to have 'crawled' along some of the ledges of Risco de Famara – the Famara cliffs – in a gale would have been foolhardy, to say the least. Yet in the pursuit of plants botanists will literally throw caution to the wind. This is an unforgiving land, majestic, stark, dramatic, precipitous, and lethal, but also fascinating botanically being the habitat of most of Lanzarote's endemic plants – species found nowhere else in the world – including these two *Aeonium* species. The cliff face, constantly moistened by ocean breezes and mists, is a veritable botanic garden with a host of unique species. One of the most obvious and striking plants is the tall, yellow, multi-umbellate giant fennel (*Ferula lancerottense*) which is related of the giant fennels of the Mediterranean. There are small, shrubby rockroses and pink-flowered everlastings, and bushy carline thistles that look rather like some of the New Zealand daisy-bushes. The local lavender (*Lavandula pinnata*) has thick, leathery, divided, grey leaves, and deep blue-purple flowers in slender spikes.

Our collecting was successful. Out of a known total of about 60 species about 50 were obtained. Of 235 gatherings made for the purposes of study, all but two arrived alive at Glasnevin gardens, thanks largely to the kindness of Captain Pope of the Yeoward liner *Alondra* in placing at my disposal an empty stateroom where the collection was spread out to the air and light.

When Praeger returned to the Canary Islands in 1927 he did not revisit Lanzarote. For four months he wandered in Tenerife, La Gomera, Gran Canaria and La Palma but found only one more new species 'and a very remarkable array of hybrids'. The 1924 visit, which covered all the main islands, yielded six new species, one being *Aeonium lancerottense* and another the very remarkable *Aeonium nobile* which is found only on La Palma. This 'massive plant, with thick, sticky leaves larger than a man's hand, a solid unbranched stem, and a large flat-topped inflorescence' was to Praeger 'undoubtedly new'. He subsequently named this handsome

111

Aeonium lancerottense blooms in midsummer, the hottest, driest part of the year. This species is locally abundant around Haria and in a few other places on Lanzarote. (© E. C. Nelson)

My notes on the flower of this plant [*Aeonium subplanum*] were unfortunately lost in a squall on a cliff on Palma . . .

One of the hazards of plant-hunting! The loss of the notes was not too much of a setback to Praeger. From memory he was able to state that 'the inflorescence and flower offered sufficiently distinguishing characters to justify the evidence of the very distinct rosettes and leaf that the plant deserves a separate name.'

The Praegers had wandered (his term) by steamer, in 'motors', on mules and camels and on foot, 'across deserts, through forests, lava-flows, gigantic craters, enormous precipices'. In those days the Canary Islands had few roads and few hotels. Unless wanderers were prepared to forsake

. . . English [*sic*] standards . . . [their] orbit [was] limited; through all their loveliest parts – and how lovely they are – only rough mule tracks lead, zigzagging over breakneck mountains and through cliff-walled gorges.

red-blossomed species *Aeonium nobile*, remarking that its

. . . flat-topped inflorescence . . . is very distinctive, that of most other of the larger [*Aeonium* species] being conical or ovoid. A remarkable and striking plant, well-adapted to its habitat on very hot rocks . . . No flower was obtained, and of about 100 plants seen only one had bloomed the previous year. The remains of other individuals that had flowered and died were at least several years old, so the plant is evidently slow-growing and long-lived.

Praeger was immensely proud of *Aeonium nobile*, and there is a familiar photograph of him standing beside a pot-grown plant, 'his best find'.

As well as the living plants carefully stowed in the stateroom on the *Alondra*, he brought back seeds which were taken care of at the National Botanic Gardens, Glasnevin. The seedlings were subsequently studied and among them several other new species were recognised including one named *Aeonium subplanum*. But . . .

Of all the places, remote and not so remote, that he saw on his Canarian wanderings, Haria is the one that seems to have impressed Praeger most, and not just because of the wild plants. He was astounded by the methods the local people used to cultivate the land, spreading a four-inch thick mulch of pea-sized volcanic gravel, *picon*, over the entire surface of the soil. This insulates the soil, preventing any moisture that is already in it from evaporating, but also attracts moisture from the air – any scanty rain and all the night-time dew is channelled down to benefit the plants. Vines, 'verdant lentils', and maize still are cultivated in this manner, as are potatoes, onions, peppers, lettuces, tomatoes and even cabbages. The desert-like aspect of Lanzarote is not deceptive, but farming is certainly not impossible – as Praeger observed the soil is 'of an amazing fertility, and only the heaven-sent gift of rain is stinted.' Today, the only change is that artificial irrigation is possible, meaning that fresh vegetables are always available.

4

ARISTOCRATS OF
THE GARDEN

4.1
'EXCELLENT AS THE CEDARS'

'And he spake of trees, from the cedar tree that is in Lebanon even unto the hyssop that springeth out of the wall . . . '. (I Kings 43: 6)

One of the champion cedars of Lebanon at Castle Forbes, County Longford, in May 1982. It is quite possible that this was one of the cedar trees seen by Nicholas Dowdall in 1682; it would have been a mere sapling then. (© E. C. Nelson)

THE CEDAR OF LEBANON is a majestic tree with a powerful aura of the sacred and the precious. The timber was much prized in the Near East during biblical times as a building material for royal palaces and religious shrines. It took King Solomon thirteen years to build a house for himself from nothing but cedar. *'He built also the house of the forest of Lebanon; the length thereof was an hundred cubits, and the breadth thereof fifty cubits, and the height thereof thirty cubits, upon four rows of cedar pillars, with cedar beams upon the pillars. And it was covered with cedar above upon the beams, that lay on forty five pillars, fifteen in a row'* (I Kings 7: 2–3). Solomon also employed cedar in the great Temple which he had built in Jerusalem: *'So he built the house, and finished it; and covered the house with beams and boards of cedar. And then he built chambers against all the house, five cubits high: and they rested on the house with timber of cedar'* (I Kings 6: 9–10).

The cedars on Mount Lebanon were ruthlessly exploited for millennia, and by the late 1500s there were, it is said, only twenty-six cedar trees left there. But the noble tree we know as the cedar of Lebanon (*Cedrus libani*) was never restricted to that one mountain in what was once Phoenicia, nor is it found only there today. There are forests of this cedar in southwestern Turkey, and two closely related cedars inhabit the Trodos Mountains of Cyprus and the Atlas Mountains of Morocco.

With its biblical associations, it is not surprising that the cedar of Lebanon also has a long history outside its native range as a cultivated tree – but not such a long one as some improbable stories suggest. There is no evidence, literary, horticultural or botanical, to confirm that it was first brought to

western Europe by returning crusaders in the twelfth or thirteenth centuries, for example. There is no antique tree of the Lebanon cedar growing anywhere west of Turkey.

Like so many other trees capable of living for centuries – oaks and yews especially – cedars are not infrequently credited with fabulous longevity. While it may be the case that very ancient trees still grow in the wild, it does not follow that every large tree in cultivation is as old as the hills. The vast majority of those in Irish gardens are not more than two centuries in the ground. While it is a hardy tree, capable of withstanding cold, there is ample evidence that trees can be fatally damaged by adverse weather: strong winds break branches, and so will a sudden heavy fall of snow. One of the most handsome of Irish cedars was the one on the lawn at Fota House, County Cork, planted about 1825, which succumbed to the storms of Christmas 1997. When I saw the last of it in May 1998, it was a pitiful pile of logs.

The introduction of the cedar of Lebanon into cultivation in Britain is usually dated to about 1640, based on 'unbroken' family tradition, not on documentary evidence. A tree planted at Childrey,

114

Left: The cedar of Lebanon on the lawn at Fota House, County Cork, in the 1980s.
(© E. C. Nelson)

Below: After the severe storm of December 1997: the Fota cedar in May 1998.
(© E. C. Nelson)

The very shapely cedar of Lebanon at Malahide Castle, County Dublin (Fingal). This tree was not recorded in the Tree Register of Ireland; its dimensions in October 2005 were girth 7.11 metres at 1.5 metres above the ground, height 20.5 metres (data by courtesy of Anne James).
(© E. C. Nelson)

Oxfordshire, by Dr Edward Pococke, presumably some time after he took up the living there in 1642, is regarded as the earliest of its species in these islands. Two decades later we encounter the earliest written record of cedar of Lebanon being grown in a garden on the western fringe of Europe. When John Evelyn addressed the Royal Society in London on 15 October 1662 he noted that the cedar of Lebanon could grow 'in all extreames' and wondered if it would 'not thrive in Old England', adding for good measure that 'I have frequently rais'd it of the seeds'. Following that, there were more, albeit occasional, references to the cedar being cultivated outdoors in England.

A famous group of cedars was planted in the Physic Garden of the Society of Apothecaries at Chelsea. The Curator of the Physic Garden, John Watts, had acquired four from the University of Leiden in the Netherlands in 1683. Sir Hans Sloane, a native of County Down and one of London's leading physicians, wrote to the Revd John Ray in 1685 exclaiming that the cedars 'thrive here (at Chelsea) so well'.

By this time, cedars of Lebanon were also being cultivated in Ireland. In 1682 when Nicholas Dowdall wrote his 'Description of the County of Longford', there was a collection of exotic trees thriving at Castle Forbes, the seat of Arthur Forbes, second Earl of Granard. According to Dowdall, Forbes had improved the demesne around the 'ancient seat', and had planted

. . . orchards, groves, hop yards, etc., and hath by such industry managed the soyle that it beareth all sorts of plants and flowers that are sett or sowed there. There is now growing there in great verdure large grows of Fir of all sorts with Pine, juniper, Cedar, Lime trees, Beech, Elm, Oak, Ash, Asp, and the famous Platanus trees, I suppose not growing any where besides in this Kingdom.

Dowdall went on to praise the 'lovely gardens of pleasure' at Castle Forbes and to add to the list of named plants: *Laburnum*, laurel, *Phillyrea*, and the sweetly-perfumed Mexican tuberose (a tender bulb which must have been grown in a heated conservatory – but that's another story).

CEDAR OF LEBANON

The list of trees grown at Lord Granard's in 1682 would perhaps not be of great interest even with the inclusion of cedar, except that to this day cedars of Lebanon are a remarkable feature of the demesne at Castle Forbes. Look at the list of champion trees published by the Tree Register of Ireland (TROI), especially that for County Longford. Of the twenty-five Longford champions no fewer than ten are cedars of Lebanon, and they all grow at Castle Forbes. No other Irish county has so many cedars among its champions. The Longford cedars are not the tallest nor do their trunks have the greatest girth, but as a *group* the trees are unbeatable.

I am not going to claim that any of the trees alive today was seen by Nicholas Dowdall: the only way that can be proved is to have each tree exactly dated by counting its growth-rings. Yet this cannot be a simple coincidence: champion trees and an early written account seem to chime together.

The Earl of Granard was not alone in acquiring – or trying to acquire – cedars in the late 1600s; they were very fashionable trees. A few days before William of Orange landed at Carrickfergus on his way to the Battle of the Boyne in 1690, Sir Hans Sloane wrote to his friend and kinsman Sir Arthur Rawdon who lived at Moira in County Down, saying that he had been to the Chelsea Physic Garden but 'the cedrus libani and cyclamen you desired, could not be sent; the one was too big, and the other could not be found . . . '. A few decades later, Judge Ward, of Castle Ward, also in County Down, was on the look-out too: 'There is no such thing as the seed or the cone of the Cedar of Lebanon to be had' in London, he was informed. The Chelsea trees had borne a single cone the previous year, 1724, but he wasn't on the favoured list of recipients for the seeds!

Most Irish cedars of Lebanon have no recorded history, or at least none that stands close scrutiny. There are many claims for priority. In *Trees of Great Britain and Ireland* by Henry John Elwes and Dr Augustine Henry, Elwes, who wrote the entry for *Cedrus libani*, stated that:

In Ireland the Lebanon cedar has been rarely planted in comparison with its frequency in England; and [Dr] Henry has not seen any large trees except one at Carton . . . said to have been the first planted in Ireland; and six fine trees at Anneville near Dundrum, Co. Dublin . . .

The Anneville trees were reported by John Claudius Loudon, writing in 1838 (and quoted by Elwes), 'to have been brought direct from the Lebanon by an ancestor of Lord Tremblestown [*sic*], and to be the oldest in Ireland'. The fine Lebanon cedar growing in front of Adare Manor is sometimes claimed to have been planted in 1645: Elwes saw this tree in 1903 and thought it was a fair specimen but did not measure it nor claim priority for it. Dr Henry evidently thought it of no exceptional merit. Writing in 1836, Andrew Coughlan, the head gardener to the Earl of Dunraven, extolled the earl's 'splendid new house' and 'some beautiful cedars of Lebanon', but the riverside cedar was not singled out for measurement like the line of 'English elm trees, more than 150ft. high, and girting 14ft. on an average', or the 40-foot tall 'yucca', or the hickory whose crown had a circumference of 90 feet. The Adare cedars were simply beautiful. Today it is the Limerick champion of champions in terms of the girth of its trunk – but we do *not* know when it was planted.

In Ireland today, there are about two dozen champion cedars of Lebanon, venerable antiques, but whether any of these dates from the 1640s is doubtful. During 2005 The Irish Lebanese Cultural Foundation initiated a programme to plant forty-seven young cedars in various towns and cities, one tree for each of the Irish soldiers who died in Lebanon while serving as United Nations' peace-keepers. In due time they will become noble cedars and future generations will surely admire them.

'From the top of the cedar, from the highest branch I will take a shoot and plant it myself on a very high mountain . . . this branch will bear fruit and become a noble cedar.' (*Ezekiel* 17: 22–23).

117

County 'champions': cedar of Lebanon (from Tree Register of Ireland).

I am grateful to the Tree Council of Ireland and to Dr Matthew Jebb (National Botanic Gardens, Glasnevin) for access to these data. Girth (@ height above ground) × height.

Antrim: Shane Castle, Antrim
8.43 @ 1 m × 21.50m
6.82 @ 1.1 m × 15.30m

Armagh: Hockley Lodge, Armagh
5.95 @ 0.6m × 24m

Carlow: Ballykealy House, Ballon
6.76 @ 1.1m × 32m
Borris House, Borris
5.99 @ 1.5m × 25.50m

Dublin: Áras an Uachtaráin, Phoenix Park, Dublin
6.40 @ 1.5m × 26.80m
Knockrapo, Goatstown, Dublin 6
6.33 @ 0.8m × 20.50m
Lyons Demesne, Newcastle
8.16 @ 0.4m × 18.50m
6.25 @ 0.6m × 22.30m
Marley Park, Rathfarnham, Dublin
5.28 @ 1.5m × 30m

Kerry: Muckross House, Muckross
6.10 @ 1m × 25m

Kildare: Carton House, Maynooth
6.85 @ 1.5m × 26m

Kilkenny: Kildalton Agricultural College, Piltown
7.80 @ 0.8m × 18.50m
7.78 @ 0.3m × 32m

Limerick: Adare Manor, Adare
9.90 @ 1m × 19m

Longford: Castle Forbes, Newtownforbes
7.67 @ 1.5m × 28m
7.50 @ 1.5m × 28m
7.44 @ 0.3m × 23m
7.28 @ 1.5m × 20m
5.78 @ 1.5m × 25.50m
5.59 @ 0.85m × 28m
5.39 @ 0.95m × 25m
5.28 @ 1.5m × 25m
5.01 @ 1.5 m × 22 m
4.73 @ 1.5 m × 25 m

Louth: Red House, Ardee
7.41 @ 1.5m × 36m

Meath: Gormanstown College, Gormanstown
6.17 @ 1.5m × 24.50m

Monaghan: Castle Leslie, Glaslough
6.24 @ 0.5m × 25.30m
5.28 @ 1.5m × 25.70m

Tyrone: Baronscourt, Newtownstewart
7.45 @ 0.7m × 20.80m
6.68 @ 0.8m × 21m

Wicklow: Charleville Estate, Enniskerry
7.11 @ 1.3m × 27m

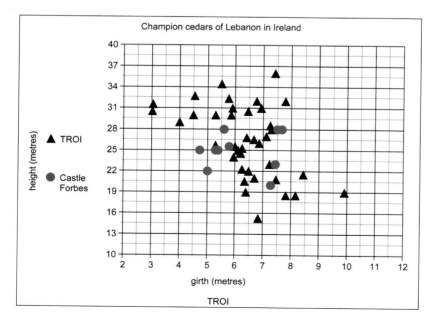

Champion cedars of Lebanon in Ireland

The cedars of Lebanon at Castle Forbes, indicated by red circles, are not the tallest in Ireland, nor are their girths the broadest.

4.2
DAVIDIA: THE 'EXTRAORDINARY AND BEAUTIFUL' HANDKERCHIEF TREE

'DAVIDIA IS WONDERFUL.' We all can agree, yet when Dr Augustine Henry wrote that simple, ecstatic sentence, perhaps only two Europeans, one of them Henry, had ever seen a living, flowering *Davidia*. Now it is a common ornament in our gardens and can be obtained readily from discriminating nurserymen. Yet this familiar tree is still wonderful – the sight of *Davidia* in full flower is something to make you stand and stare.

'Familiar' and 'common' are not adjectives that anyone could have used a century ago. *Davidia* was known only to a very select band of the most knowledgeable botanists and best-informed nurserymen as a handful of dried, scientific specimens and as rather unexciting illustrations reconstructed from those flattened specimens. *Davidia* had been named, but not introduced into cultivation.

By the spring of 1901, however, two other Europeans had managed to see this tree in its wild habitats, and by the succeeding autumn they had also both gathered seeds to send to Europe. These two men – Père Paul Farges and Ernest Wilson – were participating in one of the most extraordinary botanical races ever run and, as in any race, there would be only one winner. But neither of the participants knew the other was competing, and in this race the winner had won before the loser has started – yet the loser is the one who is best remembered.

The two original finders were not in the race. Dr Augustine Henry was home on leave and never would return to China. He had handed over the baton to a young man from Gloucestershire. The other man who was not in the race was Père Armand David, the scholarly missionary and naturalist, who is immortalised by this wonderful tree. He had died in 1900 at the age of seventy-four.

The wonderful *Davidia involucrata*; the white 'handkerchief' is formed by two unequal bracts while the true flowers, which have no petals, are clustered in the centre. (© E. C. Nelson)

Père David's other claim to fame is that he first brought the giant panda to the attention of western scientists and, most remarkably, even managed to send one animal alive to Paris where it lived for a short time.

Jean Pierre Armand David was a Basque, a native of the western Pyrenees. He entered the Lazarist brotherhood and was ordained in 1851 as a member of the Congregation of Priests of the Mission. After ten years spent teaching in Italy at a Lazarist school, he was ordered to Beijing to teach natural history and science in the Lazarist mission school. Once in China, Père David found plenty of scope for natural history – he was especially interested in ornithology but he did not neglect geology, mineralogy, ethnography and botany. He sent numerous, beautifully preserved specimens of animals and plants to the Muséum national

Dr Augustine Henry in China about the time he collected *Davidia*.

Davidia involucrata in full flower at Annes Grove, Castletownroche, County Cork; this tree, like many others in Irish gardens, was probably one of the seedlings raised from Ernest Wilson's seeds. (© E. C. Nelson)

d'Histoire naturelle in Paris. These specimens astonished French scientists, and soon the authorities in France asked the Superior General of David's order to release him from his teaching duties so that he could travel through remote regions of China collecting specimens. Remarkably, the Superior General agreed and Armand David was able to undertake three journeys into inaccessible parts of China. His first scientific mission was to the Mongolian frontier. The borderlands of Tibet were the farthest reaches on his second trip, while on the third expedition David explored the provinces of Shaanxi and Jiangxi. The second of these missions was the one that yielded the greatest botanical treasures, including the wonderful tree that was to be named after him.

David found his tree during May 1869 near Mupin (now named Baoxing), then a tiny principality, where there was a mission school run by the Société des Missions Étrangères. He arrived at Mupin as spring began, in time to experience and revel in the annual procession of blossoming flowers. There were many new birds to observe, and new plants galore. 'The large rhododendrons are in flower', he wrote, 'and I can already detect at least 7 different species.' He found a magnificent magnolia with purple flowers, 'but, as yet, no leaves.' There were so many new animals, including insects and the giant panda, that David mused in his diary: 'I realise more and more just how rich the flora of this district is, but I fear that my preoccupation with zoology will not give me time to make a representative herbarium.' David's herbarium was nonetheless very rich. He found *Davidia* in full bloom but the illustrations based on his pressed specimen show the flowers incorrectly standing upright.

Almost twenty years passed. In May 1888 Augustine Henry was in the middle of an extensive plant-hunting trip in central China, a thousand miles from Mupin. On 17 May he was riding up a river valley near the village of Ma-huang-p'o when he experienced 'one of the strangest sights he saw in China . . . a solitary tree . . . in full blow . . . waving its innumerable ghost handkerchiefs'. At the time Henry did not know the tree's name, so he collected specimens which were duly pressed and dried, and later were packed off to the Royal Botanic Gardens, Kew. But the vision of this tree so stuck in Henry's mind that in the autumn he sent his two trusted Chinese helpers back to the very tree to gather the walnut-like fruits, each of which, as we now know, usually contains seven seeds. In 1889, Dr Henry's pressed specimens and the fruits reached Kew. As Père David had not been able to collect the fruits of *Davidia*, these were the first examples seen by Western botanists. But no one thought to try to get the seeds to germinate. Instead the fruits were drawn – and then pickled.

The following year, 1890, Dr Henry came home on leave and visited Kew Gardens where he was greeted as a celebrity. By that time, the principal botanists in Kew realised that Henry's collections of plants were at least the equal of Père Armand David's. So many unknown species were in the parcels Henry had sent from central China that it seemed to be a Klondike of plant-gold! Perhaps during his visit to Kew Dr Henry talked to Daniel Oliver about his experiences in the remote hills of central China and the many plants he has seen. Perhaps Henry mentioned the remarkable tree covered with ghostly white handkerchiefs, only to be told it was not new but had been described and named by the French botanist Henri Ernest Baillon. Maybe Oliver and Henry pored over the colour plate that had been published in *Plantae Davidianae*. If they did, Dr Henry must have pointed out the error in d'Apreval's drawing – the flowers dangle from the shoots on slender stems like fluttering, white doves, they do not stand stiffly erect. And perhaps it was Henry who suggested that, as Oliver wrote, 'Davidia is a tree almost deserving a special mission to

The fluttering bracts resemble white doves, hence the name dove tree; this fine *Davidia involucrata* is in the arboretum at Fota, County Cork. (© E. C. Nelson)

Western China with a view to its introduction to European gardens.'

More time passed. Henry did not forget those wonderful ghostly handkerchiefs. When, in 1897, Dr William Thiselton-Dyer, Director of the Royal Botanic Gardens, Kew, pleaded with Henry to collect more seeds for Kew, he responded saying that he simply could not afford the time. 'Money is not what is wanted, but time, oceans of time.' And Henry continued: 'you ought to make a strong effort to . . . procure not only seeds of the Cercis [the Chinese Judas-tree], but also of Davidia. . . Why Davidia is worth any amount of money . . . Davidia is wonderful.'

'Seeds' of another kind were thus sown, ones which sprouted in 1899 when a young Gloucestershire man, Ernest Wilson, set sail for China carrying a secret set of instructions: time and money were now no object but secrecy was deemed essential. 'The object of the journey is to collect a quantity of seeds of a plant the name of which is known to us. This is the object – do not dissipate time, energy or money on anything else.'

Wilson's extraordinary instructions to collect the nameless seeds included, as a preliminary, a visit to the very remote southern Chinese town of Simao where Dr Henry was then based. It took Wilson four months to reach Simao from Hong Kong. When the

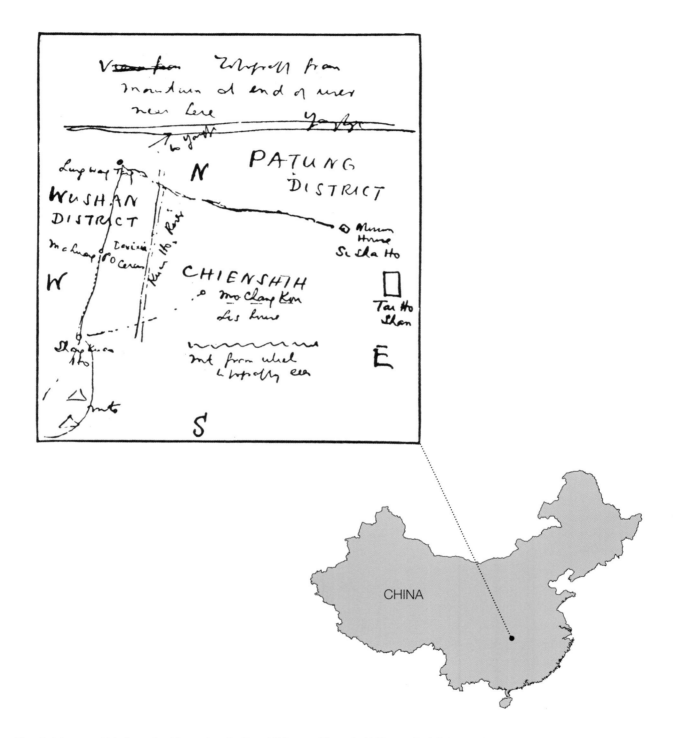

The sketch map which Augustine Henry drew for Ernest Wilson at Simao in 1899 – on the left-hand side, near the letter W (West) the words 'Davidia' and 'Cercis' can be seen. This map encompasses an area almost twice the size of the entire island of Ireland. (Reproduced from Leonard Baron, 'Chinese' Wilson – plant hunter, *The World's Work* 27: 41–52, November 1913.)

two men met, they evidently got on well together. Dr Henry had realised an ambition – at last *Davidia* would be collected and introduced into European gardens. He gave Ernest Wilson a sketch map showing roughly how to reach the valley of the handkerchief tree. Soon Wilson left Simao and travelled on into central China and eventually on 25 April 1900 arrived at Ma-huang-p'o. The first thing he did was ask for directions to the tree known as *k'ung-tung*. The locals offered to guide him, and they set off. After walking perhaps two miles, Wilson saw a rather new house, and beside it a tree-stump – he must have felt like sitting down and weeping. Henry's one and only handkerchief tree had been cut down about a year previously. The beams of the new house were made of *Davidia*! Ernest Wilson did not sleep that night.

He did not abandon his quest but went on collecting and three weeks later was rewarded, near a village called Ta-wan, with his first sight of *Davidia involucrata* in full flower. His secret mission would now succeed. He later found other trees, scattered in a area within a 100-mile radius. That autumn, Ernest Wilson returned to these trees and gathered as many fruits as he could – thousands of *Davidia* fruits were despatched to Veitch's nursery and they arrived safely in England in the spring of 1901.

Some were treated with boiling water. Some were planted in pots in a glasshouse. The woody coats of others were filed down. Everything possible was done to stimulate germination. When Wilson returned home in April 1902, a year after the *Davida* seeds, he went straight to the Coombe Wood Nursery to examine his booty. None had germinated! But there were telltale signs of life – and a month later thousands of *Davidia* seedlings sprouted in the special seed-beds. *Davidia* had been successfully introduced, and Wilson and an assistant soon embarked on the long job of potting-up 13,000 saplings.

James Veitch & Sons offered *Davidia involucrata* among it novelties in 1903. A handsome profit was ensured as every garden had to have one. But there was a disappointment too because it soon transpired that the French had pipped the English to the post.

Another French missionary, Père Paul Farges, had also gathered fruits of *Davidia* and sent them to Maurice de Vilmorin. Farges' seeds had arrived at the Vilmorins' arboretum, Les Barres, in 1897 and one – only one – germinated in 1898, a year before Ernest Wilson has sailed for China. Wilson was still immensely proud of his achievement – as he later wrote, he had been responsible for the 'introduction of *every seedling plant but one* of this remarkable tree.'

And what of Dr Augustine Henry's contribution? He had sent the first fruits of *Davidia* to Europe – it was not his fault that no one at Kew had the wit to sow them. Throughout the 1890s Henry had tried to persuade someone else to collect more seeds. Maybe, just maybe, it was Henry's fascinating little book about the economic botany of China, printed in Shanghai by The Presbyterian Mission Press in 1893, that did the trick. Did Père Farges have a copy, and did he read this passage?

> One of the most remarkable trees of Western China is *Davidia involucrata* . . . first discovered by Père David in Tibet, and of which a solitary specimen was found by me in the southern part of the Wushan district in Szechuan, on the road leading from Pei-shih inland, near Ma-huang-p'o. This tree was about 30 feet high, covered with flowers. The large white bracts mingled with the green leaves gave it an extraordinary and beautiful appearance.

I would not be surprised if that was what happened, for Henry's pamphlet was directly addressed to 'Missionaries and other living in the interior [who] are often in a position to make enquiries concerning the natural productions of China, the results of which would be of great service to science'. And, I wonder if Henry ever met the man whose tree he thought was so wonderful? Alas, history does not enlighten us. Armand David and Augustine Henry surely would have had much to talk about.

4.3
THE GOVERNOR OF NORTH CAROLINA AND A VERY SENSITIVE PLANT

I**T IS HARD TO IMAGINE** a present-day US State governor having the time, let alone the inclination, for plant-hunting or gardening – golf, maybe? Two and a half centuries ago things were evidently different – for one thing, golf was virtually unknown. His Excellency Arthur Dobbs, Esq., whose formal title was *Captain General, Governor in Chief & Vice Admiral of the Provence of* North Carolina *in America*, did have time for his garden and, being a man of great curiosity, for the Carolina flora. He went plant-hunting and seed-collecting, and consequently inflamed another man's passion.

Arthur grew up in County Antrim on his family's demesne, Castle Dobbs near Carrickfergus. As a young man, he had watched the heavens, observing such phenomena as parhelions, lunar eclipses and the aurora borealis. Ever ambitious, he became High Sheriff of Antrim and Mayor of Carrickfergus, a Member of Parliament and Surveyor-General of Ireland, but he was confounded in his attempts to advance a scheme to find the fabled Northwest Passage. By the late 1740s, approaching his sixtieth birthday, Arthur was well-settled and prosperous. Enjoying early retirement, he dabbled in his garden and kept bees.

Picture him sitting in the garden at Castle Dobbs on a sunny summer's day watching the bees entering and leaving the hives. He observed them flying to and from flowers, noting that when a bee started collecting pollen from a daisy it continued 'loading' only from daisies, ignoring clover, honeysuckle and violets. His garden contained a fine collection of wall-fruits – peaches, apricots, plums, almonds, cherries. The bees that began collecting from peaches would ignore plums, apricots and cherries, 'yet made no distinction between a peach and an almond'.

Aristotle had reported this behaviour many centuries earlier, but Arthur noticed that a bee's constancy was most rigorous when it was gathering pollen and weaker when collecting nectar. Thinking about these facts, he reasoned that bees were pollinating agents 'appointed by Providence' to carry pollen from flower to flower of the *same* species. He published his observations and conclusions in the *Philosophical transactions of the Royal Society of London*. No previous naturalist had made this connection.

But retirement with leisure to watch the bees was not to last for long. Before another decade had elapsed Arthur was living on the other side of the Atlantic, having been installed as Governor of North Carolina. Trade matters and hostilities with the French preoccupied him for a while, but he never abandoned natural history, keeping a journal while he travelled around his new domain, or gardening.

Venus's fly-trap with an almost obligatory earwig: from Benjamin Maund's *The Botanic Garden*, volume 12, plate 1064.

Governor Arthur Dobbs, Captain General, Governor in Chief and Vice Admiral of the Provence of North Carolina in America; portrait by William Hoare, engraved by James McArdall (c. 1752).

Peter Collinson.

Peter Collinson, on the other hand, was a London merchant dealing in fabrics and a keen amateur naturalist. He was a prodigious correspondent with numerous contacts in Europe and North America, and an extraordinary appetite for collecting. Standing at the shipping desk in his shop, often interrupted by his customers, he would pen his no-nonsense letters, begging, demanding any 'natural curiosity' that his friends could obtain. Around this time, Peter counted Dr Cadwallader Colden, a native of Enniscorthy and Deputy Governor of New York, and Dr James Logan of Philadelphia, one-time acting Governor of Pennsylvania, who was from Lurgan, among his numerous North American botanical friends. Before long Arthur Dobbs was to be added to that transatlantic Irish-American coterie.

In fact Dobbs and Collinson were well acquainted before Arthur sailed for America in June 1754. Already they had shared boxes of living plants sent from Philadelphia by 'our friend' John Bartram

– by the by, like Collinson, Bartram was a Quaker. After Arthur had settled into his new gubernatorial mansion at Brunswick, he took up gardening seriously. Collinson sent him cones of the cedar of Lebanon and almond seeds. 'I want much to plant almonds of the best Kinds olives and Dates here . . . and have taken a little Plantation at the sound on the sea coast [where] I intend to try oranges and Lemmones.' Arthur had already collected seeds and bulbs for Peter – among the plants Dobbs sent was the handsome Carolina spider-lily, 'a Clear white sweet flower' (*Hymenocallis crassifolia*).

But, as noted, there were hostilities against France in progress, and seeds were lost including some of the sensitive briar (*Mimosa microphylla*) – 'but my chagrin for all the seeds I had collected for you and my other Friends by their being cast away near [Boulogne] discouraged my sending over any more During the War . . . ' This information, contained in a letter written on his seventieth birthday, was as nothing to that conveyed in almost the final sentence: 'We have a kind of a Catch Fly sensitive which closes upon any thing that touches it – I will try to save the seed . . . '.

Perhaps worried about losing more letters, Arthur had entrusted this one to his son Edward who duly delivered it to Collinson during the summer of 1759. Thus came to Europe the first news of the astonishing carnivorous plant that we know as Venus's flytrap, *Dionaea muscipula*.

Arthur Dobb's brief reference to a 'catch fly sensitive' utterly mesmerised Peter who responded, no doubt standing at his office desk, demanding further information. Arthur duly obliged, on 24 January 1760, with this superb description.

> But the greater wonder of the vegetable kingdom is a very curious unknown species of sensitive; it is a dwarf plant; the leaves are like a narrow segment of a sphere, consisting of two parts, like the cap of a spring purse, the concave part outwards, each of which falls back with indented edges (like an iron spring fox trap); upon any thing touching the leaves or falling between them, they instantly close like a spring trap, and confine any insect or any thing that falls between them; it bears a white flower; to this surprising plant I have given the name of Fly Trap Sensitive.

Peter's curiosity was not quenched – far from it! Now he desired living specimens. He alerted John Bartram in Philadelphia. As it happened, John's son, William, went to live in North Carolina and in July 1761 was received at Brunswick by Governor Dobbs. Young Bartram was surely shown the remarkable fly trap and when he returned home late in 1762 he apparently brought some living plants to his father. However, before his son's return John Bartram had written to Peter describing this sensational discovery in more detail and providing another name for it – 'tippitiwitchet'.

John Bartram's letters merely tormented Peter Collinson: 'I wish I could hear it was Once in thy

own Garden & that I had good specimens. I then could forme Some Idea of the Wagish Plant as Wagishly Described.' His frustration grew, and on 5 October 1762 he sent another plea for specimens to Bartram. Not aware that Bartram was endeavouring to fulfil his demands and that a box containing samples of the 'Tippitiwitchet' had been dispatched to him, Collinson grew even more impatient – and the mails were infuriatingly slow. Towards the end of 1762, his patience nearly gave out. Writing on 10 December, he chided Bartram for teasing him with letters and omitting to send specimens: 'Whilst the Frenchman was readdy to Burst with laughing, I am ready to Burst with Desire for Root, Seed or Specimen of the waggish Tipitiwitchet Sensitive . . . if I have not a specimen in thy next letter, never write Mee more, for it is Cruell to tantalize Mee . . . '.

At last, early in May 1763, Peter was satisfied, for he received pressed leaves and flowers of the 'Wagish Tipitwitched'. With characteristic generosity, Collinson sent one leaf of this 'impossible' new plant to Professor Carl Linnaeus in Sweden: 'only to him would I spare such a jewel', he wrote, 'Pray send more specimens . . . Linnaeus will be in raptures at the sight of it.' *Miraculum naturae*, miracle of nature, was Linnaeus' exclamation.

Collinson's desire to grow the miraculous tippitiwitchet was now stronger than ever. Bartram succeeded in getting seeds which reached London about the beginning of December 1763, but none germinated. Yet Peter would not give up. He badgered Bartram and despaired of Dobbs. 'I hear my Friend Dobbs at 73 has gott a Colts Tooth in his head,' he wrote to Bartram at the end of June 1764, '& has married a young lady of 22. It is now in vain to write to Him for seeds or plants of Tipitiwitchit now He has gott one of his Own to play with.' Not for long – Arthur Dobbs died on 26 March the following year.

Four years passed. The tippitwitchet continued elusive. At last, on 6 July 1768, Peter reported to Bartram that William Young, a German plant hunter, had succeeded in bringing a few alive to

Facing page: *Venus's Fly-trap Dionæa Muscipula*'; hand-coloured engraving by James Roberts from John Ellis's pamphlet *Directions for bringing over seeds and plants from the East Indies . . .* (London, 1770).

Venus's Fly-trap.

Dionœa Muscipula.

A sensitive Plant from the Swamps of North America with a spike of white blossoms like the English Lady smock.
Each leaf is a miniature figure of a Rat trap with teeth; closing on every fly or other insect, that creeps between its lobes, and squeezing it to Death.

James Roberts sculp.

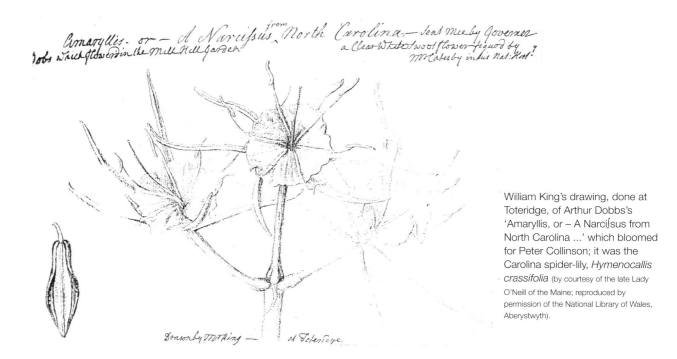

Amaryllis. or – A Narcissus, from North Carolina. – Sent me by Governor Dobbs which flowered in the Mill Hill Garden a Clear White wood flower figured by Mr Catesby in his Nat: Hist:?

Drawn by W King – at Toteridge

William King's drawing, done at Toteridge, of Arthur Dobbs's 'Amaryllis, or – A Narcissus from North Carolina ...' which bloomed for Peter Collinson; it was the Carolina spider-lily, *Hymenocallis crassifolia* (by courtesy of the late Lady O'Neill of the Maine; reproduced by permission of the National Library of Wales, Aberystwyth).

London and had sold them to James Gordon, a nurseryman, one of Peter's many friend.

Five weeks later, on 11 August 1768, Peter Collinson died. A few days afterwards one of the tippitiwitchets came into bloom. John Ellis was shown this plant and had drawings made, and in a letter to the editor of the *St James's Chronicle*, a London newspaper, Ellis gave a scientific name to the waggish 'Tippitywichit' – 'I shall call it Dionaea Muscipula, which may be construed into English, with humble Submission both to Critics and foreign Commentators, either Venus's Flytrap or Venus's Mousetrap.' Arthur's 'catch fly sensitive' was no longer a mystery.

Concluding his article, John Ellis presumed to hope that

the Name of Venus's Flytrap, as it seems most adapted to its powers, may be admitted to be the most eligible trivial Name, especially as I think myself warranted to do it from occular Demonstration of this surprising Faculty of its entrapping little Animals, such as Ear-wigs, Spiders and Flies, where they are either squeezed to Death, or remain imprisoned till they die.

Many were engaged in the task of discovering the tippitiwitchet, each making their own significant contribution. John Bartram first cultivated it and sent dried specimens to 'the curious of the old world'. Peter Collinson had persistently begged for specimens, yet died before it blossomed in London. A century later the greatest naturalist of all, Charles Darwin, threw in his mite too, declaiming it as 'the most wonderful plant in the world'.

But it was Arthur Dobbs who had made known this 'great wonder of the vegetable kingdom'. It is not difficult to imagine that the elderly Ulsterman, who years earlier had watched the bees visiting flowers in his Carrickfergus garden, crouching down in a Carolina swamp peering at the plant with leaves like 'an iron spring fox trap' and poking it with a grass stalk to trigger the sensitive lobes. Onlookers may have been dismayed that the Governor of North Carolina took an interest in plants, but he was merely fulfilling his own natural curiosity, as he had written:

I think it the Duty of every Person, who has had Time to make any Observation, which may contribute to come at the Truth . . . to throw in his Mite towards it.

4.4
AMONG THE HEATHER BRIGHT

The extraordinary flower-head of a waratah, *Telopea speciosissima*, which is the state emblem of New South Wales. Glasnevin Botanic Gardens paid the equivalent of €670 for a young plant of this extraordinary shrub in 1807. (© E. C. Nelson)

Professor Walter Wade; unsigned portrait in oils, implausibly attributed to Allan Ramsay. (Reproduced by courtesy of G. A. Kenyon)

WHEN THE DUBLIN SOCIETY established its Botanic Gardens at Glasnevin in 1795, and for the following decade and a half at least, the Gardens were the largest government-supported botanical garden anywhere in the world. The Irish Parliament, before its dissolution in 1800, voted £7,700 for the Gardens' formation: close to half a million euro in today's money. The Gardens' managers, the Society's Professor of Botany, Dr Walter Wade, and head gardener John Underwood, had an extraordinary amount of money (even by present-day standards) at their disposal for the purchase of plants, and did not stint their purchases. It is unlikely that Wade was the driving force in the programme of plant acquisition – he was not a horticulturist and is unlikely to have had a good, current knowledge of the kinds of plants that were available from nurseries. Underwood, on the other hand, had the knowledge and, I suggest, used it to acquire for Glasnevin the best, rarest and most fashionable plants.

We know little about John Underwood before he arrived in Dublin during 1798, and there is no known portrait of him. Almost the only definite information is that in January 1796 when he was proposed for election as an Associate of the Linnean Society of London, he resided in Brompton: 'a person highly skilled in the knowledge of Plants and well versed in their culture.' Significantly this was affirmed by, among others, William Curtis, proprietor of the famous *Botanical Magazine*, who

Lord Shannon's heath, *Erica shannonii*, as depicted about 1808 by Henry Charles Andrews in his magisterial four-volume work, *Coloured engravings of heaths* (plate 273). This is designated as a rare species in its natural habitats in South Africa.

The Octagon House was built to accommodate the Norfolk Island pine; in the mid-1830s, after the tree was killed, it was called the Banana House. (Drawn and engraved by J. Kirkwood, from the title-page of Ninian Niven's *The Visitor's Companion to the Botanic Garden* [1838]. Author's collection.)

had formed a nursery at Queen's Elm, Brompton, in 1789. Did Underwood work for Curtis? Perhaps. Curtis's signature was the first on Underwood's nomination paper, but we cannot be certain, especially as there were other nurseries in Brompton. His sponsors for the associateship also included John Fairbairn, the curator of Chelsea Physic Garden – did Underwood work there? – and James Dickson, a founding member of the Horticultural Society of London, who had a seed shop in Covent Garden. Given their signatures, we can be sure that John Underwood was immersed in the London nursery scene during the mid-1790s.

Within a few months of his arrival in Glasnevin, remarkable exotic plants began to appear at the Botanic Gardens. A seedling, only 15 inches tall, of the Norfolk Island pine, then called *Araucaria heterophylla* (formerly *Araucaria excelsa*) cost seven shillings and sixpence in 1798, the equivalent (roughly) of €30, a tiny fraction of the Gardens' budget. However, this sapling was so highly prized that an eight-sided glasshouse, named the Octagon House, would soon be built for it. This special greenhouse was designed so that it could be elevated, rather in the way of a telescope, to accommodate the growing tree. This famous tree, a relative of the monkey-puzzle, was to perish on a frosty night in November 1819. The pine was not that expensive, but it was only one of the newly discovered plants that Underwood acquired for the Botanic Gardens at Glasnevin. His, and Wade's, published catalogues of the collections reveal an abundance of species just arrived from 'New Holland' (an antique name for Australia) and 'C. B. S.' (*Caput Bonae Spei*, or the Cape of Good Hope).

Another example underlines the purchasing power of Glasnevin in those days. When Underwood was working in Brompton in the 1790s there was only one plant of the waratah (*Telopea speciosissima*) from New South Wales known in London; by 1807, a decade later, there were three. That is the year Glasnevin Botanic Gardens acquired one from Conrad Loddiges & Sons of Hackney; it cost ten guineas, the equivalent of around €670 today.

Where did all these plants come from? The accounts of the Botanic Gardens are vague yet revealing. In 1797, when only Dr Wade was in charge, some trees were purchased from George Smitten, nurseryman of Capel Street, Dublin; the order came to £6. 12s. 6d. (around €600). In 1798, after Underwood was appointed, it cost £98 (about €8,000) just to transport plants from the Vineyard Nursery, Hammersmith – the plants themselves cost a staggering £371 (around €31,000). The pattern repeats in succeeding years: 1799, £27 (about €1,900) for freight costs from London, presumably for more of the Vineyard Nursery's gems, but less than a third that, £8. 10s. 11d (€600), was spent on plants from Irish nurseries. In all, in the decade and a half between 1798 and 1813 the Glasnevin

Botanic Gardens purchased plants valued at £620 (equivalent to about €40,000) from the Vineyard Nursery, plus (in 1803) another £100-worth (about €7,500) from an unnamed Brompton nursery. The comparable amount spent in Irish establishments was just over £100.

The reason for this disparity was undoubtedly the fact that the Vineyard Nursery, in particular, had access to the most exciting new introductions. The proprietors, James Lee and John Kennedy, even employed their own collector at the Cape of Good Hope, and they seemed also to be favoured by other non-professional plant hunters, probably because of the nursery's reputation and connections to the likes of the Empress Josephine, wife of Napoleon Bonaparte.

There cannot be any doubt that the astonishing collection of Cape heaths (*Erica* species from the Cape of Good Hope) at Glasnevin in the early 1800s was due to the Vineyard Nursery. In Professor Wade's 1802 catalogue eighty different Cape heaths are listed. Two years later, 1804, when Underwood prepared his edition of the same catalogue the number had risen to 136. Most significantly, there are heaths listed in these catalogues by names that have never been properly published: they really were the newest of the new.

There is another possible link, albeit a tenuous one, between Ireland's new botanic garden and the Vineyard Nursery. The foreman-gardener at the Vineyard was John Cushing, about whom little is known expect that he was Irish. In 1811, the Dublin publishers Graisberry and Campbell issued the first edition of his book *The Exotic Gardener*. Its lengthy subtitle was: '. . . *in which the management of the hot-house, green-house, and conservatory, is fully and clearly delineated according to modern practice, with an appendix containing observations on the soils suitable for tender exotics, etc.*' Several later editions appeared in London, in 1812 and in 1814 at least. Were Cushing and Underwood acquaintances, I wonder? Here then is another mystery. Vineyard Nursery is credited with introducing a heather named *Erica cushiniana* about 1816; it was undoubtedly a hybrid of Cape origin, had red flowers, bloomed in

Erica shannonii, photographed in the 1960s by Ted Oliver; from one of its few known habitats, at Akkerdiskloof Pass, northeast of Stanford, Western Cape Province, South Africa. (© E. G. H. Oliver)

September and grew about two feet tall. Nothing much else is known about it except that it was listed in horticultural tomes and nurserymen's catalogues until the 1870s when it disappeared. Was it named after John Cushing – very probably, but in that case the name should be spelled with a 'g'.

Lee and Kennedy's professional plant-collector at the Cape of Good Hope was remarkably successful. His name was James Niven – he was a Scot, from Penicuik near Edinburgh (but he was *not* related to Ninian Niven who would become John Underwood's successor as head-gardener at Glasnevin in 1834). James Niven sent back hundreds of new species including countless new heaths. These tender shrubs were the horticultural rage of the late 1790s and early 1800s, so popular that one London nurseryman secretly made hybrids and passed them off as new, wild-collected species, a fact so well concealed in horticultural literature that to this day South African botanists are flummoxed by many of the *Erica* species listed in early nineteenth-century catalogues. They were also so fashionable that not a few were named after 'patrons of botany': *Erica hibbertii*, for example, which was growing in Glasnevin by 1804, was

Erica Bandonia

named after George Hibbert who had sponsored James Niven's first expedition to the Cape of Good Hope in the late 1790s.

Niven and his fellow collectors – he was not the only one gathering the riches of the Cape flora – were producing so many new plants that finding names for them proved a problem. The botanists who normally described and named new species were it seems too busy to bother with the South African novelties and so these were given names by the nurserymen who needed to sell the seedlings to make a living. Chaos ensued, as did a trend to christen new heaths after wealthy patrons. *Erica savileae*, for example, we now know was named after the Countess of Scarbrough whose personal notebooks show she had a passion for Cape heaths and tender, 'indoor' geraniums (*Pelargonium* spp). *Erica archerae* honoured (if that is the right word) Lady Sarah Archer who was so well known in London society in the late 1700s 'for her close attention to the latest fashions' that she was lampooned by the satirist James Gillray in several scurrilous cartoons.

And that is why among the company of fashionable ladies, and others of some notoriety, there are two rather unlikely Irish peers, the earls of Shannon and of Bandon: *Erica shannonii* and *Erica bandonii*. We can only guess that their lordships developed a passion for growing the heaths from South Africa, and that they were frequently seen in the nurseries around London placing lucrative orders. *Erica* "bandania" was listed in October 1808 by Lee and Kennedy as one of the firm's new introductions. John Cushing has it in the 1814 edition of his *The Exotic Garden* and it was illustrated by Henry Andrews in his sumptuous publication *Coloured Engravings of Heaths* – Andrews was married to John Kennedy's daughter, so the Vineyard Nursery connections are further enhanced. 'This Erica, named in honour of Lord Bandon, was raised from Cape seed at the Hammersmith Nursery.' Hmm . . . nothing like it has *ever* been found in the wild in South Africa, and it is 'lost to cultivation'. Lord Bandon's heath, which had purple flowers, has vanished without trace – except for Andrews'

hand-coloured engraving. The chances are it was one of the secretly created hybrids, passed off as wild-collected, simply to ensure continued income, if not profits, for a certain London nursery. The earl immortalised by this heath was the first of that title, Francis Bernard (1755–1830), of Castle Bernard, County Cork, whose wife Catherine was the daughter of the second Earl of Shannon – coincidentally?

Lord Shannon's heath is an entirely different matter. Indisputably, it still grows on hill slopes in Western Cape Province, South Africa. *Erica shannonii* is a shrub about half a metre tall, and between December and February (the southern-hemisphere summer) it produces its astonishing bottle-shaped white flowers, two to three centimetres long, much longer than the flowers of any of Ireland's native heathers. Some books say it is named after the Countess of Shannon (as *Erica shannonea*), but again Henry Andrews has the final word: 'our figure', he wrote, referring to the hand-coloured plate in *Coloured Engravings of Heaths*, 'represents a plant in the nursery of Mr. Rollisson, where we found it under the specific title of Shannonea, in compliment to the Earl of Shannon.' Given the dates, this must have been Henry (1771–1842), the third earl, who was *Custos Rotulorum* (Keeper of the Rolls) of County Cork and Clerk of the Pells in Ireland. And, given Andrews' remark about the dedication, the name must take the masculine gender – *Erica shannonii*.

Neither *Erica × bandonii* nor *Erica shannonii* is known to have been grown in Glasnevin in Underwood's day.

4.5
ARISTOCRAT OF THE GARDEN – THE SHAN LILY

THERE'S NO HURRYING A SHAN LILY. It will flower when it wants to, taking its time to perfect its extraordinary bud. Sunshine, heavy rain, wind and oppressive humidity pass the Shan lily by, and it does not wilt.

The books say that a Shan lily (*Lilium sulphureum*) can have up to fifteen flowers on a stem, but ours were content to produce a singleton each for the first few years and now have four or five apiece. The books say this is a difficult lily to grow, that it is not hardy, but ours have never been indoors and have put up with several extremely cold winters with temperatures well below freezing. The books say . . . Let's forget what the books say, mainly because they don't say very much at all, at least not the books on my shelves.

The first thing about a Shan lily that impresses you is that it is stately, superbly poised – 'essentially an aristocrat' was Ernest Wilson's phrase. The main stalk is erect and slender, dark purple-green with numerous, narrow, dark-green leaves scattered along the stem from top to bottom. The lower leaves tend to be longest. Only when the buds get to their full size does the stem show any sign of bending, and then it just bows, slightly.

Those buds! They are truly extraordinary, almost impossible to describe. They take four or more weeks to reach full size yet when they are first obvious, at the apex of the stalk, they are merely pale green pimples. When fully grown they are slender, tapering towards the more swollen tip which is slightly warty. They are pinkish, a streaky pallid, dusky pink, mixed with green, and they look like the bill of some weird, long-necked bird that has escaped from *Jurassic Park*.

The most remarkable thing about the buds is that they seem to secrete a substance – probably nectar – that is extremely attractive to ants. Every time you look at a bud there will be three or four

ants busy, scurrying to and fro. About halfway through the bud's development, when they are still only an inch or two long, on warm evenings, the local fruit flies and hoverflies also find this external secretion irresistible. Extra-floral nectaries are not reported, as far as I can discover, on lilies, but I have not made an exhaustive search. In their excellent book *The Natural History of Pollination*, Michael Proctor, Peter Yeo and Andrew Lack do record that some plants from tropical countries use externally secreted nectar to attract ants, which then protect the plants from other animals that may be nectar-thieves or corolla-munchers. I wonder if this is what is happening, although the small number of minute ants which patrol the flowers of our Shan lilies would have great trouble fending off a persistent bug. Certainly nothing else seems to crawl on the flowers and there are no holes in the buds. As for the hoverflies and fruit flies, they are harmless, as far as I know, to lily flowers.

The first sign that a bud is deigning to open is a slight splitting of the tip, and a curling of the petal tips, as if this bird-like bud is going to snarl. Then the great petals slowly separate – it takes about two days from snarl to trumpet – until the flower is a sumptuous cone of the softest cream flushed outside with dusky pink. Inside there is amber and gold. The trumpet is not brazen, but demur, nodding gently, spilling its heady perfume into the evening air where it lingers. It's a fragrance redolent of the Orient – as it should be – slightly sharp, but oh-so-sweet.

Each flower is more than 15 centimetres (6 inches) from petal tip to base, a hand's length. They have substance: the petals are thick, not flimsy. Inside there are six stamens bearing long, straight brownish-green anthers. These burst to release pollen the colour and texture of the softest soft

The Shan lily produced just one bloom in 2000. (© E. C. Nelson)

brown sugar. The stout style curves slightly and terminates in a three-sided conical stigma.

We have not allowed our Shan lilies to set seed as we are anxious not to weaken the bulbs, but they are still fecund, producing small bulbils in the axils of the uppermost leaves. Last year we missed them – the bulblets fell off before we could gather them, but this year we won't make the same mistake because we reckon we cannot have too many Shan lilies.

This pair of lilies started off sharing a square, dark blue-glazed Vietnamese pot with a pink penstemon. They cohabited happily. The penstemon has since 'passed away' but the two lilies thrive. They have not been disturbed now for ten summers. For the past five years both of the lilies have bloomed spectacularly.

There is, needless to say, a story behind the Shan lily, that makes these two plants rather special. *Lilium sulphureum* inhabits western China and northeastern Burma. It was first collected in Yunnan by the French missionary-cum-botanist Père Jean Marie Delavay during 1888 and about the same time near Kulaw in the Shan States of eastern Burma by William Boxall, presumably when he was supposed to be collecting orchids for Messrs Hugh Low, because the species was exhibited by Messrs Low at the Royal Horticultural Society's show in June 1889 when it gained a well-deserved First Class Certificate. A decade later, Dr Augustine Henry found this lily species near Mengsi in southern China, where, during the autumn of 1899, he showed it to Ernest Wilson. Three different colour-forms have been described. Henry's had a yellow throat, but pure white petals with a greenish

flush outside. Another form has pure yellow petals without any pink flush. The flowers of the Burmese plant are creamy with a deep yellow throat and the outsides are pink-flushed – as I have described.

I came across this lily, not among Henry's collections, but in the letters of Lady Charlotte Wheeler Cuffe who knew and grew the lily at Maymyo, both in her own garden and in the botanic garden which she established in that hill-town situated about forty miles northeast of Mandalay in central Burma. She sent a box full of two-year old Shan lily bulbs to the Botanic Gardens, Glasnevin, in 1920, in return for some apple scions. However, around ten years earlier she had given bulbs to her sister-in-law who lived in Cambridge and those particular lilies were mentioned in a letter that Lady Cuffe wrote to Sir Frederick Moore. The letter is dated 18 June 1913 – the Cuffes were home in Europe on leave. 'I was at Cambridge the other day', she wrote,

> and was interested to see that the Shan lily . . . which I had sent to sister in law, which was planted in the open ground had survived the winter whereas the one she put in a pot in the greenhouse died – I believe they are almost if not quiet as hardy as Candidum and more die in this country from heat than cold. There are four here which thrive splendidly in large pots in a cold house in winter, and stood out all the summer – I find they dislike being re-potted and do best by merely scraping off a little of the top soil and renewing it, and by earthing up the stems about an inch when they have grown about a foot high. You said you had found them difficult, so this may be of interest.

You will have to believe me when I say that I have only just re-read that letter, having forgotten it entirely – I did not consult it when we planted our Shan lilies. Thus, utterly by chance we have followed Lady Cuffe's advice, and our two lilies are

A decade after the bulbs were planted, the two lilies flower abundantly, producing four or five blooms on each stem.
(© E. C. Nelson)

139

as happy as can be, outdoors, in their blue pot, just thirty miles from Cambridge. They have never been in a greenhouse, and have never been disturbed!

We owe these 'noblest of all lilies' to U Aung Swe, the genial former curator of the Maymyo Botanic Garden – in fact, he is one of Lady Cuffe's successors. I met him in Maymyo, now named Pyin-U-Lwin, in his own little nursery-garden during November 1998. He gave them to me as a souvenir of Burma, and they seem to glow with the soft, golden light of that beautiful but tortured land.

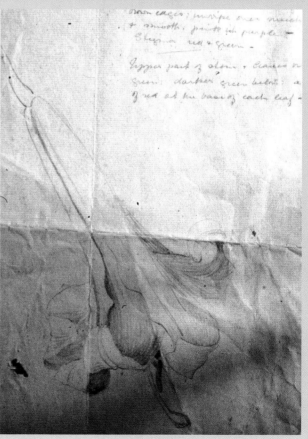

Above: One of the pair of Shan lilies in the blue Vietnamese ceramic pot, after two years' planting. (© E. C. Nelson)

Above right: The buds of the Shan lily attract insects and ants. (© E. C. Nelson)

Right: Charlotte Cuffe's pencil sketch of the flower of the Shan lily; although annotated for use in a watercolour, I am not aware if she made a coloured portrait of *Lilium sulphureum*.

4.6
JUBILEE OF A LIVING FOSSIL – THE DAWN REDWOOD

WE TAKE DAWN REDWOODS (*Metasequoia glyptostroboides*) for granted nowadays, but six decades ago they were *the* botanical sensation, a bright light in the dark aftermath of the Second World War. 1998 was the golden jubilee of the dawn redwood's arrival in our gardens, and the man responsible for ensuring that Ireland received this exciting new plant just as quickly as everyone else was an Ulsterman – one of our most distinguished horticulturists, Brian Mulligan.

This is the dawn redwood's story. In the early winter of 1941, T. Kan, a forester, noticed three leafless trees near a hamlet called Mo-tao-chi (Modaoqi) in the east of Sichuan province in central China. As there was no point in gathering twigs, Kan asked the local schoolmaster, Lung-hsin Yang, to send some specimens the following year. War erupted, and the new conifer was not a priority, but it was not entirely forgotten. In 1944, another forest botanist, T. Wang, visited the hamlet and gathered a few fragments of the new tree, but these were not quite sufficient to allow its identification. The war ended and in the spring of 1946 yet another collection was made by Chi-ju Hseh, and this time there was great excitement. Professor Wan Chun Cheng, one of China's leading botanists, realised this strange deciduous tree was a previously unknown plant, and so he sent specimens to Professor Hsen-hsu Hu in Beijing, who made another startling connection. Yes, it was new, but not quite unknown, for a Japanese botanist, Shigeru Miki, had described an almost identical fossil plant a few years earlier! So here was a living fossil, like that other remarkable tree from China, the maidenhair tree (*Ginkgo biloba*).

Realising that this exciting tree was probably of horticultural value, Hsen-hsu Hu determined to have seed collected. An expedition was mounted

One of the original seedlings of the dawn redwood: National Botanic Gardens, Glasnevin. (© E. C. Nelson)

with the help of the great American botanic garden, the Arnold Arboretum, which is situated near Boston, Massachusetts. In autumn 1947 the expedition reached the grove of three living fossils and managed to obtain a considerable quantity of good seeds. Some was kept in China and the rest was shipped to the Arnold Arboretum whence it was distributed worldwide.

The dawn redwood is a deciduous conifer, and its foliage is rather unusual. What looks like an individual, very divided leaf is in fact a small branchlet with about two dozen linear leaflets arranged in two ranks. In autumn, the entire branchlet is shed along with its leaflets. (© E. C. Nelson)

Professor Hu was a good friend of the sixth Earl of Rosse – he had met Lord and Lady Rosse when they were on honeymoon in Beijing in 1935. Lord Rosse had helped to raise funds for botanical expeditions in China before the outbreak of the war and as a result, of course, many new Chinese plants were raised in the gardens of Birr Castle, County Offaly. As soon as the war ended Dr Hu had written to Lord Rosse, describing the exciting discovery as a 'gigantic tree of 34 metres in height [and] what is most striking is that it is deciduous, like our water pine . . . and the American bald cypress'. Hu added the comment that it would be hardy, and arranged to send some seed to Lord Rosse.

Elsewhere and meanwhile, Brian Mulligan, a native of Ulster, had moved to Seattle as superintendent of the University of Washington Arboretum. He received seeds of the new conifer very soon after the first batch reach Boston, and with equal promptness sent a pinch to one of his acquaintances, Commander Frank Gilliland who lived at Brook Hall on the banks of the River Foyle outside Derry. The Commander, a somewhat cantankerous man, was very keen on conifers as the

splendid arboretum at Brook Hall testifies today and he realised that the seeds from Brian Mulligan needed special care. On 11 February 1948, Gilliland wrote to Tom Walsh, Keeper of the National Botanic Gardens, Glasnevin: 'I send a small packet of seed received yesterday from my friend Mulligan . . . It belongs to a rare, & recently discovered deciduous sequoia, called Meta-Sequoia glyptostroboides, from Szechuan . . . Please sow the seed with all care as it is rare.'

So the dawn redwood arrived at Glasnevin via Brian Mulligan and Frank Gilliland and its seeds were sown. Further packets of seed came to Glasnevin in the summer of 1948. Lord and Lady Rosse eventually also received seeds direct from Professor Hu. By 1950 there were six healthy saplings in the nursery at Glasnevin; three of these were planted in the National Botanic Gardens, and they all survive today. The others seedlings went to Avondale in County Wicklow, Ballyhaise in County Cavan, and the National Stud at Tully in County Kildare. The dawn redwoods growing today at Brook Hall and Birr Castle came from the Royal Botanic Gardens, Kew.

Above: Dr Brian Mulligan examining a tree of the Irish whitebeam, *Sorbus hibernica*, in the grounds of Trinity Hall, Dartry, in June 1983. (© E. C. Nelson)

Left: The bark of a mature dawn redwood tree. (© E. C. Nelson)

Brian Mulligan (1907–1996) was always a keen gardener and from 1924 to 1927 was a student at the Royal Horticultural Society's Garden, Wisley. About this time he cross-pollinated two relatively new Chinese candelabra primroses – *Primula pulverulenta* with dusky purple flowers and *Primula chungensis* with scented, orange flowers – creating a hybrid with bright deep-red flowers which fade to salmon- or coral-pink: he named this new primrose *Primula × chunglenta*. After working at Long Ashton Research Station near Bristol, and some years back at Wisley, in 1946 he moved to Seattle as Superintendent and acting Director of the University of Washington Arboretum. He remained Director there until he retired in 1972. Not only did Brian Mulligan develop in Seattle an arboretum which is acknowledged to be one of the top three 'living museums' of woody plants in the United States, but he also had the foresight and generosity to ensure that his native land received the dawn redwood.

4.7
HANS AND THE BEANSTALK:
A TRANSATLANTIC TALE

ONE OF THE pioneering achievements of Ireland's gardeners is almost unknown – one of our company was the first to grow a pair of nickars. Not earth-shattering, perhaps: not as difficult as the flowering of orchid seedlings, nor the creation of hybrid pitcher-plants; not on a par with the raising of a new rose or a new daffodil. But very remarkable all the same, especially bearing in mind whence that pair of nickars came.

Like the blossoming orchid seedlings and the pitcher-plant hybrids, the feat was accomplished at Glasnevin. The story is worth telling not just because of the fact that it happened so early in the history of the National Botanic Gardens, but also because the strands of the story have remarkable meanders. A baronet from the village of Killyleagh in the County Down and a general who was born in Flanders are implicated. Great natural forces are implicated too, and, ultimately, one of the threads that informed Charles Darwin's magisterial book *On the Origin of Species*.

Nickars – with an 'a'! There is nothing rude about them. Nickar is an old name for a marble, the sort we played with when we were children, made from glass or sometimes pottery. The seeds called nickars look like glazed, porcelain marbles, the resemblance enhanced by the hair-like cracks that encircle them. They can be grey, or more rarely yellow, or very exceptionally brown, and they are as hard as porcelain too.

A Kerry lady gave me some seeds two years ago, that she had picked up on some shore; they were of a grey blue colour, except one that was yellow: they were about the size of marbles, and globular, highly varnished, and the kernels or seeds rattled within.

So wrote General Charles Vallencey, a leading light in the (Royal) Dublin Society and a somewhat eccentric individual, in a letter to Sir Joseph Banks, the man who had been with Captain James Cook when Botany Bay was discovered and who was by the first decade of the nineteenth century the director in all but title of the Royal Gardens at Kew. Vallencey took more than a passing interest in the Dublin Society's newly created Botanic Gardens at Glasnevin, and evidently decided that the grey, marble-shaped seeds from Kerry should be sown there: 'Of the grey, I gave a gentleman some, & sowed some in our hothouse; they proved to be runners, our Gardiner thinks from Africa', he added. The gardener had also managed to raise a seedling from one of the yellow seeds: 'the yellow seed proved to be a shrub, unknown to all our Irish botanists', crowed the general. In the spring of 1802 that plant was flourishing: 'it is full vigour', Vallencey told Sir Joseph, 'and about twice the size of the drawing enclosed . . . [which] I made a month since'. 'Probably you will know this shrub and give me a name for it', he added, enquiringly.

Banks must have responded, naming the plant 'Bonduca', for in November 1802, General Vallencey sent another bulletin: 'The Bonduca, from the seed found on the coast of Kerry, is in a very flourishing state, beginning to grow bushy', and adding that another seed had been found on the coast of Londonderry and it too had been planted, '& I hope will succeed'. The following month, December 1802, the octogenarian general scandalised Dublin by marrying a 'fair housemaid' and so became the butt of a caricature sold by Dublin booksellers. The Professor of Botany at Trinity College, Dublin, Dr Robert Scott, commented to an English colleague: 'apropos the old man, I am sorry to tell you [he] has compleatly played the fool by marrying

Like nickars, sea-hearts can remain afloat for many years, and as they bob about in the ocean sometimes goose-barnacles become attached. I also found this sea-heart with goose-barnacles at Dog's Bay in 1986. (© E. C. Nelson)

Inset: Nickars can float for more than a year. This one was stranded on the beach at Dog's Bay, near Roundstone, in Connemara during 1986. The nickars collected in Ireland are usually grey. (© E. C. Nelson)

The four different drift-seeds that are most frequently found on beaches in the west of Ireland: sea-heart (top right), horse-eye (or hamburger) bean (lower right), nickar (lower left) and Mary's bean (upper left). (© E. C. Nelson)

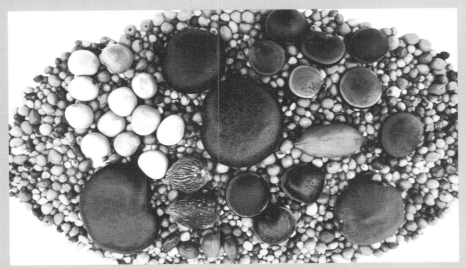

Left: Over many years, a dedicated beachcomber can collect thousands of tropical seeds from a west-facing Atlantic beach in Ireland or Great Britain. These are some of the seeds that Alma Hathway has gathered from one beach in Cornwall. The countless small seeds come from such plants as sea bindweed, moonflower and beach morning-glory (members of the bindweed family, Convolvulaceae) as well as sea pea (*Lathyrus japonicus* subsp. *maritimus*). The twelve grey seeds are nickars, the four largest, heart-shaped ones are sea-hearts; there is also a cluster of six horse-eye (or hamburger) beans. All of these seeds have the potential to germinate. (© E. C. Nelson)

a servant maid. This occurrence took place last week. I was thunderstruck when I heard of it. He is I am assured 84 years of age & this adds not a little to the <u>extraordinaries</u> attending Him.'

Back to botany – almost nothing else is known about the Glasnevin nickar bushes. They were reported in the first catalogue of the Botanic Gardens published in 1802: 'Our Bonduc was raised from seed picked up on the coast of Ireland, and sent to the garden by GENERAL VALLENCEY, 1801.' That they flourished for a few years is likely: perhaps one or other blossomed although the flowers are less remarkable than the spine-encrusted pods. But a seedling raised from a seed

Above (both photographs): Flowers of the horse-eye bean, *Mucuna sloanei*. (By courtesy of Ed Perry)

Facing page: Sir Hans Sloane, the Ulsterman after whom the horse-eye bean was named. (Portrait by Clifford Hall, after Stephen Slaughter; reproduced by courtesy of the Ulster Medical Society, Belfast.)

collected on a Kerry beach growing in the Glasnevin hothouse? This was a tropical plant, not a hardy, Irish native.

Nickars (*Caesalpinia* species) and a couple of dozen other seeds including those called sea hearts (*Entada gigas*) and hamburger beans (*Mucuna* species) have remarkable life-histories. Those that are stranded and sometimes collected on Irish beaches have travelled thousands of miles from their native lands, simply by floating in ocean currents. The first person to make this point was the man whose birthplace was Killyleagh, Sir Hans Sloane. This Ulsterman is best remembered nowadays as the founder of the British Museum in London. He also ensured that Chelsea Physic Garden, one of the oldest botanic gardens in the world, survived into this millennium. Sloane was the most fashionable physician in London during the early 1700s; he made his fortune and obtained a baronetcy. He was also no mean botanist.

As a young man, Dr Hans Sloane had gone to Jamaica as physician to the island's governor. While living on that Caribbean island during the late 1680s he indulged his passion for natural history, especially botany, and eventually wrote a natural history of Jamaica. Only someone with this experience could have proceeded to make the globe-encircling connection between some extraordinary seeds washed up on Irish and Scottish beaches and the shrubs and vines that grew naturally beside Caribbean beaches. Sloane did exactly that, when he returned home from Jamaica. In a paper published in the prestigious *Philosophical Transactions of the Royal Society of London* during 1698, he reported that he had heard about strange beans 'thrown up by the Sea . . . pretty frequently in great Numbers' on the beaches of Scottish islands and also on 'the Coast of *Kerry* in *Ireland*'. 'How these several Beans should come to the *Scotch* Isles, and one of them to *Ireland*, seems very hard to determine', he continued. But he knew the answer. 'It is very easie to conceive' that they fell onto their native tropical beaches, were washed into the sea, and then floated across the Atlantic Ocean, propelled by wind and ocean currents.

These tropical seeds still make this voyage and still come ashore in untold numbers. If you go down to any beach on the west coast, between Cape Clear and Malin Head, in autumn, winter and spring, especially after a period of strong, on-shore, westerly winds, I guarantee that you will be in the presence of such seeds – you may not see them instantly, but poke around on the high-tide mark, among the flotsam and jetsam, and they will be there. Sea beans of all sorts are lucky objects, if you find them.

One of the lucky seeds that is washed ashore on Irish beaches is called *Mucuna sloanei* – its

Flowering shrub of
Caesalpinia bonduc,
the grey nickar nut,
and some nickars
and a pod.

(By courtesy of Ed Perry)

Bondue

Right: The sketch of the seedling raised in the Glasnevin Botanic Gardens about 1800.
(Reproduced by courtesy of The Natural History Museum, London.)

common names include horse-eye bean, donkey's eye, sea bean, and (a modern invention from Florida) hamburger bean but you may have to strain your powers of imagination to see the connection. Needless to say, *Mucuna sloanei* was named after Sir Hans. Like the nickar, the horse-eye bean is a member of the bean or legume family – they are tropical 'cousins' of sweet pea, *Wisteria*, clover and even shamrock.

Unlike nickars, there are no reliable early reports of any *Mucuna sloanei* seeds having been germinated in Irish gardens. Yet this *Mucuna* is as capable of germinating after its year-long voyage across the Atlantic as the nickar. Four plants were raised at Glasnevin in 1988. Nineteen weeks after they had germinated, those *Mucuna sloanei* seedlings were six feet tall and 'still growing vigorously'. Of course, they were cosseted in the warmest greenhouse, but eventually perished. In Florida, on the other hand, it is possible to grow Hans Sloane's horse-eye bean outdoors – like Jack-and-the-Beanstalk's bean, it is a very rapid, twining vine, growing as much as six inches a day! Given plenty of light and a tree to climb, a *Mucuna* vine can blossom and fruit within a year of germination, as my friend Ed Perry has proven. The clusters of yellow flowers are succeeded by wrinkled pods, each of which contains at least one hamburger bean.

Sir Hans, General Vallencey and Sir Joseph have made their entrances – what about Charles Darwin? He was fascinated by the possibility that ocean currents could be a mechanism by which viable seeds, and consequently plant species, were distributed around the globe. He knew that some seeds could float and even tried an experiment with a horse-eye bean and the much larger sea-bean (*Entada gigas*): 'I have now floated them for 10 days and they float as well as ever'. Ten days is not enough time – any object floating in the North Atlantic Ocean, moved along in what is commonly called the Gulf Stream, needs at least twelve months to make the journey from the Caribbean to western Ireland. Nickars can stay afloat for at least thirty years, whereas Sloane's bean only lasts around five years – that is still more than enough time.

It is an incontrovertible fact that for many millennia nickars, sea hearts, hamburger beans and perhaps two score more, have been crossing the Atlantic from west to east on the Gulf Stream and the North Atlantic Drift, the current that warms our western shores. I like to imagine a band of Neolithic beachcombers, alive long before St Brendan set off from Kerry or Christopher Columbus visited Galway, gathering such tropical American seeds from Irish beaches and wondering what they were. They could never have guessed.

4.8
THE JOURNEY OF A ROSE

I LOOKED ACROSS THE LAKE, over ruffled water to the wooded mountains on the opposite shore. The sun was setting behind the peaks and sunlight shafts lit patches of sweet chestnut and beech. In the far distance, snow gleamed on higher Alps. There was a small town dimly visible when the nearest of the hills merged with the lake. I looked at my map, curious to find the town's name and something chimed in my memory: Baveno. There was a familiarity about the name but for a while I couldn't fathom it.

Later, driving through the twisting, narrow streets of the town where I was staying, I spotted a rose bush in full bloom and instantly recognised it, and suddenly the nagging puzzle of the name of the lakeside town resolved itself. Threads of stories that I had unearthed in old nursery catalogues, and in *Irish Gardening*, the gardening monthly that flourished between 1906 and 1922, came into focus. I was near the place where a lovely rose had been found early in the twentieth century.

The poet Walter de la Mare, in 'All that's past', summed up the story of many a rose:

> Oh, no man knows
> Through what wild centuries
> Roves back the rose. . .

Yet some of the history of this particular rose, and its journey to Ireland, is known and can be told.

The rose is most familiar under the name *Rosa chinensis* 'Mutabilis' but that is not its first name. It is a wonderful rose that blooms from late spring into autumn with delicate, single flowers that open from slim, pointed buds.

The petals on their first day are pale creamy-apricot. On the following day they turn to a soft pink tinged with copper. On the third day, before the petals fall, they go crimson. Thus a vigorous,

Rosa 'Tipo Ideale', also known as *Rosa* 'Mutabilis'. (© E. C. Nelson)

healthy bush, which can be at least two metres tall (or even taller when grown against a wall), is spattered at the same time with flowers of apricot and pink and crimson. The flower colours are most intense in hot weather, but this is not a tender rose and it will withstand hard winters.

Let us return to the lakeside town. Baveno is situated on the western shore of Lago Maggiore in the north of Italy where the Alps suddenly end. Like the nearby towns of Stresa and Pallanza, Baveno has been a mecca for tourists for many decades – the lake and the mountains combine in a memorable landscape. Offshore, between Pallanza and Baveno, lie the islands of Isola Madre, Isola Bella and Isola dei Pescatori, the property of the Borromeo family, one of Italy's richest dynasties.

On Isola Madre there is a dignified villa surrounded by a fine garden containing many interesting plants, of which the glory is a magnificent, gigantic Kashmir cypress (*Cupressus torulosa* 'Cashmeriana'), its branches curtained with grey-blue

149

The single, five-petalled flowers of 'Tipo Ideale' change colour as they mature, from apricot, to pink to crimson.
(© E. C. Nelson)

foliage. Isola dei Pescatori is crowded with a village for fishermen (hence the island's name). On Isola Bella there is a sumptuous palace with marble floors and lofty corridors, hung with tapestries, that lead you out into a stupendous, formal garden, stepped in terraces and embellished with statues and obelisks. White peacocks strut there and fountains splash into shell-shaped pools. The gardens of Isola Bella were completed in the 1690s and are regarded as among the finest Baroque gardens surviving in Italy.

Early last century, Sir John Ross-of-Bladensburg and his wife visited Lago Maggiore, and according to Lady Moore, Lady Ross noticed this lovely rose growing in a small market garden at Baveno. She purchased a plant and brought it home with her to Rostrevor in County Down. Needless to say, that eagle-eyed nurseryman and rose enthusiast Tom Smith, of Daisy Hill Nursery in nearby Newry, saw the Baveno rose and obtained cuttings from Rostrevor. Smith introduced it in about 1929 under the name 'Tipo Ideale', the name given to it apparently by Sir John himself and first used by Lady Moore in 1921 in an article in *Irish Gardening*. She was describing the garden at Rostrevor House:

A little further up the path on a trellis of larch poles a single climbing rose of unusual colour and shape is flourishing. Some years ago Lady Ross saw this remarkable rose in a small market garden . . . in Italy and wisely brought home a plant. . . the flowers are not the usual cupped shape, but flattened with undulating petals something like rose 'Anemone', but flatter. The stems are very slender with delicately shaped leaves. It is flowering so freely one wondered where the cuttings so generously promised by Sir John Ross were to come from, but they have arrived. The name of this delightful rose is R. 'Tipo Ideale'.

So 'Tipo Ideale' had reached Rostrevor from Baveno, and I thought that it would be amusing to see if I could find it growing there. It was clear that Baveno was a good place for gardening. Every wall was encrusted with ferns just as in Ireland. An exotic weed, the Mexican daisy *Erigeron karvinskianus*, sprouted in profusion from the walls too, and in gardens everywhere Chusan fan-palms (*Trachycarpus fortunei*) were thriving, each tree bearing custard-coloured trusses of blossom. But, the rose was nowhere to be seen. Mind you, the

Even on a wet day, a bush of *Rosa* 'Tipo Ideale' looks as though it is covered with a flock of butterflies.
(© E. C. Nelson)

incessant rain, as wet and as discouraging as Irish rain, didn't make rose-hunting a pleasant activity.

I was soaked through in half an hour and decided to give up the chase. But, as I have said, the rose is still grown in the region. As in every plant-hunting story, Murphy's law was in operation and I spotted it in a villa garden within a hundred yards of my hotel in Pallanza, on the opposite shore of Lago Maggiore.

To repeat, 'Tipo Ideale' is most familiar by the name 'Mutabilis', and this Latin name confirms the link with Lago Maggiore. The Swiss horticulturist and alpine enthusiast Henri Correvon published a description and an illustration of the rose in 1934 (more than a dozen years after Lady Moore had written about it). Correvon named it *Rosa mutabilis* (it is now listed as *Rosa × odorata* 'Mutabilis'). In his article he mentioned how he had first encountered the rose. He had obtained a plant, under yet another name, *Rosa turkestanica*, in 1895 from Prince Gilberto Borromeo, the owner of the island-gardens of Isola Madre and Isola Bella, both little more than a 'stone's throw' from Baveno.

There can be no doubt that 'Mutabilis' – or 'Tipo Ideale' as I prefer to call it – is a splendid garden plant. It has been described by the famous rose expert, the late Graham Stuart Thomas, as a bedding rose with endless possibilities, its varied tone ensuring that it can fit into almost any colour scheme. He suggests planting it with blue cranesbills, such as *Geranium himalayense*, perhaps especially 'Irish Blue', or 'Johnson's Blue'. It goes well with red and orange and yellow – try it with red-hot pokers (*Kniphofia*). The mature leaves of the rose are rich green, while the young shoots and the young foliage are dark plum, so it can also be combined with silvers and greys – rue and perhaps *Buddleja fallowiana* 'Alba'.

We will probably never know how 'Mutabilis' came to be grown in Baveno, or for how long Italian gardeners had admired it before Lady Ross-of-Bladensburg saw it. Prince Gilberto Borromeo did not know anything about the history of the rose yet the name he had for it suggested that it had come from central Asia, from the vague place called Turkestan. Perhaps it had journeyed thence along the Silk Road, for rose experts accept that 'Mutabilis' is a cultivar or perhaps a hybrid of the China rose, *Rosa chinensis*. Could it have travelled in the 'sponge bag' of a trader following in Marco Polo's footsteps?

Rosa 'Mutabilis'; this illustration accompanied an article about the rose's origins written by Henri Correvon (from *Revue horticole* 1934; by courtesy of the Hunt Institute for Botanical Documentation, Pittsburgh ©).

5

MAINLY ABOUT PEOPLE

5.1
THE LAST ROSE OF SUMMER

'Tis the last rose of summer,
Left blooming alone;
All her lovely companions
Are faded and gone.

WE ALL LIKE A GOOD STORY, so here are three for the price of one. (Two were told in my original article, as follows; the third in the note on p. 157).

Thomas Moore, 'The Irish National Poet', was fond of amateur theatricals and every year, in October, he would go to Kilkenny to take part in a local festival. One year, about 1805, or 1810, he was at the Kilkenny theatricals and staying in Jenkinstown House. In the garden he saw a rose bush still in bloom. At that period, a rose that flowered in autumn was rather unusual, and this bush inspired him to put pen to paper and compose his love-lorn ballad.

By 1950 both the house and the rose bush had disappeared, but Lady Elaine Bellew, who had lived in Jenkinstown House, had propagated the rose and on 15 June 1950 the Thomas Moore Society presented a cutting, taken from that rose bush, to Dr Tom Walsh, Keeper of the National Botanic Gardens, Glasnevin. This cutting was accompanied by a certificate attesting its authenticity, signed by Herbert O. Mackay, President of the Thomas Moore Society. I know all this is true, because that framed certificate hung in my office when I worked at Glasnevin.

That's the first story. When I was 'unwise enough' to tell it on RTÉ's *Sunday Miscellany* radio programme during the 1980s, I was politely informed that I was wrong, and I was told the second story by that most hospitable man, the late Dermot Kinlen, who became a High Court judge, and so I now relay his version of the 'true' story.

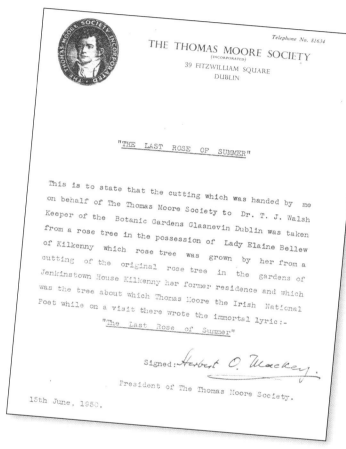

The letter from
The Thomas Moore Society authenticating the
cutting provided to the National Botanic Gardens, Glasnevin.

John Philpot Curran, Ireland greatest barrister, had his country house in Rathfarnham. The grounds were extensive and included a ruin known as The Priory. Curran was a widower by the early 1800s and his eldest and favourite daughter had also passed away and was buried in a grave in the Abbey grounds. Over her grave was a special rose and Curran tended this lovingly. He was prone to bouts of melancholy and when these beset him he would go down to his daughter's grave at night and sit there playing the 'cello. Curran and Thomas Moore

"The last rose of summer", *Rosa chinensis* 'Old Blush', the authentic plant in the National Botanic Gardens, Glasnevin. (E. C. Nelson ©)

were good friends, and one evening when Moore was dining at Loreto Abbey he heard Curran playing the plaintive air that became the tune for the verses that Moore then composed, about the rose over the young girl's grave, 'The last rose of summer'. By the 1930s, this graveside rose had gone wild, and the nuns who then lived in Loreto Abbey and taught the kindergarten would point it out to their young charges as the rose that inspired the poem.* (See note on p. 157)

That is the second story and, who knows, there may be other roses in long-decayed gardens that are also the prototypes for 'The last rose of summer'. And Dermot Kinlen concluded his story by noting that others claimed the poem was written in Wexford, or Wicklow . . .

For a long time, almost a century, this 'last rose of summer' has been identified as an antique China rose that is correctly named *Rosa* 'Old Blush' (or 'Old Blush' China rose). Tom Smith, who founded Daisy Hill Nursery in Newry, County Down, in 1886, used to make this claim and he was a rosarian of renown. Phylis, Lady Moore, a redoubtable plantsman, also accepted this identification, and she was also a rose enthusiast.

'Old Blush' is not an Irish rose but one that originated in China, and it was first cultivated widely in Ireland and other European countries

from about 1800. It is a semi-double, pink rose that blooms repeatedly through the summer. 'Old Blush' is believed to have come to England in 1789, introduced through Joseph Banks, the 'director' of the Royal Garden at Kew, and to have bloomed first in a garden belonging to one Mr Parsons at Rickmansworth, near London; hence it is sometimes called 'Parson's Pink China'. This history is not confirmed and, as Graham Stuart Thomas points out, it is just possible that the rose was brought from China by Lord Macartney and Sir George Staunton following their famous embassy to China that concluded in the autumn of 1794 (the date is still acceptable). Macartney and Staunton were Irish; Macartney was a native of Antrim and Staunton came from Galway.

'Old Blush' surely came to Ireland not long afterwards, and must have been planted in fashionable gardens.

It is impossible today to claim beyond all doubt that the 'Old Blush' China rose was the variety which, growing at Jenkinstown House or wherever, inspired Thomas Moore, but it is a most likely candidate. At the beginning of the 1800s European gardeners did not have a wide choice of roses. In particular they did not have many that would blossom throughout the summer into autumn and even – especially in mild years – into winter. In 1789

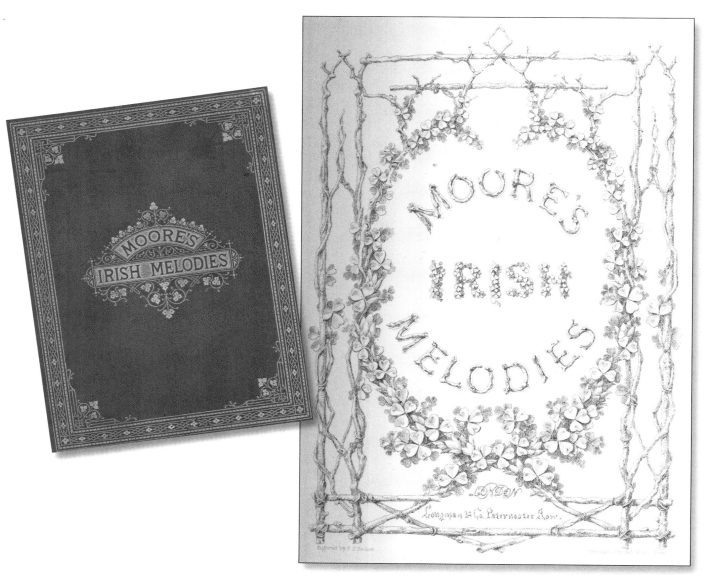

a new type of rose came to western Europe from China, a derivative of two wild Chinese species, the true Chinese rose (*Rosa chinensis*) and the tea rose (*Rosa gigantea*). This new import had the ability in our climate to blossom from May until October, and when crossbred with other roses passed on that remarkable characteristic.

You can grow you own 'last rose of summer': 'Old Blush' is readily available from nurseries specialising in old-fashioned roses. It thrives in almost any good garden soil. Before planting make sure that the place where the rose is to be grown is well and deeply dug, and incorporate some well-rotted compost into the loam (peat may be desirable too, especially in very heavy, sticky clay). An annual mulch of well-rotted compost is an excellent way of providing the nutrients the rose will require for vigorous, healthy growth. 'Old Blush' should not be pruned vigorously; aim to maintain a many-stemmed bush about one metre tall. Remove old shoots after three or four years (shoots become too woody and will not yield abundant blossom) and spur-back the softer shoots.

Of course, the 'certified genuine' Last Rose of Summer from Jenkinstown House still flourishes in the National Botanic Gardens, Glasnevin.

Facing page, above and right: Cover and pages from "Moore's Irish Melodies".

* Alas, what the nuns told their pupils was nonsense. Suffice it to note that Curran was never a widower; his marriage disintegrated and his wife deserted him, but she was still alive, as also was their eldest daughter, Amelia, in October 1817 when he died in London. The Currans' fourth daughter, Gertrude, who died on 6 October 1792 at the age of twelve as the result of a fall from one of the windows of The Priory, was indeed buried in the demesne in unconsecrated ground and for a long time her grave was marked by a stone slab which has long-since vanished. Thomas Moore was a friend of Curran's son, Robert, and his ballad 'She is far from the land where the young hero lies' is reputed to celebrate the love that Robert Emmet, one of the leaders of the United Irishman who was executed in Dublin in September 1803, had for Sarah, the Currans' youngest daughter, an affair that scandalised her father. Sarah died aged twenty-six in 1808 and was laid to rest in the Curran family vault in Newmarket, County Cork. Finally, The Priory, Curran's house and long-since demolished, was so-called because he was the 'Prior' of a drinking club called 'The Order of Saint Patrick'; it must not be confused with Loreto Abbey, originally Rathfarnham House, which at the end of the eighteenth century was the home of the Reverend John Palliser.

5.2
QUID PRO QUO – A NASTURTIUM PARASOL FOR A VARIEGATED FUNKIA

Did you know that if you have a large surplus of garden nasturtiums, you can turn them into parasols? Bonnets of honeysuckle, lace of sweet pea and even mittens of nettles are also possible, although I cannot provide patterns. This is not as absurd as it might appear, and so-called 'botanical lace' made from such unusual plants was all the rage during the 1850s. Threads were spun from the stem-fibres of bindweed, nasturtium, honeysuckle, nettle, marsh-mallow, oxeye daisy, Solomon's seal and sweet pea in exactly the same way that fibres from the flax plant are spun into thread for making linen. These 'botanical' threads were used by Irish lace-makers, especially at Bailieborough, County Cavan. Viscountess Doneraile, of Doneraile Court, County Cork, wrote: 'Mrs Veevers (a lady, whom I don't know personally, but with whom I have been in active correspondence about these laces as she superintended their construction) . . . approves strongly of the marsh mallow, & the nettle for the purpose, as they both yield two crops a year . . .'

If that sounds far-fetched, then consider this: Lady Doneraile donated examples of Irish lace made from these rarefied threads to the Royal Botanic Gardens, Kew, and they remain today among the treasures of its Economic Botany Museum. This unique collection of nineteenth-century, hand-made lace has no counterpart in Ireland, and its preservation owes everything to Lady Doneraile's acquisitiveness – her passion for plants. In return for the samples, she got at least one *Funkia*, with variegated leaves, for her garden in County Cork, possibly the first ever seen in Ireland. (*Funkia*, by the way, is a former name for *Hosta*.)

Mary Anne Grace Louise Lenox-Conyngham married the Honourable Hayes St Leger on 20 August 1851. Upon the death of his father, the third

viscount, in March 1854, Hayes St Leger succeeded to the title and inherited Doneraile Court. The fourth viscount became a celebrity when he died in August 1887 – he was bitten by a tame fox and caught a fatal dose of rabies. After her husband's unfortunate demise, Lady Doneraile moved to France and lived in a chateau at Grésy-sur-Aix, where she created a fine flower garden. The Dowager Viscountess Doneraile died from pneumonia at Nice on 24 February 1907, having survived her husband by almost thirty years.

It is clear that Lady Doneraile kept a close eye on the garden at Doneraile Court, although, like most ladies of that period, it is rather improbable that she did any of the routine work, leaving that to the bevy of gardeners employed on the estate. During visits to London she often went to the Royal Botanic Gardens, Kew, where she struck up a friendship with affable director, Sir William Hooker.

While in residence at Doneraile Court, May Doneraile (as she signed her letters) corresponded with Sir William about her garden, seeking his advice on various matters. After the head gardener at Doneraile Court died unexpectedly during a visit to London, Lady Doneraile asked Hooker's opinion about a replacement, and also consulted James Veitch of King's Road Nursery in Chelsea. A suitable person was found, and one of his early tasks was to sow some rhododendron seeds which Sir William had given Lady Doneraile. He also had to bring from Kew to Cork a load of plants which Hooker was 'so good as to say you thought you could spare me . . .' Lady Doneraile tactfully jogged Sir William's memory – her 'wants list' included striped-leaved kinds of lily-of-the-valley, variegated fuchsias, and variegated *Funkia*. But the new gardener was not a success. He made the mistake of letting some of the Kew plants perish, and was dismissed.

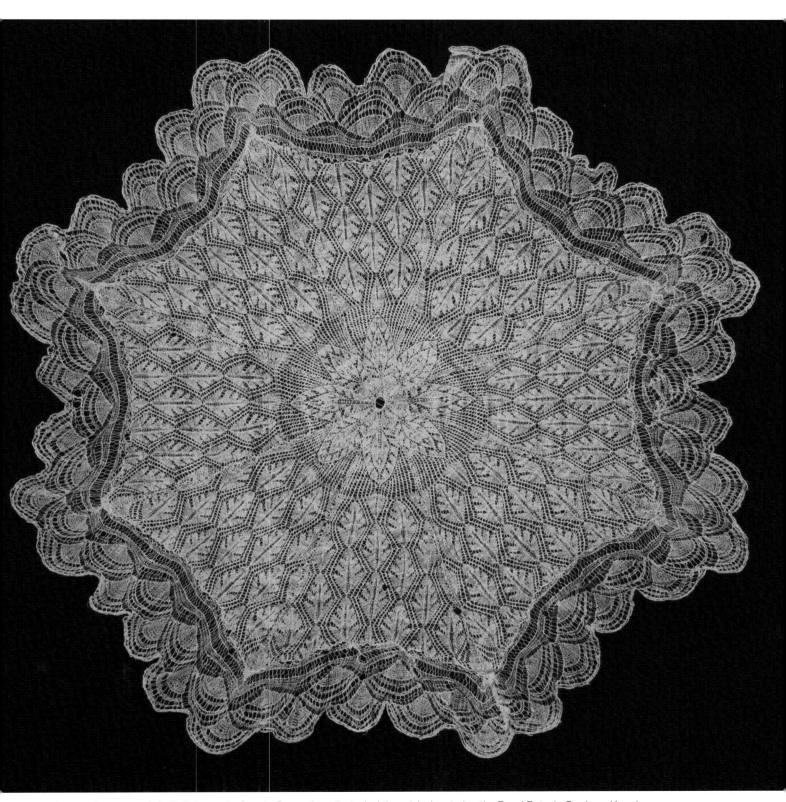

A parasol cover made in Bailieborough, County Cavan, from 'botanical threads', donated to the Royal Botanic Gardens, Kew, by Viscountess Doneraile. (Reproduced by permission of the Royal Botanic Gardens, Kew).

Mary Anne Grace Louisa St Leger, Viscountess Doneraile, was elected a Fellow of the Royal Horticultural Society of London on 24 May 1861. (Portrait by A. Weigall, from *The Court Album. A Series of Portraits of the Female Aristocracy* [1854]. Author's collection)

Botanical lace was manufactured from threads that included such plants as Solomon seal.

Sir William Hooker did not give away variegated fuchsias and funkias for nothing, not even to a viscountess. The deal that May Doneraile struck with him was that he would give her choice plants in return for articles made in Ireland from various plant products.

Dear Sir William

I venture to send you for your museum as I fancy it condescends to accept even very trifling things made from vegetable productions, a specimen of lace made in some parts of this country from the fibres of plants. The lace can be & is manufactured from almost any kind of plant, but generally from the nettle, as being more easily procured than any thing else. The accompanying piece of lace is however of the fibres of 'Solomon's Seal' I am told, & they make it I think smoother & finer than those of the nettle. All our Kew plants are, you will be happy to hear, doing remarkably well both as to growing & flowering, Many thanks to you for them. Lord Doneraile desires me to remember him to you & I remain yrs very sincerely

May Doneraile

It goes without saying that Lady Doneraile did not make the lace herself: that is where Mrs Veevers enters the picture. In the late 1840s during the Great Famine and into the early 1850s, Letitia Veevers was engaged in charitable work, helping to distribute famine relief provided by the Quakers around Mohill in County Leitrim. In the early 1850s she was living at Bailieborough in County Cavan where her husband, John, was the Resident Magistrate, and that was where she established a lace-making venture.

Handmade 'botanical lace' was one of the attractions of the Dublin Exhibition of 1853. A commentator wrote:

In exchange for samples of Irish hand-knitted lace Lady Doneraile received such plants as variegated *Funkia*, otherwise *Hosta*.

Lady Doneraile's 'wants list' included jasmine.

Let not even the botanist flatter himself that the iron foot of utility will not tread down his parterre. Here are shawls, scarfs and various other articles of ladies' apparel woven from the fibres of the commonest wild plants, as well as the choicest and most fragrant flowers of the garden. What would be thought of the handsome belle who would make her appearance in all the equipment of her gaiety, wrapped in a shawl of daisies, or a scarf of nettles, or a polka of japonica or marsh mallow, defying old Sol with a parasol of sweet pea, or nasturtium or convolvulus; or encased in a habit of wild bog-down?

So the 'trifling' lace that Lady Doneraile exchanged with Hooker for variegated hostas and other choice plants was made in the Bailieborough area from all sorts of wild and garden plants. A parasol cover was one of the pieces sent to Kew, but in 1855 an 'enlightened' member of the public stole it and Lady Doneraile obligingly replaced it with another. The largest pieces still in the Kew Museum are in fact two splendid, octagonal parasol covers; one is described as having been made from stinging nettle with a border made from Solomon's seal, while the other was made from nasturtium. A bonnet or cape, perhaps the finest item in the collection, is said to have been made from 'japonica', the precise identity of which is uncertain. Eight smaller pieces, best described as samplers, have equally unusual origins and were recorded variously as having been made from bindweed, nasturtium, honeysuckle, nettle, marshmallow, oxeye daisy and sweet pea. Skeins of thread reputedly spun from such plants accompanied the lace.

Lace was not the only product that Lady Doneraile found to exchange for living plants – insoles for shoes made from the down of bog-cotton, and some fine pieces of bog-oak jewellery were also bartered for treasures for the Doneraile garden. In November 1854, May Doneraile thanked Hooker for a 'very kind contribution to our hothouses', adding that the range of glasshouses had just been enlarged. Orchids and tender aquatics were growing in the range, and there was soon 'a miniature Kew arrangement for the ferns along the bottom of the houses.' Repeatedly she cajoled Hooker. 'You will not forget I am sure the Sikkim Rhododendrons, as well as the young yuccas, & deodars though I think they were all written down in your book so that I have no business to trouble you with mentioning them again.' The rhododendrons and deodars were certainly very choice, having only just been raised from seeds collected in the Himalaya by Sir William's son, Dr Joseph Hooker. These plants soon reached Doneraile:

> We have planted out a few of your oaks & Deodars, & put the rest, as well as the yuccas, into the nursery-ground for the present, till we have decided on some more places to put them, a matter of grave deliberation always here as we have already so many large and fine trees about the grounds.

On one occasion, Sir William sent six beautiful seedling the current horticultural sensation, the giant redwood, then called Wellingtonia. There were already several flourishing Wellingtonias in the demesne – 'they as well as all pines & firs do so well here that I was anxious to increase my stock', wrote Lady Doneraile.

Sir William Hooker evidently greatly admired Viscountess Doneraile, and in December 1858 he dedicated the 84th volume of the famous *Curtis's Botanical Magazine* to her, applauding her as 'a great admirer and successful cultivator of plants'. Her reaction is not known but we do know that she was delighted with her acquisitions from Kew, telling Sir William that

> You can't think what admiration some of the leaves of the variegated 'Funkia', which I got from you a couple of years ago, have made within my nosegays this season in London at balls. Nobody knows the plant & at night the leaves are lovely.

Lady Doneraile is now largely forgotten in gardening circles, yet two fine garden plants were named after her. *Begonia* 'Viscountess Doneraile', a hybrid raised and named by Messrs James Veitch, suggests she was a regular visitor at the Chelsea nursery. This begonia had very dark blood-red flowers, 'the darkest-flowered variety we have yet seen', and it received a First Class Certificate from the Royal Horticultural Society's Floral Committee in July 1876. It is extinct. On the other hand, the large, pure white wood anemone called *Anemone nemorosa* 'Lady Doneraile' is still in cultivation; its origins are unknown, but we can assume she found it at Doneraile Court.

As for Letitia Veevers, one can only wonder where she obtained the large supplies of nasturtium, sweet pea, bindweed, Solomon's seal, marshmallow and nettle stems for the lace-maker's threads. Nettles and bindweed are rampant weeds, but someone must have cultivated the others at least on a modest scale. Yet the idea that crops of nasturtium, sweet pea and marshmallow were planted in the fields around Bailieborough in the 1850s seems rather incredible.

Among the plants that came to Doneraile Court from Professor William Hooker was the tree rhododendron, *Rhododendron arboreum*.

5.3
'DEAR MR DARWIN': LETTERS FROM IRISH GARDENS

CHARLES DARWIN was a prodigious correspondent. Between the age of twelve in January 1822 and his death sixty years later in April 1882, he wrote at least 7,800 letters and received no fewer than 7,000 – he may well have written and received many, many more, for undoubtedly innumerable letters have not survived. Darwin used his correspondence network as a means of gathering the information he needed to establish and solidify his ideas and theories – it was the Victorian equivalent of the Internet, but letters have the immense virtue of being more permanent than e-mails.

Darwin's correspondents lived in places as far apart as County Donegal and New Zealand. They would answer his questions or send him unsolicited information after reading about his work in newspapers, or, like Blanche and Alice (of Liverpool), simply ask for his autograph – and those two polite girls wrote back thanking him for it. Of the almost 15,000 letters to and from Darwin that are known still to exist, just a few were addressed to Ireland or were sent by Irish correspondents. Some correspondents were fellow naturalists, but others were merely helpful amateurs.

Today Charles Darwin is famous above all for one book, his astounding best-seller *On the Origin of Species by Means of Natural Selection*, yet that was only one of his books. He also wrote *Insectivorous Plants*, *The Movement and Habits of Climbing Plants*, and *The Various Contrivances by which Orchids are Fertilized by Insects*. For these, and indeed for several other books, as well as for his numerous publications, Darwin assiduously garnered information through his correspondence network.

Facing page: The Australian sundew *Drosera binata* has forked leaves; from *Curtis's Botanical Magazine* (plate 3082).
(Reproduced by courtesy of the National Botanic Gardens, Glasnevin)

On the origin of species

Darwin's most famous book, *Origin of Species* – 'my unlucky book ' – was published on 22 November 1859; all 1,250 copies of the first edition were sold that day at fourteen shillings apiece, and a second edition had to be prepared immediately. Darwin became a household name. He was 'drenched' with letters in the days following publication and for months, indeed years, afterwards.

This 'wicked book' provoked strong, opposing opinions. Among those who found the ideas set down in *Origin of Species* untenable was Professor William Harvey, the Royal Dublin Society's Professor of Botany, also more recently appointed Professor of Botany in Trinity College, Dublin. Harvey was Ireland's most eminent botanist at that time, and was evidently a regular visitor to the Royal Dublin Society's Botanic Gardens at Glasnevin. He took a while to react to *Origin*, finally making his 'hit' in *The Gardeners' Chronicle* on 18 February 1860. Harvey notoriously disparaged Darwin's theory of evolution in a lecture given in Dublin which afterwards he foolishly had printed. Darwin was shaken by Harvey's siding with his opponents but, in the end, it was Harvey's arguments that were defeated. The two men agreed to disagree, Harvey thanking Darwin for his patience and good nature, assuring him that he did not want to engage in a controversial correspondence

Climbing plants

Despite their fundamental difference of opinion, Darwin and Harvey exchanged letters about various matters including climbing plants. Darwin's studies of plants which had the capacity to climb started in the early 1860s. When confined to his room by illness, he occupied himself by watching hop shoots twining – it took two hours and eight minutes for the tips of the shoots to make a full rotation,

'.J.H del.t   Pub by S.Curtis Glazenwood Essex July 1.1831.   Swan S.c

Charles Darwin in the early 1870s (from *The Life and Letters of Charles Darwin . . . edited by his son Francis Darwin*, volume 1 [1896]).

Darwin teased the native sundews by feeding them and watching the reaction of their gland-dotted leaves; (clockwise from top left) round-leaved sundew (*Drosera rotundifolia*), greater sundew (*Drosera anglica*) and oblong-leaved sundew (*Drosera intermedia*).
(© E. C. Nelson)

he discovered – without the aid of time-lapse photography. Darwin patiently timed other plants as they twined, some moving with the sun and other against the sun.

From Harvey, Darwin obtained information about some very unusual plants growing in the glasshouses at the Botanic Gardens in Glasnevin. In November 1864 he provided Darwin with examples of South African plants which in their native habitats formed compact, bushy shrubs less than 18 inches tall, yet behaved differently under cultivation. While Darwin only mentioned that the species were cultivated or raised 'near Dublin',

Harvey's letters reveal that Glasnevin was the location. One such plant was a member of the bindweed family then named *Ipomoea argyreoides* (its current name is *Turbina oenotheroides*): the Glasnevin seedlings 'twined up sticks above 8 feet in height.' Darwin also reported that two (unnamed) species of the bizarre, usually succulent, genus *Ceropegia* 'as I hear from Prof. Harvey . . . in their native dry South African home generally grow erect from 6 inches to 2 feet in height . . . when cultivated near Dublin, they regularly twined up sticks 5 or 6 feet in height.'

Pinguicula grandiflora, large-flowered butterwort which is native in southwestern Ireland. (© E. C. Nelson)

Facing page: The tropical orchid *Sobralia macrantha* which the Dungarvan bumblebee pollinated. (© Aishling O'Donoghue)

Insectivorous plants

When we come to Darwin's book on insectivorous plants, Irish references are rather more numerous. Darwin had begun investigating plants that appeared to trap insects in the summer of 1860 while recuperating in his cousin's house in Ashdown Forest where he had easy access to lots of sundews (*Drosera*), the leaves of which glisten with red, stalked glands that Darwin often referred to as 'tentacles'. He exclaimed to his friend Joseph Hooker that 'I have done nothing here; but at first amused myself with a few observations on the insect-catching powers of Drosera; and I must consult you some time whether my "twaddle" is worth communicating to the Linnean Society.' He pursued the twaddle for a few years, gave it up, and returned to the subject in the 1870s. Darwin fed

sundews with all sorts of substances to see what their reactions would be. His admiration for *Drosera* grew. It was more sensitive in detecting substances than forensic chemists. A dose of opium knocked out its sensitive powers for several hours. He obtained some plants of the great sundew (*Drosera anglica*) from Ireland, without being specific about the collector. Fed a bit of roast meat, the tentacles began to move a minute of so later. When fed dead flies, the tips of the leaves curled over so that twenty-four hours later the corpses were 'embraced and concealed'.

So much for native sundews – Darwin needed to know about the exotic ones: could they also catch flies? There is an Australian species called *Drosera binata*, with handsome, forked leaves up to half a metres (20 inches) long. It was not a common garden plant. Lady Dorothy Nevill grew it in her famous Hampshire garden (where she employed thirty-four gardeners!). There was plants in the Royal Botanic Garden, Edinburgh, and probably also in Glasnevin. And Thomas Copland, who was a first-class clerk in the Accountant's Department of the Office of Public Works in the Custom House, Dublin, also cultivated it. He read about Darwin's experiments in *The Echo* and decided to write to the great man about his plant. 'Mr. Copland informed me that the leaves of a plant which he kept for some years were generally covered with captured insects before they withered.' Copland certainly did not have thirty-four gardeners to assist him – in the early 1870s he and his wife Anne and family lived at 53 Sandymount Road, Dublin. Presumably that is where he grew his sundews. He admitted to Darwin that he had killed his plant by trying to grow it in Irish sphagnum moss – why he did not succeed is a mystery because an article had been published in *The Garden* magazine recommending sphagnum. 'This Sundew may be grown to a large size', advised James McNab, Curator of Edinburgh Botanic Garden, 'and will flower abundantly, either under basket culture in Sphagnum Moss or in pots covered with Sphagnum and placed in a sunny situation or in shallow pans of water.' McNab did add that when cultivated outdoors the plants generally become

'black with dust and insects'. I wonder if Thomas Copland knew he would become remembered by virtue of a single sentence in one of Darwin's books. Did he ever read the book? We will probably never know.

Insectivorous plants were also a speciality at Glasnevin's Botanic Gardens in the 1870s under Dr David Moore. Darwin had asked for Moore's assistance and received it. Moore packed the tiny bladders of the native greater bladderwort (*Utricularia vulgaris*) carefully, along with a plant of the Portuguese sundew (*Drosophyllum lusitanicum*) and posted them to Darwin and they arrived in 'perfect condition'. Moore was able to tell Darwin that the greater (or Kerry) butterwort (*Pinguicula grandiflora*) was much easier to cultivate that the common butterwort (*Pinguicula vulgaris*). At Glasnevin, the Kerry one grew 'freely and flower[ed] annually without dying out'. Strangely, Darwin received plants of *Pinguicula grandiflora* from Cornwall where it is certainly not a native species.

As for common butterwort, Darwin's niece, Lucy, who had married Matthew Harrison, RN, a few months previously, was staying at Rathmullan on the western shore of Lough Swilly during the late summer of 1874, and on 22 August she went butterwort-hunting. 'Another friend', wrote Darwin with strange reticence, 'examined on August 22 some plants in Donegal, Ireland, and found insects on 70 out of 157 leaves; fifteen of these leaves were sent me, each having caught on an average 2.4 insects. To nine of them, leaves (mostly of *Erica tetralix*) adhered; but they had been specially selected on this latter account.'

Orchids and bees

Down at the other extremity of Ireland, one day in July 1871, the Rector of Dungarvan was out in the vicarage garden cutting flowers and was followed indoors by a bumblebee. The bee flew to the parlour window which, as it happened, led into the rector's orchid house. This contained a collection of tropical orchids – *Dendrobium*, *Cattleya*, *Coelogyne* and *Sobralia* were among the rector's treasured plants. *Sobralia macrantha* happened to be in bloom – that

species from central America has short-lived, fragrant, purple-pink flowers at least 15 centimetres across. The bumblebee flew straight for the orchid and, with the rector's assistance, found the nectar deep inside the flower. Having supped, the bee backed out and in the process triggered the orchid's remarkable pollination mechanism – the bumblebee emerged with two large pollinia (pollen masses) stuck on its back. According to the rector, the pollen-laden insect looked around to see if there were other flowers worth visiting, saw none, and promptly returned to the orchid. Back inside went the bee, had a quick rummage around for more nectar, and then re-emerged without the pollinia which had been transferred to the orchid's stigma. Pollination was achieved although this was not supposed to happen.

Henry George Cavendish Browne, Rector of Dungarvan from 1860 to 1881, is not renowned as an orchid grower, let alone a gardener, yet like his Dublin contemporary Thomas Copland he has achieved immortality in the publications of the great Darwin. One might suppose that Darwin would not be impressed by the promiscuous habits of a Dungarvan bumblebee, but he was, and he gave the affair a full paragraph in the second edition of his book with the splendid title *The Various Contrivances by which Orchids, British and Foreign, are Fertilized by Insects*. Unless you happen to know that the Reverend Cavendish Browne once lived in Dungarvan, you would be quite unaware of the Irish connection, because Darwin does not reveal where the bumblebee encountered the orchid.

Darwin kept the letter from Dungarvan Vicarage, and so the conclusion of the story can also be told. The large, dusky yellow bumblebee stretched out its legs and lay down on the flower, overcome. According to Darwin, 'The nectar of this Guatemala Orchid seemed too powerful' for the Waterford bee. But it was only having a nap. An hour later the bee was bumbling about, as bumblebees do when trapped in a greenhouse, banging against the glass trying to escape. I hope the rector let it out to find less exotic nectar and pollinate the native flora of Dungarvan.

5.4
A RICH BACHELOR AND MOLLY-THE-WITCH

FOR AROUND FIFTY YEARS in the late 1800s and early 1900s, the garden at Belgrove was renowned for its plants and its 'Master'. Its situation was most favourable, towards the eastern side of Great Island in Cork Harbour, a short distance from Cobh (then named Queenstown) and about the same from Fota. Thus Belgrove had an 'unusually mild and genial' climate. William Robinson, the great Irish horticulturist, wrote that 'Belgrove is dominated by a personality at once independent and critical . . . The Master of Belgrove has for a long time been known as an energetic amateur gardener . . . '. Turning to *Joys of the Garden*, a small and little-known book written by a fellow plantsman, the Reverend Dr Henry Kingsmill Moore, I found this description of the Master of Belgrove: 'W. E. Gumbleton . . . was a rich bachelor, addicted to music and flowers.'

William Edward Gumbleton has left a considerable horticultural legacy, although his garden has long since ceased to be the sort of botanical paradise described by William Robinson: 'No pains, personal labour, or reasonable expense has been spared in the acquirement of botanical rarities from home or abroad . . . '. Among 'flowers', he was addicted to begonias, pampas grass, Montbretia and red-hot pokers which were once familiarly called torch lilies – 'Among other of the hobbies indulged in by the Master of Belgrove is a special liking for the Torch lilies, or Flame flowers (Kniphofias), and for all the best green-leaved and variegated Cortaderia or Pampas grasses.'

The Master of Belgrove – Gumbo, for short, but only in family circles! – was succinctly described as a small, partly bald and very pompous individual. He was peculiarly sensitive to criticism but very willing to cavil at the opinions of others! He did not

William Edward Gumbleton. (Reproduced by courtesy of W. E. G. Bagwell. © E. C. Nelson)

Belgrove garden about 1900, showing the numerous small beds that contained Gumbleton's choicest plants, and a clump of pampas grass. (© E. C. Nelson)

Pampas grass was one of Gumbleton's favourite plants; this clump was photographed at Belgrove in the late 1970s. (© E. C. Nelson)

Facing page: Three new French cultivars of Monbretia (*Crocosmia × crocosmiiflora*): 1. 'Bouquet Parfait'; 2. 'Gerbe d'Or'; 3. 'Étoile de Feu' – that were cultivated in Belgrove and painted by Miss Travers: from *The Garden*, 28 May 1887. (Reproduced by courtesy of the Manchester Museum)

suffer fools yet, it seems, had an impish sense of humour. Needless to say, he was not universally liked. He was a veritable eccentric who also collected paintings and fine books and it can be argued that the best gardeners need more than a touch of eccentricity in them to make them great. Without a shadow of doubt, Gumbo was a great gardener.

One of William Edward Gumbleton's legacies was a botanical library, the gems of which now form part of the library at the National Botanic Gardens, Glasnevin. His books were often handsomely bound, and the very best contained outstanding examples of botanical illustration. Not surprisingly for a connoisseur of plants and art, Gumbleton

possessed a complete 'run' of *Curtis's Botanical Magazine* which William Curtis began publishing in 1787 – it is still being published by the Royal Botanic Gardens, Kew. To Gumbleton, these books and periodicals were not museum pieces, but working reference books and often he annotated them in pencil.

Canon Moore remembered Gumbleton's passion for novelties especially a particular yellow lobelia, 'a poor weak thing, it did not long persist.' Another 'thing' which did not persist long had intense reddish-orange flowers and turned out to be a new species of *Arctotis*, a genus of daisy confined to southern Africa. Somehow Gumbleton had acquired seeds and he grew and flowered the species, sending samples to the Royal Botanic Gardens, Kew, for identification. The daisy had no name, so it was dubbed *Arctotis gumbletonii* by Sir Joseph Hooker, and soon was illustrated in *Curtis's Botanical Magazine*. It is a bit of a mystery how an African daisy with very limited distribution ended up in Belgrove. (If you want to try to see it in the wild it can be found in Namaqualand, in the northern corner of the Western Cape, near Springbok and in the Khamiesberg.) As far as I know, *Arctotis gumbletonii* has not been grown in Ireland since Gumbleton's day and it is not even well known to South African gardeners.

Turning to more mundane plants, Belgrove boasted a splendid walled garden that was well stocked, an apple orchard and a vinery. Gumbleton apparently enjoyed collecting unusual fruiting shrubs as much as the rarest flowers. William Robinson recorded loganberry, raspberries including a black raspberry from the United States named 'Lovett', a white blackberry called 'Iceberg', numerous different strawberries, and the dewberry named 'Lucretia'. Belgrove's fruit garden contained 100 distinct gooseberries – that's one more than the number of cultivars for sale today from nurseries and garden centres. There was also a crimson-stemmed rhubarb which had come from the Californian horticulturist, Luther Burbank, from whom Gumbleton had also acquired two hybrid walnuts, 'Royal' and 'Paradox'. The former tree may

1

3

2

well still survive – in 1978 it was 57 feet tall with a trunk 14 feet 7 inches in circumference.

Belgrove was nothing if not a plantsman's garden with 'many things on probation', to quote Robinson again. Most of the ornamentals were grown in the multitudes of flower-beds – more than sixty in 1909 – that were ranged in the lawns near the house, while others presumably resided in one or other of the greenhouses. Waterlilies, another of Gumbleton's passions, were kept in specially constructed tanks which were raised above ground-level so that the flowers could be better appreciated. Rare crocus species were given special treatment, as Moore recalled, each little group being 'cased in a metal pocket, an interesting but scarcely a beautiful sight.'

Given his passion for rarities and new plants, Gumbleton could claim several firsts. *Buddleja colvilei*, one of the most handsome of the butterfly bushes with large clusters of crimson bell-shaped flowers quite unlike the very familiar *Buddleja davidii*, bloomed at Belgrove from the first time in cultivation in 1891. The splendid white-blossomed foxtail lily, *Eremurus himalaicus*, flowered in Gumbleton's garden in 1881, the first occasion in Europe, much to the chagrin of another Cork gardener, one John Smyth: 'I am a bit jealous over this plant as I was the first to grow it from seed . . .', he grumbled.

Gumbleton's passion for rare plants was mirrored by his extreme opinions about bad ones. For example, in November 1911, he wrote to Charles Ball, Assistant Keeper of the Botanic Gardens, Glasnevin, complaining that a New Zealand daisy-bush he had purchased 'from the ignorant most presumptuous Gauntlett . . . was utter Tush' – 'Tush' really was underlined twice and had a capital T, and was the ultimate put-down! Another nurseryman who was marketing a blue marguerite at two shillings per rooted cutting was described as '<u>hum</u> <u>bugging</u> puffer', underlined! The particular plant, in Gumbleton's view, was 'not worth more than 3 or 4 shillings a dozen at most,

only the general public don't know this and think a blue Paris Daisy must be a most desirable plant.'

There is a well-known story about Mr Gumbleton's first call on Frederick Moore shortly after he had been installed as curator of the Glasnevin Botanic Gardens following the death of his father, Dr David Moore. Fred Moore was only in his early twenties, a mere boy, and was confronted by a delegation comprising three horticultural *éminences grises*, Gumbleton, John Bennett-Poë from Nenagh in County Tipperary, and Edward Woodall from Scarborough in England. Gumbleton was irritated by the way Moore pronounced some of the Latin plant names, so he corrected him, thumping the flagstones with his umbrella to make his criticisms more pointed. Outside the Curvilinear Range, Gumbleton spotted a plant that he deemed to be inferior. Again, his umbrella came into play, and the plant was swiftly annihilated – no doubt Gumbleton proclaimed it was 'utter Tush'. Moore was unable to do anything but protest timidly, and he must have quaked whenever Gumbleton repeated the same act of extermination, as he often did even in his own garden.

Fortunately, many plants were spared extinction by umbrella. Gumbleton was also extremely generous, giving countless choice new plants to Glasnevin. Unfortunately no exact records of his own collections have survived although there are numerous notes and articles written by Gumbleton scattered through the horticultural periodicals of the period. One of the best, albeit rather select, indicators of the richness of Belgrove is the list of plants illustrated in *Curtis's Botanical Magazine* and a few other horticultural journals from specimens sent by Gumbleton. A splendid painting of *Magnolia campbellii* was published in *The Garden* in 1904. The species had first bloomed in cultivation across the Harbour, at Lakelands, William Horatio Crawford's garden in Cork city. The Belgrove tree was more than 69 feet tall in June 1978 with a trunk 13 feet around – one of the largest in these islands. I hope it still is going strong. Gumbleton had feared that

Facing page: Another of the Belgrove plants which Miss Travers painted for *The Garden* – this shows the beautiful *Buddleja colvilei*: from *The Garden*, 10 June 1893. (Reproduced by courtesy of the National Botanic Gardens, Glasnevin)

Azara microphylla 'Variegata', which was once called *Azara microphylla* 'Belgroveana', apparently originated in Gumbleton's garden. (© E. C. Nelson)

Molly-the-Witch – *Paeonia mlokosewitschii*. (© E. C. Nelson)

this magnolia would not do well in 'our uncertain climate' – how wrong he was, and fortunately he never used his umbrella on it. *Nerine bowdenii*, the now-familiar, hardy, pink-blossomed Guernsey lily, was figured in *Curtis's Botanical Magazine* from Gumbleton's collection – he shared a passion for these bulbs with Moore and Bennett-Poë. The splendid Californian lady's-slipper orchid (*Cypripedium californicum*) was another. It probably had shared space in the conservatory which, Robinson recalled, was always filled with 'a blaze of colour and redolent with perfume' from tuberous begonias, indoor geraniums, cannas and 'choice composites' such as *Arctotis*, 'in their season'. 'For begonias Belgrove was famous,' wrote Henry Kingsmill Moore, 'its owner seemed to think he had introduced them. He certainly was one of their first cultivators.'

William Edward Gumbleton was 'one of a kind', rich and passionate. His passion was not for shrubs and trees, although he tolerated many, and certainly admired the best, and to him we owe the handsome variegated *Azara microphylla*, which originally bore the name *Azara microphylla* 'Belgroveana' – since that name has been abandoned there is nothing now commemorating the garden. Rather his passion was for tender annuals and bulbs, as well as herbaceous perennials

– indeed, he shared many enthusiasms with Frederick Moore, including *Nerine, Lachenalia* and herbaceous peonies. And that is where Molly The Witch enters the story. *Paeonia mlokosewitschii*, named after a Polish soldier and naturalist Ludwik Franciszek Mlokosiewicz, is a splendid perennial with beautiful yellow flowers 'like sophisticated buttercups'. Mlokosiewicz had found it in the Caucasus at the end of nineteenth century and Gumbleton had lost no time in acquiring it (from another equally passionate gardener, Max Leichtlin), nurturing it and bringing it into bloom so that it could be painted and featured in *Curtis's Botanical Magazine* in 1908. Superlatives abound about this peony. Graham Stuart Thomas writes that this is 'undoubtedly one of the most wonderful flowers of the early year'. Helen Dillon called it enthralling: 'when in bloom it is indeed the goddess of the garden.' The irrepressible Reginald Farrer penned this instruction: 'This pleasant little assortment of syllables should be practised daily by all who wish to talk familiarly of a sovereign among Paeonias.' One wonders how many times Gumbo banged his umbrella on the flagstones when *mlokosewitschii* was mispronounced.

5.5
'RIP VAN WINKLE' AND WILLIAM BAYLOR HARTLAND

EACH SPRING A LITTLE DAFFODIL pops up to remind me of one of Ireland's most endearing gardening characters, William Baylor Hartland, a Cork man through and through. He was a veritable eccentric, and so too, one can say, is the little daffodil. 'Rip Van Winkle' was the name Hartland bestowed on his diminutive narcissus. It has very double flowers with several series of long, pointed, light yellow segments, tinged with green, interspersed by shorter, deeper yellow ones. In some rich soils the long segments can be almost entirely green. 'Rip Van Winkle' is hardly 6 inches tall at full maturity, so it can be grown in troughs and rock gardens, but is vigorous enough to thrive in the front of borders and increases well.

William Baylor Hartland, whose Ard Cairn nursery was situated on the south side of Cork city, adored daffodils. He must be reckoned the father of the flourishing Irish daffodil industry, and also of the now-extinct Irish tulip industry. Over a century ago, in 1885, Hartland published an outlandish catalogue of daffodils with the pretentious, mock-antique title *Ye Original Little Booke of Daffodils in Great Variety . . .* ; each copy cost one shilling. This seemingly innocuous list of Cork-produced daffodils gave several well-known, opinionated gardeners apoplexy. A daffodil-besotted Wiltshire vicar, George Herbert Engleheart, was so enraged that he unleashed a fusillade of invective against Hartland in *The Gardeners' Chronicle*. Engleheart accused Hartland of doing his best to make the lamentable confusion of daffodil names even worse, and that was only the beginning. The fantastic cover of *Ye Original Little Booke of Daffodils*, which was probably designed by Hartland himself, really irritated Engleheart. The catalogue was embellished, Engleheart fumed, with a damsel 'entangled in a growth of impossible daffodils'. She floated, wand in hand, over the famous Jacobean botanist John Parkinson and his

William Baylor Hartland, 'a lover of daffodils and tulips'.
(Reproduced by courtesy of the National Botanic Gardens, Glasnevin)

companion, 'a short-sighted gentleman whose botanical studies are being much impeded by a swarm of bees hovering round his bald head'. The vicar concluded his tirade with this advice to Hartland: 'before you publish another catalogue you should consult authorities in such matter as languages, living and dead, aesthetics and daffodils.'

William Baylor Hartland was not deflected by intemperate clergymen. In fact he probably relished the publicity. That same year, he also staged a superb advertising coup. When the Prince and

Princess of Wales visited Cork, Princess Alexandra entered the city wearing a cluster of Mr Hartland's daffodils – he had himself placed them in the royal carriage at Ballyhooly railway station, just in case . . .

Hartland had been encouraged to start collecting daffodils by Frederick Burbidge, curator of Trinity College Botanic Garden at Ballsbridge in Dublin. He searched for whatever daffodils survived in old gardens, and then increased the stock until he had sufficient bulbs to market them. Hartland took to this with some gusto, and even described how he had used a pickaxe and crowbar to extract bulbs from a derelict garden at Bishopstown. Those particular bulbs yielded a distinctive daffodil which Hartland named 'Bishop Mann'. Perhaps Hartland's most famous daffodils were 'Ard Righ', a large, yellow trumpet, and 'Colleen Bawn' described as a 'small trumpet daffodil, white, tinted pale primrose yellow, especially the corona, which is turned back at the mouth and much frilled'. Of the 100-odd daffodils that Hartland is credited with only my little double-blossomed 'Rip Van Winkle' is still readily available; none of the others is listed by present-day daffodil growers.

William Baylor Hartland did not have all his eggs in one basket which was a lucky thing because on the night of 17 November 1892 a fire, which started in some outbuildings at Ard Cairn, spread to the bulb-house and half of Hartland's 'rare collection of Trumpet White Daffodils [was] entirely lost, some very valuable and scarce. One lot of "Colleen Bawn", probably the most beautiful of all (600 bulbs), just removed from the warehouse for planting, [were] a great loss.' He also propagated and sold tulips – almost sixty are attributed to him including a lovely, yellow-blossomed cottage tulip named 'Mrs Moon' that had come to Trinity College Botanic Garden from a 'lady amateur gardener in the West of Ireland'. Presumably Burbidge gave it to Hartland who advertised it as his own 'original introduction'. Again, none of Hartland's tulips is in current lists.

Hartland's begonias were also famous. In the late 1890s, he claimed that 'over 300 new varieties of double begonias have been raised at Ard-Cairn

Narcissus 'Rip Van Winkle'. (© E. C. Nelson)

Facing page: *Helianthus* 'Soleil d'Or', which Hartland claimed to have introduced; this is a tall autumn-flowering perennial sunflower. (© E. C. Nelson)

within three years'. Once again, none survives, not even 'Electric Light' (a very large-flowered pink and white) or 'Grace O'Malley' (bright pink). There's more. Among other, now-lost Ard Cairn plants was an auricula with indigo flowers called 'Empress of India', and a 'giant oxlip' named 'William of Orange': 'The powerful fragrance of Mr Hartland's Cowslips and Oxlips is remarkable; in this respect they are superior to Polyanthuses.'

However, this is not a tale of utter extinction. There are Hartland plants that deserve to be better known – indeed to be made popular once again – including a hybrid goat's-rue that even bears his name, *Galega* × *hartlandii*. It is right and proper that *Galega* × *hartlandii* 'Alba' has gained the Royal Horticultural Society's Award of Garden Merit because it is in every way an excellent garden plant. This is a vigorous perennial, reaching 6 feet in height by the end of summer. When the young stems and leaves first appear above the soil in the late spring they are variegated with pale yellow, but this soon disappears and for the rest of the summer the leaves are rich green, an excellent foil for the

179

Galega × hartlandii 'Alba'. (© E. C. Nelson)

Hartland's hybrid goat's-rue, *Galega × hartlandii*. (© E. C. Nelson)

flowers. The stems branch freely bearing erect, elongated spires of white pea-flowers. Hartland's original form had blue-mauve and white flowers, and silver-variegated foliage. Frederick Burbidge, who seems to have noticed it at Ard Cairn before Hartland did, reckoned this goat's-rue was 'one of the best summer border plants for colour'. *Galega × hartlandii* was a chance acquisition by Hartland who promised that his 'lovely new Goat's Rue, when plentiful, will be launched and sold by all Market forces in the Kingdom'.

I sowed a packet of mixed seed I had from France, about twelve years since, and planted out the seedlings, which gave seed freely. Later on I sowed again, with the result that one plant was a bicolor or tricolor form, a chance from the cross fertilisation of bee action, and I now venture to introduce it to all lovers of herbaceous plants . . . It is highly decorative, with a touch of *Wistaria sinensis*, with variegated foliage when starting into growth in the spring.

Hartland's other enduring introduction, dating from the early 1890s, is a perennial sunflower, *Helianthus × multiflorus* 'Soleil d'Or'. The brilliant yellow, semi-double flower-heads have quilled 'petals'. Referring back to *Galega × hartlandii* Hartland wrote: 'May I claim some small authority over the introduction of this beautiful hardy plant, the same as I did some years ago over that now most popular

180

Azara microphylla 'Variegata': after William Edward Gumbleton's death, Hartland acquired the original shrub and sold it to Richard Beamish of Glounthaune House, Glounthane, County Cork.
(© E. C. Nelson)

Apple 'Ard Cairn Russet' (© E. C. Nelson)

Sunflower Soleil d'Or, when spreading it with difficulty through the gardens of Europe.' 'Soleil d'Or' grows to about two metres in height and forms healthy clumps of dark green foliage. It blooms in late summer and early autumn and is an excellent tall perennial for the back of a border.

There is one other handsome, ornamental plant with a Hartland connection, which can be added to his credit. The origins of *Azara microphylla* 'Variegata' are not recorded, but Hartland sold the original at auction in 1911 among a collection of plants from the garden of a recently deceased plantsman, William Edward Gumbleton. The *Azara* was actually listed by the name *Azara microphylla Belgroveana*, which suggest it arose in Gumbleton's own garden, Belgrove, at East Ferry, County Cork. Hartland sold the shrub to another great Cork plantsman, Richard Beamish, who presumably planted it in his garden at Ashbourne House, Glounthaune. *Azara microphylla* 'Variegata' is a splendid evergreen shrub with tiny leaves that are irregularly margined with creamy white. Like the species, it has inconspicuous, sweetly-scented flowers in spring. A mature plant is a splendid sight, a creamy froth of delicate foliage.

William Baylor Hartland's other claim to enduring horticultural fame is as a promoter of Irish apples. 'Ard Cairn Russet', a very tasty and attractive dessert apple, is one of about a dozen that were marketed by him. This was not raised at Ard Cairn but was found in 'an out-of-the-way orchard in this County some years since'. Hartland took every opportunity to promote 'Ard Cairn Russet', even

Hartland's nursery catalogues often carried a world map showing Cork, 'The true home of daffodils', at the centre.
(Reproduced by courtesy of the National Botanic Gardens, Glasnevin)

with illustrations replete with shamrocks. It is a late apple, golden brown and covered with russet. At its prime in January and February, the flesh is firm, yellowish white, and sweet, tasting 'like a banana'. Another very old Cork apple, much loved by Hartland, is 'Gibbon's Russet', also called 'Ould Devil' or 'Cherry Brandy'. This sweet, early dessert apple had been 'known to the Blackwater cider men years ago' and was 'so perfumed in the fruit house that its odour excludes all other'. So good was 'Gibbon's Russet', and so popular, that Hartland was obliged to note in one copy of his catalogue for 1903 that 'all my dishes were eaten and stolen at the last show here [in Cork]. All the old men said it was the favourite in the Room and they were Right.'

William Baylor Hartland was no ordinary nurseryman, and he could have taught his successors a thing or two about the arts of selling plants and blowing one's own trumpet at the same time. He was a marvellous self-publicist, fearless, opinionated

and pompous. Being a Corkonian, he was determined to ensure that he put Cork on the horticultural map of the world – and he succeeded! On the back page of his catalogue there was indeed a map of the world with Cork, writ large, at the very centre. On an enlarged map of the British Isles, the only place marked was Cork, the only name printed was Cork, and the legend proclaimed that Cork was 'The true home of daffodils'. From this great metropolis of *Narcissus*, shipping routes were marked to all corners of the globe, including two to Siberia, bearing for good measure the inscription 'Hartland's seeds, daffodils and bulbs of all sorts, for all parts of the world'. Did the icebound gardeners of northern Siberia really buy bulbs and seeds from Cork? No matter – as the Latin motto proclaimed, as the Trojan hero Aeneas once did, *Quae regio in terris nostri non plena laboris*. In other words, what region on earth is not full of our toil, and Hartland's daffs!

5.6
MOTORING AFTER REMARKABLE TREES

A GREAT STORM from the southwest raged across Ireland on Thursday 26 February 1903 – it was the worst for more than sixty years but not so bad as to enter folklore as the truly memorable pre-Famine 'Big Wind' of 1839. All the same, thousands of large trees were toppled like skittles and countless branches snapped off like matchsticks. The Phoenix Park in Dublin suffered huge damage with around 1,700 elms felled.

Four days after the storm, Henry John Elwes arrived in Ireland on a mission – he had come in search of remarkable trees and it is very likely that his two-day trip was occasioned by news of the storm. He saw some of the damage, and in his diary he recorded the storm's aftermath.

March 2 got to Ireland and went to Castlecomer . . . an old place with some fine timber,

The hand-coloured title-page of *The Trees of Great Britain and Ireland* designed by Florence Woolward.

especially silver firs which are said to be 200 years old & over 100ft tall . . . the heavy gale after a great deal of rain had torn the trees right out of the ground. I saw a hornbeam with a trunk 4ft round or more & 50ft high torn right out of the ground & the stem twisted by the force of the wind.

March 3 On the way to Dublin . . . stopped & drove to Powerscourt where the gale has not done so much harm as elsewhere. However a number of very fine beech, Scots pines & others blown over. One of the latter near the house was an immense tree 10–12ft in girth, & Lord P promised me a piece of its wood. His conifers are good but nothing very special for size, so far as I saw, but the beech avenue is perhaps the best in Ireland & worth photographing.

At Dublin I called on Mr Moore at Glasnevin after dark; he told me that many fine trees had been blown down & promised me samples of timber from some of them.

Elwes, traveller, sportsman, plantsman, naturalist, was a friend of Frederick Moore, Keeper of the Glasnevin Botanic Gardens. He moved in the same circles as Ireland's other notable gardeners, men like William Edward Gumbleton of Belgrove in County Cork, and Frederick Burbidge of Trinity College Botanic Garden. He was one of the luminaries of the Royal Horticultural Society, a Fellow of the Royal Society, and a wealthy landowner who indulged himself by hunting – and hunting for plants – in remote regions of the world: his destinations had included Tibet, Asia Minor, China, Mexico, Siberia and Chile. Seeds and bulbs that he collected yielded new plants: a snowdrop from Asia Minor, *Galanthus elwesii*, is his most familiar botanical memorial. Moreover he had

Henry John Elwes (seated) and Dr Augustine Henry; frontispiece in volume 7 of *The Trees of Great Britain and Ireland*.

sufficient money to publish lavish books: *Monograph of the genus Lilium* (1880), illustrated by Walter Hood Fitch, remains an authoritative work.

Henry Elwes' visit to Ireland in March 1903 coincided with a start of a new venture that culminated in another superlative book. This time his co-author was Dr Augustine Henry, who had returned not long since from China. Their partnership yielded *Trees of Great Britain and Ireland*. Dr Henry's share of the work was largely (but not solely) the botanical sections, descriptions and nomenclature; Elwes gathered data on commercial uses and remarkable specimens growing in Ireland and Britain.

The seven volumes, issued one by one between 1906 and 1913, together compose one of the most luxurious books about the cultivated and wild trees ever issued, the text being printed on thick, cream-coloured paper. The volumes were illustrated with more than 400 luminous black-and-white photographs, 23 portraying trees growing in Ireland. Volume 1 appeared on 14 November 1906; volume 2 on 3 July 1907. Five months after volume 3 was issued on 12 February 1908, Elwes returned to Ireland. He covered great distances in a few days – Dublin to Castlewellan in County Down, back to Dublin, then Kilmacurragh in County Wicklow and on to Fota and Castlemartyr in County Cork in search of trees to measure and record. This rapid journeying was possible only because he used a novel and rare form of transport – a motor car. His first stop, on 6 July, was Glasnevin, this time in daylight, and again he made copious notes in his diary. He inspected the splendid weeping cedar (*Cedrus atlantica* 'Pendula') – 'very remarkable erect for about 25ft then lateral for 20ft, trained up as youth' – and the Caucasian elm (*Zelkova carpinifolia*): 'a good tree about 70ft × 10ft'.

'Started in car 5pm & went via Ashbourne . . . to Oriel Temple', outside Collon in County Louth. A century earlier this had been the home of the Hon. John Foster, a very keen collector of trees and the 'founding father' of Glasnevin Botanic Gardens. In 1903 the demesne still contained some exceptional trees:

Weeping beech, *Fagus sylvatica*, in the garden at Florencecourt, County Fermanagh; this seems to be a unique variety but has not been given a distinctive name. (© E. C. Nelson)

The mother tree of all Irish yews which are characterised by their barrel-shaped form, erect (fastigiate) branches, and red fruits. The original tree was spotted at Carrick-na-madadh on the slopes of Cuilcagh Mountain by George Willis about 1740. He brought this to his landlord, and it was planted in the demesne which was later named Florencecourt. This matriarch still survives, and all true Irish yews are descended from it. (© E. C. Nelson)

Above: The weeping cedar, *Cedrus atlantica* 'Pendula', in the National Botanic Gardens, Glasnevin. (© E. C. Nelson)

Above right: The same Caucasian elm photographed before 1914: *The Trees of Great Britain and Ireland* plate 249.

The best thing here are 3 very old Cupressus Lusitanica . . . Also a large old Picea abies 'Clanbrassiliana' 12ft high, 43ft round, very like big beehive [and] a very fine large Birch . . . 58ft × 7ft 4ins, bole about 12ft, bark very like a cherry with small bars across it not scaling.

Onwards to Daisy Hill at Newry – 'Found Smith Junr in the nursery where I saw a lot of rare trees shrubs & plants' – and thence Rostrevor House where the 'gardener showed me a lot of rare trees & shrubs including a very curious large-leaved sweet chestnut said to have very large fruit and the young leaves now purple are said to be copper colour in autumn'. This was *Castanea sativa* 'Purpurea'.

Next morning was very wet yet Elwes 'managed to get a few photos' of some of the trees in Castlewellan. 'There are a great number of rare trees, shrubs & plants here', he noted, including a 79-foot *Cupressus macrocarpa*, a 'fine specimen', and a Lawson cypress named 'Gracilis Aurea', 'a very

handsome variegation', which had originated in Ogle's nursery in Hillsborough.

Elwes returned to Dublin and went with Moore to the College Botanic Gardens, Ballsbridge: 'The only thing of notice I saw was Betula utilis from Himalaya about 25ft high' – the mother tree of the white-stemmed birch, *Betula utilis* 'Trinity College'.

'Motored on . . . to Ashford where I visited Rosannagh, . . . most kinds of trees grow uncommonly large & fine especially ash, oak & chestnut.' Elwes photographed 'a line of very fine beech trees planted on top of a bank in old avenue now exposing 3ft or more of roots.' And, not wasting the opportunity, also paid a visit next door to Mount Usher: 'At the bottom of the park is a most wonderful garden belonging to Mr Walpole full of every sort of rare shrub & plant many very tender & growing luxuriantly.'

Next day, Moore took Elwes to Kilmacurragh, 'a very dilapidated old place but full of rare & good trees & shrubs'. They measured about forty of the more remarkable trees including 'a very fine variegated oak whose second growth leaves are conspicuous by their bright red colour'. On the wall of the Kitchen Garden was *Magnolia campbellii*, 'large trunk 3ft girth' – it is still there!

'11 July Motored via Dungarvan to Castle Martyr. In the Camellia garden . . . is a very fine Tulip tree 75ft × 11ft 4ins barked by rabbits all round 2 years ago but still covered with leaves & flowers.' Elwes reached Fota later that afternoon: 'The trees here are certainly finer than any place in Ireland and the general run of Oaks Elms Beech & Ash remarkably good.' The Himalayan dogwood *Cornus capitata* was 'a wonderful tree covered with bloom, with 7 stems about 45ft round branches 74 paces . . . largest trunk is 3ft 11ins in girth.' Cypresses and gum-trees caught his attention too, while 'Cryptomerias grow finer here that at any place I have seen . . . even in very wet ground'. *Pinus montezuma*, a 'splendid tree . . . 50ft × 7ft 3ins at 3ft, 52 paces round forked at 15ft', was also photographed, and he noted several more tulip trees (*Liriodendron tulipifera*) including a 'variety . . . called contortum with curious twisted leaves.'

On 12 July, 'Went to Belgrove after breakfast & found Gumbleton' but there was little of note there, so returning to Castlemartyr, Elwes

> . . . went to what is called the Deer Park about 2½ miles off . . . In a hollow are a quantity of fine Araucarias some 50ft high or more . . . I lunched with the Miss Arnotts 2 very nice girls and afterwards Foster got 3 photographs of Tulip tree, Araucaria and castle.

The following day, Elwes called on Captain Walker at Tykillen, near Wexford, who showed him 'a very fine Cupressus . . . supposed to be macrocarpa . . . with perfectly horizontal branches'.

Volume 4 came out on 1 February 1909, and in July following Elwes came to Ireland yet again. He drove via Enniskillen, visiting Castle Coole, Colebrooke and then Lough Eske Castle near Donegal, to Strabane and thence Barons Court 'the finest place in north west Ireland, with a lot of fine

The Caucasian elm, *Zelkova carpinifolia*, in the National Botanic Gardens, Glasnevin, in the early 1980s. (© E. C. Nelson)

large timber but no trees of special interest or size'. Returning to Enniskillen, 'motored to Florencecourt . . . some very handsome weeping beeches which look like seedlings'. Here Elwes paid his respects to the original Irish yew, 'a poor & rather shabby old tree . . . only about 25ft high & is not very fastigiate in habit'.

He motored on through Manor Hamilton to Sligo, and at Markree Castle 'there are a lot of fine old trees' including oaks, elms, yew, poplar and 'some very large Copper beeches of which the best is 100 × 9ft 8ins'. Lissadell possessed 'very interesting gardens full of rare alpine plants, and a large collection of Narcissus grown for sale', but there was no need to linger as there were few notable trees. '17 July had a long motor journey through Claremorris to Limerick . . . The country flat all the way & uninteresting'. At Adare Manor Elwes saw 'a very fine spreading walnut . . . 30 paces diameter might be photographed in winter, finest seen in Ireland . . . and a Cedar of Lebanon large branching tree close to house'.

Continuing on to Killarney, Elwes observed the native yew woods and wild strawberry trees. 'The Arbutus rarely exceed about 30ft × 12ins with several stems often leaning. I saw no young seedlings. The largest Arbutus figured in our book

Spanish chestnut, *Castanea sativa*, at Rossanagh, County Wicklow: *The Trees of Great Britain and Ireland* plate no. 236.

is about 40ft on Dinas island.' From Killarney, his itinerary took in Fermoy, Lismore and Waterford.

20 July . . . drove to Curraghmore . . . a very fine place, in a sheltered glen with large woods of natural oaks all round which are much larger than any seen elsewhere . . . A lot of splendid tall clean Scots pine said to be about 100 years old with very clean boles. The best is 118ft × 9ft 2ins clean to about 75ft . . .

'Then motored on via Ballyhale to Inistoge.' At Woodstock 'the woods . . . are extensive & very fine'. Oak, Ash, Beech are all very tall & well grown and no rabbits, so lots of natural seedlings.' There were several avenues of exotic conifers: 'A long avenue of Abies Nordmanniana planted 1879 average about 40 × 48 yards wide (much too close)

alternate trees cut out . . . of Abies nobilis glauca, [and] of Araucaria both 25–30 years.' The giant redwood had attained 93ft × 12ft, while the coast redwood was 95ft × 14ft. 'In Crow island . . . splendid Ash best figured volume 4 116ft × 17ft.'

The last three volumes of *Trees of Great Britain and Ireland* were issued in subsequent years: volume 5 on 27 May 1910, volume 6 on 15 October 1912 and volume 7 on 14 July 1913. The project was completed in October 1913 with a slim index volume. Only 300 copies of Elwes and Henry's *Trees of Great Britain and Ireland* were printed – it is very much a collector's item these days with copies advertised for high prices: at auction as much as £6,000. Dr Augustine Henry's own, heavily annotated copy is one of the treasures of the National Botanic Gardens, Glasnevin.

5.7
THE PORTERS: THE EVERYDAY STORY OF AN ULSTER HEATHER FAMILY

Ambling through the Heather Garden at the Royal Horticultural Society's Garden, Wisley, in early autumn, some of the late heathers were still in full bloom especially a sumptuous pink ling (*Calluna vulgaris*) named 'Peter Sparkes' – one of the several heathers called after members of the Sparkes family of Worcestershire.

That set me thinking about the Porter family from Ulster who in their heathery incarnations enliven many a winter garden. Sure enough, I found them in separate beds, Jenny and Margaret and 'J. W.' – James Walker. They were not in blossom but were covered with promising buds. Come springtime, and the Porters are in full bloom. The Porters are among the best of all the winter- and spring-blooming heathers, hardy, easy to accommodate, and two of them bear the Royal Horticultural Society of London's prestigious Award of Garden Merit.

Jenny, Margaret and James were from a family of twelve, brought up in Ballymacarett, one of Belfast's eastern suburbs. James, or 'Jimmy', was a bright lad, but nothing in his early life suggests that one day he would be a breeder of brilliant heathers and recognised internationally as an authority on them. He studied chemistry at the Royal College of Science in Dublin, gaining a silver medal in 1912. When the First World War broke out, he went to Arklow to work for a munitions company. By 1920 he had returned to Belfast, employed as an industrial chemist by the Ulster Linen Company, and four years he later became a part-time lecturer in Belfast College of Technology. Eventually, J. Walker Porter became Senior Lecturer in Chemical Technology in The Queen's University, Belfast, retiring in 1955. As his business card indicates,

Eileen and James Walker Porter on the occasions of their silver wedding. (Reproduced by courtesy of Heather Dobbin.)

throughout his adult life he preferred to use his second name, Walker.

I have a tape-recording – how old-fashioned that sounds! – made in June 1959 of a conversation between Walker Porter and his doctor, Dr Clarence Wilfred Musgrave. Porter starts by explaining the origins of his enthusiasm for heathers.

I've been interested in growing hardy heathers since 1920. I was away from Belfast for ten or twelve years and when I came back in 1920 I had a garden in which I could do such things. Now the reason I was interested in heathers was this – if you make a proper selection you can have them in flower every month throughout the year.

At first Walker presumably grew only the heathers then generally available from nurseries, a not very exciting selection. But things were to change. In December 1927, he married Eileen Gee, and on the

Some of the Porter family, including Anne Dobbin, granddaughter of Eileen and James Walker Porter. (© E. C. Nelson)

following St Patrick's Day, Eileen and Walker were strolling on Collin Mountain, to the west of Belfast, when they spotted a coloured shoot on a plant of the ubiquitous ling which had been burnt but not killed. Carefully he removed this shoot, made a 'slip' out of it, and this rooted. The Porters named their discovery 'Saint Patrick'. When grown in shade 'St Patrick' was a 'dirty green' but in full sun 'bright terracotta in spring and a terracotta red in winter'. Alas, it is extinct. Their next discovery was a bell heather (*Erica cinerea*) named 'Pure Gold'. Eileen Porter told me it came from Squire's Hill, another of the crags that overlook Belfast. She was the first to spot this one, and it looked just like its name. On this occasion Walker dug the plant out very carefully. He always carried a carving knife with him on trips into the countryside, as he found it was the most suitable implement for digging heathers out of the sinewy peat. (Nowadays such activities would be frowned upon, and in any case transplanting heathers from the wild is *very* rarely successful.)

Walker Porter had a passion for growing plants from seed – this is an affliction that often attacks keen plantsmen with beneficial results for the rest of us! The Porters' garden in Carryduff was stuffed with seed-raised conifers, maples and other trees and shrubs, yet heathers were always his first love. He gathered seed from his own heathers with great care.

> You have got to watch them day by day at the stage where the seed becomes ripe . . . and as soon as the seed turns brown, or is even showing signs of turning brown, then you can collect [it] . . . and I generally keep mine, and allow it to dry, in a very fine muslin bag so that

the air gets through it and there is no chance of the seed being lost.

For sowing, Porter recommended a frame against a west wall, and lime-free compost for which he had a special recipe. He also invented his own seed-sowing equipment: a test tube fitted with a cork and a very narrow glass tube (that was the experimental chemist in him) through which a mixture of sand and seeds could be sprinkled thinly.

> Now the seedlings take different times to flower: some of the seedlings will flower inside three years – the tree heathers generally require six or seven years – and that is the most exciting part of the game as far as I am concerned, to see the first flowers.

The Porters' garden contained many different heathers, including winter heath (*Erica carnea*) which he called Swiss mountain heather, Irish or Mediterranean heath (*Erica erigena*), tree heather (*Erica arborea*) and Cornish heath (*Erica vagans*). In his conversation with Dr Musgrave, Walker explained the flowering seasons and recollected one special heather of his own.

> The Swiss mountain heather flowers right through the whole of the winter. I have been fortunate enough in producing one heather, the only heather ever to have got a double Award of Merit, which will flower for seven months continuously from the beginning of October until the end of April, and, if the weather's cold in May, it'll continue blooming so long as the weather is cold.

190

Erica carnea 'Eileen Porter'. (© E. C. Nelson)

Erica × darleyensis 'Margaret Porter'. (© Allen Hall)

Erica × darleyensis 'Jenny Porter'. (© E. C. Nelson)

Erica × darleyensis 'J. W. Porter'. (© Allen Hall)

This award-winning 'Swiss mountain heather' is still in cultivation – Walker named it after Eileen. *Erica carnea* 'Eileen Porter' was raised at Dundonald, where the family were living in 1934, from seed collected from 'Praecox Rubra'. After it blossomed for the first time in 1936, Porter sold layers to an English heather nursery for £10 – plant breeders' right were not available at that time, so this was his only recompense. 'Eileen Porter' has carmine-pink flowers and is low-growing; 'she' has a reputation for being slow and a trifle difficult to propagate.

I have no doubt that this success spurred on Walker Porter to continue raising heathers from seed. Some of his seedlings were new hybrids and he was especially successful in raising *Erica × darleyensis*, a hybrid that had arisen by chance in Darley Dale, Derbyshire, when *Erica mediterranea* (as it was then; now *Erica erigena*) and *Erica carnea* were cross-pollinated accidentally, perhaps by bees.

> Well now, Erica mediterranea and Erica carnea hybridise naturally, and a very large number of hybrids are known. I have one hybrid, a white-flowered one, which is often in flower at Christmas and will flower from the beginning of January, or thereabouts, until the end of April and sometimes into May, and generally can get later flowers on the north side of a plant where it doesn't get so much light.

I am not sure what heather this was, and it may not have been one of his own seedlings. However, Porter did have one white-flowered Darley Dale hybrid which he named 'Carryduff', a remarkable,

191

but extinct, cultivar which was fertile (hybrids are almost invariably sterile).

Many of Walker Porter's heather seedlings were given away or sold, but he kept the best plants and named a few before his death in 1963; others were selected for naming after that by his widow. His first *Erica × darleyensis* cultivar was the rosy-purple blossomed 'W. G. Pine' raised in 1943. The original plant survived until at least 1966 when it was 1.2 metres in diameter and about 0.4 metres tall. *Erica × darleyensis* 'Archie Graham', with pale lilac-pink flowers, is another of Porter's cultivars, named after his friend the one-time superintendent of Belfast Botanic Garden Park.

A remarkable characteristic of these Darley Dale hybrids (and of other *Erica* hybrids, as we now know) is the bright and unusual colour of the young shoots during the spring and early summer – yellows, reds, oranges, not greens. Porter recognized this and seems to have tried to select heathers that showed especially good 'spring-tip' colour.

> In the case of the hybrids between carnea and mediterranea the colour of the foliage is more intense than the colour of the flowers and most people cannot believe that it is coloured foliage. Most people take it for the colour of the flowers, and it is really a sight to see these heathers.

As well as the lime-tolerant winter-blooming heaths, Porter worked on raising new cultivars of ling, *Calluna vulgaris*, the heather that paints the mountains purple in late summer.

> Now, one particular race of heathers which I think I am the only one to have produced – I have some very miniature forms of the common heather . . . I have one particular one at the present time, it hasn't exceeded an inch in ten years, and some of these miniatures flower very freely. . . Also amongst the Callunas there is a variety which I call Calluna vulgaris 'folio-colorata' – in other words it has got coloured foliage – and I have got a great range

of those with the most marvellous colours of foliage. This foliage only starts at the beginning of the season . . . about March, April, May, and then the colour gradually fades and merely leaves a tip of colour on each leaf.

It is likely that 'Saint Patrick' was in the lineage of Porter's coloured lings, one of which was named 'Flame of Fire'.

After her husband's death in 1963, Eileen Porter maintained her keen interest in heathers. She was responsible for ensuring Walker's plants were propagated and distributed, 'J. W. Porter' and 'Margaret Porter' being named at her suggestion. She also resumed that fascinating task of hunting for unusual heathers in the wild, and about 1969 near Killybegs in County Donegal gathered two dwarf ones, a ling and a bell heather. She named both after her granddaughter: *Erica cinerea* 'Little Anne' is extinct, but *Calluna* 'Anne Dobbin' grows with her grandparents and great-aunts in the heather beds at Wisley.

James Walker Porter never achieved his ambition to produce a white, double-flowered Corsican heath (*Erica terminalis*) yet his name will not be forgotten as long as he and his two sisters and his wife Eileen continue to be admired by discerning gardens. 'Jenny Porter', introduced in 1966, has pale cream spring-tips and pale lilac flowers: it is widely available and has the coveted Award of Garden Merit. 'Margaret Porter' produces shell-pink flowers in profusion. 'J. W. Porter', also an AGM plant, had red and cream spring-tips and heliotrope-pink flowers.

Let J. W. Porter have the last word about his beloved heathers:

> They are wonderful things . . . and I can recommend everybody who wants an interesting garden to try out heathers: you can make hedges of them; you can make windbreaks out of them; and you can produce a wonderful show of colours by bedding them out and you can get any, any kind of combination you like.

5.8
GARDEN CRIME AND SOME RATHER ORIGINAL MURDERS

SHEILA PIM (1909–1995), the daughter of Frank and Margaret Pim, was born in Dublin and educated at the French School in Bray. In October 1928, after a period at La Casita, a finishing school in Lausanne, Switzerland, she went up to Girton College, Cambridge, where she studied Modern Languages, obtaining her BA degree in 1931. Subsequently Sheila worked for a while in the Royal Dublin Society, but then devoted most of her life selflessly to keeping house for her parents – her mother died in 1940 and her father in 1958 – and her disabled brother, Tom.

Encouraged by her father, Sheila spent her spare time writing; she became well known as a horticultural journalist and as a novelist, although nowadays she is best remembered for *The Wood and the Trees*, her biography of the plant hunter and dendrologist Augustine Henry. Some of Sheila's early gardening articles, which originally appeared in the magazine *My Garden*, were gathered into a volume entitled *Bringing the Garden Indoors* (1949). In these, Sheila recounts and explains her gardening activities, month by month, linking them to household activities including flower-arranging, cooking, preserving fruits and vegetables, and keeping children occupied and entertained. That slim book and Sheila's novels form a literary 'time capsule', a social history of gardening in Ireland in the 1940s and 1950s when, for example, courgettes were 'new', young nettles were not despised as a vegetable, but garlic was shunned by many – 'We don't want that in the garden. But I only mean to lay in a small store for cooking', she asserted. At the time the Pims lived at Campfield, Dundrum, County Dublin, where Sheila commanded the 'old-fashioned, not-too-tidy, half-acre of garden and a few surrounding fields.' It was a time when cowslip balls could still be made – 'as well as a toy

Sheila Pim (1909–1995), a portrait (1945) by her close friend Brigid Ganly who also designed some of the dust-jackets for Sheila's novels.

(Private collection; reproduced by permission. Photograph © David Davison)

they make a table decoration, either in bowls, or hanging from an overhead light fitting' – and when fashionable young women, off to the theatre, trimmed their matinée hats with fresh flowers.

I knew Miss Pim well, working with her on the revised edition of her biography of Dr Henry. In the 1980s she was a frequent visitor to the National Botanic Gardens, Glasnevin. There was always something slightly 'Miss Marple'-ish about her: the almost pixie-like, slender, stooped, very deaf lady who wore a plain tweed coat and sturdy brogues and drove a small, temperamental car. Sheila could, have walked straight off the pages of a 1930s'

193

Sheila Pim, as biographer of Augustine Henry, was often asked to plant commemorative saplings, usually of the handkerchief tree, *Davidia involucrata*, as during the visit by the Irish Garden Plant Society to the campus of the (New) University of Ulster, Coleraine, on 24 April 1984.

Clonmeen: summer 1943. Set in a 'village on the hem of the outskirts of Dublin', it tells of the sudden death of Lady Madeleine Osmund, murdered, it turns out, by eating adulterated horseradish with some cold, left-over roast beef for Sunday lunch. Grated root of aconite had been added. It wasn't winter aconite with buttercup-like flowers that burst into bloom around Midwinter's Day, but the more deadly root of the blue 'Arabian' monkshood (*Aconitum ferox*) which was growing in a neighbouring garden having been raised from seeds sent home by Mrs Nichol-Jervis' son who was serving with the Ninth Army in the Middle East. To cut a long story short, it was . . . but I can't spoil the mystery! . . . who murdered Lady Madeleine.

Meanwhile, Clonmeen is preparing for the annual flower show, and we are treated to a gentle satire of early 1940s Ireland – specifically the Irish Free State of the Emergency years when fuel was rationed, commercial vehicles ran on charcoal, and there was even a shortage of manure – and of a local horticultural society and its multifarious members. 'Old Miss Milfoyle . . . was a retiring person with mainly antiquarian interests; a collector of old rose varieties, and the "Irish" double primroses.' Indeed Miss Milfoyle, we're told, could 'not get interested in any variety until it was in danger of being lost to cultivation.' You all know that type of gardener, I'm sure: many a Miss Milfoyle still flourishes in Ireland!

detective novel. I suppose it might have been an impression born from what someone had once whispered to me in her presence: 'You know, Miss Pim once wrote murder mysteries!'

It never seemed to chime with her other principal character, that of a committed Quaker. But, like the best mystery story, the truth is, perhaps, stranger than fiction. Sheila was indeed a novelist whose novels were exactly what they were whispered to be – 'crime' mysteries with unexplained deaths, even murders, and horticultural twists. They were firmly set in Ireland, and I have recently enjoyed reading them.

COMMON OR GARDEN CRIME (1945)

I wonder what Sheila's reaction was when she saw a copy of this, her first novel, enclosed in its black and dark-green dust-wrapper on which nine yellow winter aconite flowers sparkle – the wrong aconite! You soon notice a skull concealed in one of the blooms – murder! She must have chuckled at the error which no gardener would have made . . . or was it a joke? Sheila Pim's murder mysteries are never without humour.

Sheila's books are witty: 'Lady Madeleine Osmund walked in, and all of a sudden the drawing-room smelt like the Carnation Classes under canvas on a hot day.' One doesn't quite know whether that is a compliment or a devastating put-down – the answer, as we will see, is found in *Bringing the Garden Indoors*. Home-grown vegetables were 'a great standby', and the bottling of the seasonal gluts of fruits was an essential task. *Common or Garden Crime* is not a gardening manual, but it contains some gems of wisdom. Asked if she'd seen Ivor anywhere, Mrs Nichol-Jervis smiled. 'I saw him during *The Soldier's Song*', she said, 'kissing my daughter behind the honeysuckle trellis. I always say it's hard to get *Lonicera* to thicken into a really satisfactory screen.'

CREEPING VENOM (1946)

Brainborough, June 1945: the first flower show since the end of the War/Emergency is the setting. 'One novelty was the class for Medicinal Herbs ("Class for Noxious Weeds, I call it," said old Miss Hampton).' So this, Sheila's second novel, opens with a flower show, and both of the prize-winning exhibitors are later revealed to have been cheating.

The central character is 'wonderful' Miss Hampton of Hampton Court , 'a very littery old lady', wealthy, opinionated and very protestant. Needless to say, Miss Hampton was a keen gardener and enjoyed showing her garden to visitors. There were old roses, lupins, a greenhouse full of arum lilies and a bed of new hybrid irises, her 'greatest treasures', which had been raised from crosses she had made herself. These irises had not yet flowered – Miss Hampton never saw them in bloom. She mysteriously dies after a lunch of *escargots à la poulette* which she herself had prepared. We are treated to the recipe. 'Drop the snails into boiling water . . . ', and so on. Miss Hampton had bought the edible snails (which, incidentally, had been imported from Cheltenham) at the auction following the flower show – no one else wanted them, of course!

This is altogether a saucier book than *Common or Garden Crime*: 'Mushroom sauce was a thing she was rather fond of, but how to tell which of the lumps were mushrooms and which were snail?' The mystery is more convoluted, and the red herrings more numerous, and there are splendid glimpses of some of our gardening prejudices and foibles. Miss Hampton didn't like people taking 'bits' from her garden and so when Miss Tench was revealed to have broken off 'half the bush' of 'Rosa Mundi', the old lady, in pure horticultural revenge, presented her with a root of variegated coltsfoot and advised Miss Tench to give it a good position on the rockery. 'I don't suppose she'll ever quite get it out again,' chuckled the satisfied Miss Hampton, before she was murdered.

But even if she stole 'bits' from other ladies' gardens, Miss Tench was not a murderer. No! The murderer was a much slippier and, accidentally, more venomous creature and the poison was deadly nightshade (*Atropa belladonna*).

A BRUSH WITH DEATH (1950)

Dublin, 1950. The 'season' begins with the annual exhibition at the Royal Hibernian Academy. Everyone who is anyone goes there to be seen, *not* to view the pictures. We are treated to a satire of the pretensions of Dublin 'society', and a splendid story about shenanigans in the world of artists and art dealers, with some gentle digs as the Gardaí.

Gardening and flowers aren't omitted. An 'Old Master' flower-piece, signed 'Jan Van Huysum, 1737', is noticed to be a forgery because of 'a snail in it, crawling up the stem of a dahlia'. There is an impassioned plea for the preservation of old varieties of apples. 'Apples, man, apples. Every intelligent person ought to take some interest in apples. You eat them, don't you? Then you ought to see that you get the best. I suppose you'd never think of asking for White or Scarlet Crofton, Sam Young, Gibbon's Russet, Cockle and Whitmore Pippin, Cluster Pearmain, Cat's Head, Nonesuch, Hall Door, Cockagee?' Half of those apples are antique varieties of Irish origin – or at least with a distinctive Irish history. 'Cockagee' (or 'Cackagee'), for example, is a cider apple, first listed as long ago as the 1720s.

And, in between the paints and paintings, we learn that 'Cockle Pippin' will keep till April.

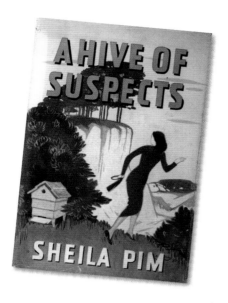

A HIVE OF SUSPECTS (1952)

Drumclash: June, and the bees are going about their business. Retired mine-owner Jason Prendergast keeps bees. After tea with bread and his own honey, he drops dead. The bees are suspected of gathering nectar from the rhododendrons in local gardens, and, as the ancient Greeks knew, rhododendron honey is poisonous. But, it wasn't the bees that caused old Mr Prendergast's death – it was his business partner, and a honeycomb deliberately laced with arsenic. Miss Pim was most ingenious!

THE SHELTERED GARDEN (1964)

In her final novel Sheila returned to the subject of gardens, specifically the public opening of private gardens for charitable purposes. There are other threads in the weave of the story, but it is the agony which the event causes to the owner, Mrs Sloperton, that is paramount. Her son, Gervaise ('Ger'), happens to be an intrepid plant hunter and botanist who travels abroad searching for new plants which he sells to wealthy patrons who subscribe to support his expeditions. Some of the seeds end up in his mother's garden. He happens to have found a new species, a yellow-flowered Chilean fire-bush, which has attracted the attention of the press and been shown on television. It was to be called *Embothrium slopertonii*. There's more to the story, of course . . .

If you want yellow-blossomed *Embothrium*, try 'Eliot Hodgkin' (if it still exists). Sheila's Latin name was pure fiction.

'THANK YOU, MISS PIM'

But let's revisit the Carnation Class. One day, Sheila relates in *Bringing the Garden Indoors*, she went with a 'highly fastidious' friend to the theatre. It was hot. Her friend grew restless, complaining: 'I shall simply have to keep on smoking cigarettes. There is somebody near me wearing some dreadful cheap perfumery, and I cannot bear the smell.' Sheila sympathised, but at the interval when all the seats nearby were empty, the annoying fragrance persisted. ' "It must be something they use to spray the theatre" ', said my friend, but I knew better. The scent was the scent of real carnations, with which, in a moment of abandon, I had adorned my matinée hat.'

And that, I am sure, is what actually happened.

SOURCES

SOURCES

CHAPTER 1

1.1. Once Upon a Time . . . 10 (9: 2001): 46–48.

1.2. 'By a Little Industry Brought to Perfection': John K'Eogh's *General Irish Herbal*; 13 (7: 2004): 50–53.

1.3. 'Charming Views Every Way: & Sweet Inequalities': Design Desk 1765; 15 (6: 2006): 70–73.

1.4. 'The Prettiest Orangery in the World'; 17 (5, June 2008): 60–63.

1.5. 'When the Swift Appears, Turn out the Greenhouse': Cranmore And John Templeton, Ulster's Pioneer Plantsman; 13 (4: 2004): 56–59.

1.6. '. . . 'Mongst the Green Mossy Banks & Wild Flowers': Cork Botanic Garden 1808–1828; 17 (3, April 2008): 56–59.

1.7. Forty Shades of Green and White; 7 (8: 1998): 48–51.

1.8. A Garland from an Irish Glebe; 7 (10: 1998): 4–9.

CHAPTER 2

2.1. The Short-Styled Bristle-Fern from Killarney: 10 (7: 2001): 66–69.

2.2. Blue Thunderbolts and Wooden Enemies; 6 (2: 1997): 38–40.

2.3. 'My Love's an *Arbutus*' – Strawberry Trees; 8 (8: 1999): 16–19.

2.4. A Saintly Heather; 8 (7: 1999): 42–44.

2.5. Dr O'Kelly, I Presume?; 7 (4: 1998): 44–45, 47.

2.6. The Archbishop of Dublin's Mistletoe; 16 (10: 2007): 54–57.

2.7. The Eighth Joy of Gardening: Ferns; 16 (4, May 2007): 62–64.

CHAPTER 3

3.1. Dr Browne's Firecrackers; 4 (4: 1995): 28–30.

3.2. Thomas Drummond and the Pride of Texas. 9 (4: 2000): 76–79.

3.3. On the Trail of the Big-Cone Pine; 3 (4: 1994): 30–32.

3.4. The Most Splendid Victorian Vegetable and a Feather-Flower Bed; 17 (9: 2008): 50–53.

3.5. William Robinson's Little Tour in the Alps, 1868; 17 (8: 2008): 54–57.

3.6. 'From Sea to Shining Sea': William Robinson Crosses North America, 1870. 12 (8: 2003): 54–57.

3.7. 'Painting Pictures' in 'Beautiful, Laughing Burma'; 7 (1: 1998): 38–40.

3.8. Floral Gems from the Celestial Empire; 15 (8: 2006): 56–59.

3.9. 'The Way that I Went': Praeger's Footsteps in the Canary Islands; 11 (7: 2002): 50–53.

SOURCES

CHAPTER 4

4.1. 'Excellent as the Cedars'; 15 (5: 2006): 68–71. [Includes Optional Table].

4.2. *Davidia*: The 'Extraordinary and Beautiful' Handkerchief Tree; 10 (3: 2001): 72–75.

4.3. The Governor of North Carolina and a Very Sensitive Plant; 12 (3: 2003): 64–67.

4.4. Among the Heather Bright; 14 (4: 2005): 70–72, 75.

4.5. Aristocrat of the Garden – The Shan Lily; 11 (8: 2002): 52–54.

4.6. Jubilee of a Living Fossil – The Dawn Redwood; 7 (2: 1998): 44–45.

4.7. Hans and the Beanstalk: A Transatlantic Tale; 13 (8: 2004): 52–55.

4.8. The Journey of a Rose; 8 (6: 1999): 42–44.

CHAPTER 5

5.1. The Last Rose of Summer: 9 (9: 2000): 46–48.

5.2. Quid Pro Quo – A Nasturtium Parasol for a Variegated Funkia; 16 (6, July 2007): 54–56.

5.3. 'Dear Mr Darwin': Letters from Irish Gardens; 14 (8): 54–57.

5.4. A Rich Bachelor and Molly-The-Witch; 11 (1: 2002): 52–55.

5.5. 'Rip Van Winkle' and William Baylor Hartland; 9 (3: 2000): 68–70.

5.6. Motoring after Remarkable Trees; 15 (9: 2006): 59–61.

5.7. The Porters: The Everyday Story of an Ulster Heather Family; 16 (2: 2007): 62–65.

5.8. Garden Crime and Some Rather Original Murders; 15 (4: 2006): 70–73.

INDEXES

PLANT INDEX

Numbers in **bold** indicate illustrations; names in parentheses following these provide the full botanical or horticultural names of the plants shown in the respective illustrations.

PLANT INDEX

torch lily 171
Trachycarpus 150
Trichomanes **40–44** (*speciosum*)
tuberose 115
tulip 177, 179
tulip tree 187
Turbina 167
turnip 22
tutsan 35
Tweedia 35, **36** (*coeruleum*)

Utricularia 170

Vaccinium 23
Venus's flytrap **124**, **127**, 128
Venus's mousetrap 128
Verticordia 86, **87** (*grandis*)
Viburnum **104** (*utile*)
vine 9, 35, 91, 95, 96, 97, 112
Viola **36** ('Molly Sanderson'), 37, 88, **91** (*biflora*)
violet 14, 34, 37, 124
viper's bugloss 109, **111**
Viscum 60

walnut 10, 172, 187
waratah **130**, 132
water avens 76
waterlily 3, 174
watermelon 95
wattle 30
Wellingtonia 162
Welsh poppy **67**, 70
willow 13, 14, 30, 106
winter aconite **194**
Wisteria 148
wood anemone 37, **45–46**, 70
woodbine **16**, 70, 78
woodruff **5**
wood sorrel 70
wood-violet 91
worts 3, 5
wych-hazel 38

yarrow 3
yellow loosestrife 73
yew 22, **185**, 187
yucca 117, 162

Zelkova 185–**187**
Zephyranthes 78

GENERAL INDEX

Numbers in **bold** indicate illustrations.